Jennifer Kutzleb

The concept of the "case" is a basic feature of social science research, and yet many questions about how a case should be defined, how cases should be selected, and what the criteria are for a good case or set of cases are far from settled. Are cases preexisting phenomena that need only be identified by the researcher before analysis can begin? Or are cases constructed during the course of research, only after analysis has revealed which features should be considered defining characteristics? Will cases be selected randomly from the total pool of available cases? Or will cases be chosen because of their unique qualities? To what degree must cases be comparable? Is the logic of quantitative research, using a large number of cases, fundamentally different from that of qualitative research, using only one or a few cases?

These questions and many others are addressed by the contributors to this volume as they probe the nature of the case and the ways in which different understandings of what a case is affect the conduct and the results of research. The contributors find a good deal of common ground, and yet they also express strikingly different views on many key points. In his introduction, Charles Ragin provides a framework for distinguishing four fundamentally different approaches to case-based research. These approaches are organized around two dichotomies in how cases are conceived: whether they are considered to be empirical units or theoretical constructs and whether they are understood as examples of general phenomena or as specific phenomena. Each approach involves procedural and analytical guidelines that will affect the course of research and the conclusions the research draws. As Ragin argues and the other contributors demonstrate, the work of any given researcher often is characterized by some hybrid of these basic approaches, and it is important to understand that most research involves multiple definitions and uses of cases, both as specific empirical phenomena and as general theoretical categories.

What is a case?

WHAT IS A CASE?

Exploring the foundations of social inquiry

Edited by
Charles C. Ragin, *Northwestern University*
and
Howard S. Becker, *University of Washington*

CAMBRIDGE
UNIVERSITY PRESS

PUBLISHED BY THE PRESS SYNDICATE OF THE UNIVERSITY OF CAMBRIDGE
The Pitt Building, Trumpington Street, Cambridge, United Kingdom

CAMBRIDGE UNIVERSITY PRESS
The Edinburgh Building, Cambridge CB2 2RU, UK   http://www.cup.cam.ac.uk
40 West 20th Street, New York, NY 10011-4211, USA   http://www.cup.org
10 Stamford Road, Oakleigh, Melbourne 3166, Australia
Ruiz de Alarcón 13, 28014 Madrid, Spain

First published 1992
Reprinted 1994, 1995, 1997, 2000

Printed in the United States of America

Typeset in Palatino

A catalog record for this book is available from the British Library

Library of Congress Cataloging in Publication Data is available

ISBN 0 521 42050 4 hardback
ISBN 0 521 42188 8 paprback

Contents

v

Contributors

Andrew Abbott is Professor of Sociology at the University of Chicago. His research spans occupations and the professions and basic issues in social science methodology. His book *The System of Professions* won the Distinguished Contribution to Scholarship Award of the American Sociological Association in 1991.

Howard S. Becker is Professor of Sociology at the University of Washington. His publications include *Outsiders, Boys in White, Art Worlds, Doing Things Together,* and *Writing for Social Scientists.* He has taught at Northwestern University, the Visual Studies Workshop, and the Museu Nacional (Rio de Janeiro).

Douglas Harper is Professor of Sociology and Chair of the Department of Sociology at the University of South Florida. His works include *Good Company* and *Working Knowledge: Skill and Community in a Small Shop.*

Stanley Lieberson is Abbott Lawrence Lowell Professor of Sociology at Harvard University and Past President of the American Sociological Association. He is the author of numerous articles and books, including *Making It Count: The Improvement of Social Research and Theory, A Piece of the Pie: Blacks and White Immigrants Since 1880,* and *From Many Strands: Racial and Ethnic Groups in Contemporary America.*

Jennifer Platt is Professor of Sociology at the University of Sussex. She has been editor of the journal *Sociology* and President of the British Sociological Association. Her research interests are in the history of sociological research methods and in analytic methodology, especially the logic of case studies.

Charles C. Ragin is Professor of Sociology and Political Science at Northwestern University. His writings on methodology span macro-sociology and comparative politics; his substantive work addresses ethnicity and political economy. His book *The Comparative Method: Moving Beyond Qualitative and Quantitative Strategies* won the Stein Rokkan Prize for comparative research.

John Walton is Professor of Sociology and Anthropology at the University of California, Davis. He has published various books and articles in the fields of Third World development, historical sociology, revolution, and collective action, including the award-winning *Reluctant Rebels: Comparative Studies of Revolution and Underdevelopment*. His chapter in this volume is a reflection on the research that led to his 1992 book *Western Times and Water Wars: State, Culture, and Rebellion in California*.

Diane Vaughan is Associate Professor of Sociology at Boston College. Her research areas include the sociology of organizations, deviance and social control, transitions, and qualitative methods. She is the author of *Controlling Unlawful Organizational Behavior: Social Control and Corporate Misconduct* and *Uncoupling: Turning Points in Intimate Relationships*. Currently she is writing a historical ethnography explaining the *Challenger* launch decision and a book that develops the ideas presented in this volume.

Michel Wieviorka is Directeur d'études at the Ecole des Hautes Etudes en Sciences Sociales in Paris and Deputy Director of the Centre d'Analyse et d'Intervention Sociologiques. He is the author of several books, including *The Workers Movement* (with Alain Touraine and François Dubet), *Sociétés et terrorisme* (English translation forthcoming from the University of Chicago Press), and *L'espace du racisme*.

Harrison White is the author of the forthcoming *Identity and Control: A Structural Theory of Social Action* (Princeton University Press, 1992), as well as books on vacancy chains, on the rise of the French Impressionists, and on role structures, plus articles modeling social networks, industrial markets, and social mobility. Currently he chairs the Department of Sociology at Columbia University.

Introduction: Cases of "What is a case?"[1]

CHARLES C. RAGIN

The precept of case analysis

Social science methodology is anchored by a number of basic precepts
that are rarely questioned by practitioners. One precept that is central to
the logic of analysis is the idea of having *cases*. Social scientists use terms
like "*N* of cases," "case study," and "sample of cases" with relatively
little consideration of the possible theories and metatheories embedded
in these terms or in the methods that use cases and make conventional
forms of analysis possible. For example, we may describe an investigation as a case study because it involves ethnographic research in one
setting, without ever considering what constitutes a case study or whether
there are methodologically decisive differences between case studies
and other kinds of studies. Another example: In quantitative research,
we use the terms "cases" and "units of analysis" interchangeably without considering the problems that might come from conflating data
categories and theoretical categories (Ragin 1987:7–9). One researcher
may use *families* as data-collection sites in a survey study; another may
write a book called *What Is Family?* (Gubrium and Holstein 1990). A
third example: A study that uses interviews of employees to construct a
picture of the informal organization of a firm looks superficially like one
that uses interviews of employees to address variation in job satisfaction. Both studies use interviews of employees as the primary data
source, but the first is about the firm as a whole, while the second is
about employees' subjective states. In short, the term "case" and the
various terms linked to the idea of case analysis are not well defined in
social science, despite their widespread usage and their centrality to
social scientific discourse.

Implicit in most social scientific notions of case analysis is the idea
that the objects of investigation are similar enough and separate enough
to permit treating them as comparable instances of the same general
phenomenon. At a minimum, most social scientists believe that their

1

methods are powerful enough to overwhelm the uniqueness inherent in objects and events in the social world. The idea of comparable cases is implicated in the boundary between dominant forms of social science and other types of discourse about social life (e.g., journalism and, in many quarters, history). The audiences for social science expect the results of social scientific investigation to be based on systematic appraisal of empirical evidence. Use of evidence that is repetitious and extensive in form, as when it is based on observations of many cases or of varied cases, has proved to be a dependable way for social scientists to substantiate their arguments. Social scientists who conduct case studies argue that their cases are typical or exemplary or extreme or theoretically decisive in some other way. Thus, even in case-study research the principle of repetition is often implicated in statements concerning the relation between the chosen case and other cases. [For an extended discussion of this issue, see Feagin, Orum, and Sjoberg (1991) and especially Sjoberg et al. (1991).]

No matter which case or unit investigators use in their empirical analyses, they typically invoke additional units in the presentation of their research. An analysis of individual-level survey data from a sample of adults in the United States, for example, provides a foundation for statements about individuals and about the United States (in addition to the range of units in between these two poles – e.g., communities, cities, social classes). A study of this type can be seen both as an extensive analysis of many cases (the sample of individuals) and as an intensive case study of the United States. Further, the United States may be seen as a case in several different senses. For example, it may be seen as a member of a larger set of broadly defined objects (e.g., advanced societies), or as an instance of an important theoretical concept or process (e.g., partial implementation of meritocratic principles), or as an intrinsically interesting historical or cultural entity in its own right (e.g., a country that is changing in historically specific or decisive ways). This example shows as well that while it is tempting to see the case study as a type of qualitative analysis, and perhaps even to equate the two, virtually every social scientific study is a case study or can be conceived as a case study, often from a variety of viewpoints. At a minimum, every study is a case study because it is an analysis of social phenomena specific to time and place.

When presenting their results, investigators manipulate both empirical cases and theoretical cases, and these different cases may vary by level, as when they are nested or hierarchically arrayed, and they may vary in specificity. A given body of empirical evidence also can be constructed into a variety of different substantive cases (a case of mismanagement, or a case of overwhelming external pressures, or a case of inertia, etc.). To the question "What is a case?" most social scientists would have to give multiple answers. A case may be theoretical or empirical or both; it may be a relatively bounded object or a process; and it may be generic and universal or specific in some way. Asking "What is a case?" questions many different aspects of empirical social science.

Conceptions of "cases" and social science discourse

The various usages and meanings of the term "case" have far-reaching implications for the conduct of social science; this fact alone is enough to justify questioning its status. The issue also deserves careful consideration because different conceptions of the term "case" are central to the enduring gulf between quantitative and qualitative social science. The term "case" is one of many basic methodological constructs that have become distorted or corrupted over time. The typical pattern is for a key methodological term to gain multiple and sometimes contradictory meanings. Consider, for example, the term "cause." A fundamental rule of quantitative social science is that "correlation is not causation." Yet social scientists routinely make statements that one variable *causes* variation in another, when the evidence is based entirely on correlational patterns. The term "cause" has been permitted multiple, non-overlapping meanings. It is only when critics challenge a researcher who uses correlational evidence that "cause" in the sense of documented empirical connections is addressed (see Becker's discussion, Chapter 9). The term "control" offers another example. Originally, "control" referred almost exclusively to experimental designs, where causal factors are directly manipulated by the investigator (hence the appropriateness of the term "control"). Today we use the term "control" to refer as well to arithmetic adjustments based on assumptions of causal linearity and additivity in analyses of naturally occurring data. [A conceptually oriented overview of these practices is offered by Lieberson (1985).] Thus, we say that we control statistically for the effect of parental social class when we assess the effects of public-versus-private-school attendance on student performance, when in fact we have no real control at all over who attends which school. The term has been broadened in meaning to refer to very different research activities.

The same holds true for the term "case." The view that quantitative researchers look at many cases, while qualitative researchers look at only one or a small number of cases, can be maintained only by allowing considerable slippage in what is meant by "case." The ethnographer who interviews the employees of a firm in order to uncover its informal organization has at least as much empirical data as the researcher who uses these same interviews to construct a data set appropriate for quantitative assessment of variation among employees in job satisfaction. Both have data on employees and on the firm, and both produce findings specific in time and place to that single firm. Further, both researchers make sense of their findings by connecting them to studies of other firms. Yet the ethnographer is said to have but one case and to be conducting a case study, while the quantitative researcher is seen as having many cases.

In this light, much of what is considered large-N research also must be seen as case-study research, and the tendency to conflate *qualitative study* and *case study* should be resisted. To apply the same term to vastly different methodological constructs serves only to increase the perception that the different kinds of social science are irreconcilable and that their practitioners speak mutually unintelligible languages. We need to strive for greater clarity in what we mean by "case" and differentiate its various meanings. This emendment of current practices will simplify the task of linking qualitative and quantitative research and bring greater richness and unity to the conduct of social science (Ragin 1991).

Consider this book a first step in confronting this important task. Collectively, the contributors have questioned the term "case" from a variety of viewpoints; their contributions to this volume can be seen as the groundwork for future efforts toward refining the various meanings of "case." As the contributions show, it is difficult to ask "What is a case?" without addressing other bases of social scientific methodology. Asking this question initiates a long-overdue conversation about the foundations of social science and the meanings of the terms we use to describe what we do.

Conversations about "What is a case?"

The conversation about the term "case" presented in this volume had its origins in other conversations. The issue of cases came up often in a logic-of-analysis workshop that Howard Becker and I conducted in the winter and spring of 1988. This particular workshop had its origins in still other exchanges, based on our shared reaction to the unexamined status of the case in social science methodology.

This peculiar status of the "case" was clear to me in my work *The Comparative Method* (Ragin 1987). In that work I showed how conventional variable-oriented comparative work (e.g., quantitative cross-national research), as compared with case-oriented comparative work, disembodies and obscures cases. In most variable-oriented work, investigators begin by defining the problem in a way that allows examination of many cases (conceived as empirical units or observations); then they specify the relevant variables, matched to theoretical concepts; and finally they collect information on these variables, usually one variable at a time – not one case at a time. From that point on, the language of variables and the relations among them dominate the research process. The resulting understanding of these relations is shaped by examining patterns of covariation in the data set, observed and averaged across many cases, not by studying how different features or causes fit together in individual cases.

The alternative, case-oriented approach places cases, not variables, center stage. But what is a case? Comparative social science has a ready-made, conventionalized answer to this question: Boundaries around places and time periods define cases (e.g., Italy after World War II). In comparative and historical social science, there is a long tradition of studying individual countries or sets of theoretically or empirically related countries conceived as comparable cases. The conventionalized nature of the answer in macrosocial inquiry made it simple to contrast variable-oriented and case-oriented approaches. It could just as easily be argued, however, that not countries but rather parallel and contrasting event sequences are cases (see Abbott's contribution, Chapter 2), or that generic macrosocial processes, or historical outcomes, or macro-level narratives are cases. "What is a case?" is problematic even where researchers are confronted at every turn by big, enduring, formally constituted macrosocial units such as countries.

The problem of "What is a case?" is even more crucial when the contrast between variable-oriented and case-oriented approaches is transferred to other research domains, because in most research areas the answers are less conventionalized. Is a social class a case or a variable? (See Platt's discussion in Chapter 1.) This is not a trivial question for scholars interested in social movements and the future of inequality. Is an analysis of United States census data a study of many cases (individuals) or one case (the United States)? As I pushed my ideas about case-oriented research into new substantive areas, I found that I had a lot of new questions about cases. The logic-of-analysis workshop provided a good setting for exploring these questions.

Howard Becker brought many questions about cases to the workshop, too. His concerns overlap with mine, but also differ qualitatively (see Chapter 9). In the workshop, and later in the symposium where the essays in this volume were first presented, he persistently pulled the rug out from under any possible consensus about "What is a case?" From his perspective, to begin research with a confident notion of "What is a case?" (or, more precisely, what *this* – the research subject – is a case of) is counterproductive. Strong preconceptions are likely to hamper conceptual development. Researchers probably will not know what their cases are until the research, including the task of writing up the results, is virtually completed. What *it* is a *case of* will coalesce gradually, sometimes catalytically, and the final realization of the case's nature may be the most important part of the interaction between ideas and evidence.

In short, Becker wanted to make researchers continually ask the question "What is this a case of?" The less sure that researchers are of their answers, the better their research may be. From this perspective, no definitive answer to the question "What is a case?" can or should be given, especially not at the outset, because *it depends.* The question should be asked again and again, and researchers should treat any answer to the question as tentative and specific to the evidence and issues at hand. Working through the relation of ideas to evidence answers the question "What is this a case of?"

Thus, while I hoped the workshop would bring the start of an answer to my questions about cases, Becker, my co-conspirator, hoped to keep the question on the floor, unanswered. These contrasting orientations made for a lively workshop, with some participants sharing my concern for answers, however tentative and incomplete, and others sharing Becker's concern for keeping the question alive. Still, we all left the workshop with a strong sense of unfinished business. This sense that there was much more that could be mined from the topic was our primary motivation for organizing a symposium on the topic.

We decided to keep the conversation about cases going by posing the question to a select group of eight social scientists in the fall of 1989, to be followed by a symposium on the topic in the following spring. Our primary selection principles were diversity and originality. Convincing eight diverse social scientists to come to Northwestern University and offer their thoughts on "What is a case?" was easier than we had anticipated. Potential participants were eager to take a crack at our question. As a lure we suggested the following topics to our participants as possible issues for discussion:

1. Alternative definitions of cases, of case study, and of case analysis.
2. The contrast between observational and explanatory units and the implications of this distinction for research findings as representations of social life.
3. The hierarchical nature of units and the implications of this structure for case analysis and the goal of generalization.
4. The place of theoretical and purposive sampling in social science and the relation between these sampling strategies and case study.

5. The relationship between analysis of cases and analysis of research literatures.
6. The different uses of case studies in social science.
7. The boundary between social science and other forms of discourse and the place of the concept of the case in supporting this boundary.
8. What is a good case study?

Our lure produced a collection of contrasting answers to the question "What is a case?" and an avalanche of new questions as well. During the two-day conference, which involved not only the invited scholars but also many of the original workshop participants and a lively group of students and faculty from Northwestern and other universities in the Chicago area, it was difficult to separate our questions about cases from a wide array of issues concerning the foundation of modern social science methodologies.

The present collection of essays includes all eight prepared specifically for the symposium. However, the essays have been modified in response to the discussion at the symposium and in response to each other as well.

Starting points for answering "What is a case?"

Before discussing the different responses, it is important to note that none of the symposium participants offered what might be considered conventional answers to the question. For example, no one pushed methodological individualism or the idea that social life can be understood only from the perspective of individual actors. Nor did any of the participants attempt to defend textbook treatments of cases – the idea that there are populations of cases (observations) "out there" waiting for social scientific analysis. (However, acceptance of this position is implied in Lieberson's essay; see Chapter 4.) Nor did anyone endorse the idea that the definition of a set or population of cases was the purely practical task, specific to each research endeavor, of defining the universe of possibly relevant or comparable observations. When sampling came up for discussion at the symposium, the primary focus was on theoretical or purposive sampling, not random sampling from a population. Correspondingly, there was little discussion of issues in estimating population parameters. The concept of "the case" is logically prior both to the concept of "the population" and the concept of "the variable." In a context where the concept of "the case" is made problematic, these other concepts appear impenetrable.

While the answers to "What is a case?" were diverse, they displayed common themes. Participants agreed that the precept of case analysis is fundamental to the conduct of social science and that it has a special, unexamined status. They agreed that individual social scientists answer the question "What is a case?" in remarkably different ways and that answers to this question affect the conduct and results of research. And all agreed that cases may be multiple in a given piece of research: What the case is may change both in the hands of the researcher (during the course of the research and when the results are presented) and in the hands of the researcher's audiences.

This general agreement on the importance and indeterminate nature of the term "case" should not be taken as evidence that striking differences in emphases do not exist among the eight responses. In fact, the differences are dramatic. At the most general level, the contributions differ in whether the question stimulated a critique of current practices or a reflection on research experiences. Four of the eight contributions focus on critiques of common practices, and four focus on their own experiences. Crosscutting this descriptive dichotomy, however, are more fundamental differences which reflect different starting points for answering the question. To understand these different starting points, consider two key dichotomies in how cases are conceived: (1) whether they are seen as involving empirical units or theoretical constructs and (2) whether these, in turn, are understood as general or specific.

The first dichotomy (whether the question of cases involves empirical units or theoretical categories) is common in discussions of social science methodology and overlaps with the philosophical distinction between realism and nominalism. Realists believe that there are cases (more or less empirically verifiable as such) "out there." Nominalists think cases are theoretical constructs that exist primarily to serve the interests of investigators. A realist sees cases as either given or empirically discoverable. A nominalist sees cases as the consequences of theories or of conventions.

The second dichotomy concerns the generality of case categories. Are case designations specific (e.g., the "authoritarian personality" or the "anti-neocolonial revolution") and developed in the course of research (e.g., through in-depth interviews or historical research) or are they general (e.g., individuals, families, cities, firms) and relatively external to the conduct of research? In many areas of research, generic units are conventionally treated as cases, and case categories are neither found nor derived in the course of research. They exist prior to research and are collectively recognized as valid units by at least a subset of social scientists. Specific case categories, by contrast, emerge or are delineated in the course of the research itself. What the research subject is a "case of" may not be known until after most of the empirical part of the

Table I.1. *Conceptual map for answers to "What is a case?"*

Understanding of cases	Case conceptions	
	Specific	General
As empirical units	1. Cases are found (Harper)	2. Cases are objects (Vaughan)
As theoretical constructs	3. Cases are made (Wieviorka)	4. Cases are conventions (Platt)

consider this

project is completed. To a limited extent, this second dichotomy overlaps with the qualitative-quantitative divide in social science. The cases of quantitative research tend to exist as conventionalized, generic categories independent of any particular research effort. The cases of qualitative research tend to coalesce as specific categories in the course of the research. "What is this – the research subject – a case of?" is a question that is best asked in qualitative social science.

The cross-tabulation of these two dichotomies (Table I.1) yields four possible starting points for answering the question "What is a case?" Consider the nature of "cases" from the perspective of each cell of the cross-tabulation:

Cell 1: Cases are found. In the first quadrant, researchers see cases as empirically real and bounded, but specific. They must be identified and established as cases in the course of the research process. A researcher may believe that "world systems" (networks of interacting and interdependent human societies) are fundamentally important empirical units for understanding the history of human social organization and therefore may seek to determine the empirical boundaries of various historical world systems (verifiable, e.g., through evidence of trade in bulk goods between peoples of differing cultures). Researchers who approach cases in this way see assessment of the empirical bounding of cases as an integral part of the research process. Among the eight contributions, the clearest advocate of this view of cases is Douglas Harper (Chapter 6). Harper makes the empirical unit "community" problematic and attempts to delineate communities inductively, through individuals. Communities are bounded in different ways depending on their nature, and the boundary of a single community may be fluid and ever-changing.

Cell 2: Cases are objects. In the second quadrant, researchers also view cases as empirically real and bounded, but feel no need to verify their existence or establish their empirical boundaries in the course of the research process, because cases are general and conventionalized. These researchers usually base their case designations on existing definitions present in research literatures. A researcher interested in explaining contemporary international inequality, for example, would accept nation-states (as conventionally defined) as appropriate cases for his or her analysis. Often coupled with this view is an instrumental attitude toward cases – they exist to be manipulated by investigators. Diane Vaughan's contribution (Chapter 8) offers the best example of this approach. Her empirical cases are conventional units such as organizations and families. She argues that by exploring generic processes (e.g., misconduct) across different types of generic empirical units (e.g., families and formal organizations), it is possible to develop better theories.

 Cell 3: Cases are made. Researchers in this quadrant see cases as specific theoretical constructs which coalesce in the course of the research. Neither empirical nor given, they are gradually imposed on empirical evidence as they take shape in the course of the research. A cell-3 investigator interested in tyranny, for example, would study many possible instances of tyranny. This investigation might lead to an identification of an important subset of instances with many common characteristics, which might be conceived, in turn, as *cases* of the same thing (e.g., as cases of "patrimonial praetorianism" or as cases of "modern tyranny"). Interaction between ideas and evidence results in a progressive refinement of the case conceived as a theoretical construct. At the start of the research, it may not be at all clear that a case can or will be discerned. Constructing cases does not entail determining their empirical limits, as in cell 1, but rather pinpointing and then demonstrating their theoretical significance. Michel Wieviorka's contribution (Chapter 7) offers a good example of this understanding of cases (as does John Walton's; see Chapter 5). Wieviorka's essay shows how the interaction of ideas and evidence in his research on terrorism made it possible for him to identify its sociologically decisive features.

 Cell 4: Cases are conventions. Finally, in the fourth quadrant, researchers see cases as general theoretical constructs, but nevertheless view these constructions as the products of collective scholarly work and interaction and therefore as external to any particular research effort. A researcher, for example, might conduct research on "industrial societies," recognizing that the assignment of empirical cases to this theoretical category is problematic and that the theoretical category itself exists primarily because of collective scholarly interest. In this view, cases are general theoretical constructs that structure ways of seeing social life and doing social science. They are the collective products of the social scientific community and thus shape and constrain the practice of social science. This view of cases is the basis for Jennifer Platt's contribution (Chapter 1). Among other things, she shows how the cases of a given study may shift over time as intellectual fashions change in social science and past work is selectively reconstructed by the social scientific community.

This fourfold division of case conceptions is not absolute. A researcher could both use conventionalized empirical units, accepting them as empirically valid (cell 2), and try to generate new theoretical categories or case constructs (cell 3) in the course of his or her research. Frustrations with conventional case definitions and practices (cell 4) could lead researchers to intensify their empirical efforts and to define cases and their boundaries in a more inductive manner (cell 1). In fact, most research involves multiple uses of cases, as specific or general theoretical categories and as specific or general empirical units. These multiple uses occur because research combines theoretical and empirical analysis, and the two kinds of analyses need not use parallel cases or units. The point of Table I.1 is not to establish boundaries between different kinds of research, but to establish a conceptual map for linking different approaches to the question of cases.

[handwritten margin note: Key]

The eight answers

As noted, independent of starting point, the contributions split equally into two main groups. The first four are critiques of conventional practices. The second four are analyses of research experiences.

Jennifer Platt (Chapter 1) searches broad expanses of the terrain of social research in her effort to explore the diverse ways sociologists use the term "case." This sweep includes both qualitative and quantitative empirical research from the past and present. She uncovers surprisingly little consistency. Both empirical and theoretical cases are multiple within most research efforts, and investigators only occasionally seem concerned to match theoretical cases and empirical cases. For example, much theorizing about social classes as cases has occurred over the history of sociology and political science. Yet many recent efforts to study classes empirically use survey data from samples of residents (often males only) and infer classes and their characteristics by aggregating the characteristics of individuals. The distance between these artificial statistical constructions and the theoretical categories are obviously great, especially when viewed from the Marxist perspective of classes as historical actors. Yet this way of studying classes has become conventionalized (Platt 1984). Another confounding factor in social scientists' uses of cases is whether investigators see the research setting itself as a meaningful historical case (e.g., Great Britain in the 1970s) or as just one among many possible equivalent settings for research (a postindustrial society). Platt also notes that in many studies crucial arguments depend on evidence about other cases in other studies; thus the evidence used to support a conclusion may be secondhand or even thirdhand. Researchers may construct arguments from contrasts between their own cases and those of other researchers, even when this contrast involves using secondary cases in ways that conflict with their original uses. This feature of social research underscores the communal nature of case use in social science.

Andrew Abbott's critique of conventional practices (Chapter 2) focuses on the tendency for most social scientists to conflate the dichotomy of "population" (or large N) versus "case study" with the dichotomy of "causal analysis" versus "narrative account." He argues that social scientists should conduct narrative analysis across many cases. After dissecting several "population/analytic" studies (large-N, variable-oriented investigations), Abbott concludes that these conventional forms of analysis cannot systematically address action, agency, and complex event sequences. These studies describe cases as acting only in crude and ad hoc ways. For example, some version of the rational actor model may be invoked to explain an anomalous statistical relationship. Abbott contends that investigators should ask "What do cases do?" first and that narratives, as cases, are the appropriate units. Inductively, the investigator constructs narrative accounts and explanations from events, which in turn are found in colligations of occurrences and other evidence. Thus, narratives can be discerned in specific empirical evidence. The end product is not a mere collection of narratives, however. Abbott points to the possibility of building generic narrative steps and generic plots from the events and sequences that make up individual narratives [see also Abbott and Hrycak (1990) on patterns and sequences of events].

Harrison White (Chapter 3) bases his analysis of social scientists' use of cases on an examination of "worldly" conventions in their use – how nonscientists use them. He finds three basic worldly uses: (1) to establish identity, (2) to explain or resolve by invoking general principles, and (3) to account for why events unfold in one way and not another, with the idea that such knowledge can be used to control situations or to fix them in some way. These different worldly uses of cases are paralleled in different kinds of social scientific work. An example of the first type is Immanuel Wallerstein's *Modern World System* (1974), which establishes the world capitalist system as a singular and fundamental unit for social scientific thinking. An example of the second type is Barrington Moore's *Social Origins of Dictatorship and Democracy* (1966), which accounts for a range of political outcomes with a single explanatory framework. Jane Mansbridge's *Why We Lost the ERA* (1986) offers an excellent example of the third type. White shows that there is no simple correspondence between these different goals in the use of cases and the kinds of evidence or types of empirical units used in a study. Mansbridge's book, for example, a classic "control" case study in White's framework, includes survey data on individuals showing broad-based support for the equal-rights amendment and the ideas it embodied. White argues forcefully that scholarly recognition of these worldly conventions in the use of cases would improve social scientific thinking.

The relative utility of different types of empirical units for formulating or testing causal arguments is Stanley Lieberson's key concern (Chapter 4). He is troubled by what might be called pseudo-causal analysis (Mill's method of agreement and his indirect method of difference) mechanically applied to small numbers of cases. Researchers working with small N's have argued that Mill's methods permit rudimentary causal analysis [see, e.g., the exchange between Nichols (1986) and Skocpol (1986)]. Lieberson disagrees and frames his contribution to this volume as a cautionary tale: Although it may be tempting to do causal analysis of small N's using Mill's methods, the end product will be a seductively deterministic, and probably faulty, causal generalization. Lieberson attempts to demonstrate that when N's are small, the possibility of formulating causal statements that are both general and reasonable (e.g., "state breakdown is a cause of social revolution") is greatly diminished. The problems that crop up resemble those that occur in quantitative analysis when researchers attempt to maximize the proportion of explained variation (Lieberson 1985). While this cautionary tale bypasses discussion of the ways in which Mill's methods have been superseded (e.g., Ragin 1987:85–123), it is significant because much of the discussion of "What is a case?" focuses on small N's. Lieberson's implicit message is that investigators who want to make valid causal generalizations should use generic empirical units and conduct large-N, variable-oriented investigations. Lieberson illustrates his arguments not through analyses of examples of small-N research, but by showing what might happen if these methods were applied mechanically to artificially constructed, generic empirical units – automobile accidents contrasted with nonaccidents.

John Walton (Chapter 5) argues that cases are made by invoking theory. The process of justifying a case – as a case of something important – involves showing that the case belongs to a specific family of phenomena. This family, in turn, is important because of its relevance to general social scientific thought ("theory"). This theoretically grounded character of cases explains both why they are central to the advancement of theory – why case studies appear prominently in the history of social thought – and why cases can be made and remade as new theories are applied to known cases (a point also made by Jennifer Platt in Chapter 1). What cases are "cases of" may change as our theories change. To demonstrate his arguments, Walton describes how "the case" shifted in his own study (Walton 1991) of "California's little civil war," an episode of conflict between the residents of Owens Valley and the City of Los Angeles over rights to the valley's water. The case had obvious historical significance, but its sociological significance was at first elusive. Moving back and forth between theoretical ideas and historical evidence, Walton eventually found a suitable theoretical context for framing his case sociologically.

Douglas Harper's contribution (Chapter 6) offers a clear example of how cases are conceived in much of qualitative sociology. He plumbs the boundaries of communities through intensive study of individuals. In effect, the individual provides a window on the community. In the process of finding communities through individuals, empirical limits are established. For example, through ethnographic investigation of "Willie," a rural handyman, Harper (1987) unearths a complex web of formal and informal exchanges and interdependences. Willie's skill in making repairs and creating useful objects out of refuse is a feature of this community, not simply an aspect of Willie (i.e., Willie's human-capital endowment). Harper's answer to "What is a case?" argues, in essence, that cases can be found inductively, pieced together from the lived experiences of individuals. When collaborating with researchers who see communities as givens (i.e., defined by formal political boundaries or census tracts), Harper chafes and struggles because he feels that an important part of the research – finding and delimiting cases – has been assumed away.

Michel Wieviorka opens his discussion (Chapter 7) by examining the factors that make something a "good case," focusing first on the peculiar status of the good case in medicine. A medical case is "good" when it is both rare and diagnosable; it embraces both an individual, the patient, and an important or new category in the professional literature. Wieviorka then moves to the contrast between good cases in history and sociology. What makes a case good in history often differs from what makes it good in sociology, even though the two approaches may be applied to the same historical facts. A historical case is good because of its significance for subsequent events; a sociological case is good because of its theoretical significance. These two don't always go hand in hand, however; the sociologically decisive aspects of the case may not be relevant to questions about why the case followed one historical path and not another. To illustrate his arguments, Wieviorka presents his own work on terrorist groups, where his primary concern was to identify their theoretically decisive character (i.e., a feature that was general to these groups and that clearly differentiated them from other groups) (see Wieviorka 1988). This search led to the development of a new theoretical case or construct, which in turn allowed him to differentiate among terrorist groups. As Wieviorka explains, some groups which originally had been classified as terrorist in journalistic accounts could now be seen to differ from terrorist groups marked by the presence of theoretically decisive features. Thus, the end result of empirical research for Wieviorka is a new or refined theoretical case.

Diane Vaughan's contribution (Chapter 8) focuses on general empirical units as cases – families, organizations, nation-states, and so on. But she sees in this diversity of empirical units a great possibility for studying specific processes in vastly different types of settings. She opens by noting that the typical academic career requires social scientists to know more and more about less and less and that this specialization also often entails a focus restricted to a single empirical unit (e.g., the family). This restriction impedes theory development and elaboration because many of the phenomena that interest social scientists and their audiences appear in many different types of empirical units, at various levels of complexity and size. Patterns observed studying a phenomenon in small units (e.g., misconduct in families) can lead to theoretical and analytic insights in the study of the same phenomenon in larger units (e.g., organizations). This creative symbiosis is further strengthened because different kinds of evidence are available in different types of units. For example, it is difficult to do an in-depth interview of a formal organization, but possible to do so for the members of a family [as in Vaughan's study (1986) of couple breakups using principles from organizational theory]. Formal organizations, by contrast, leave many written records of their day-to-day operations; families, relatively few. Thus, Vaughan's answer to "What is a case?" celebrates the diversity of generic empirical units and the many opportunities for social scientists this affords.

Looking ahead

One of our authors commented at the symposium that the question "What is a case?" was like a Rorschach test and capable of producing a variety of responses from social scientists, even like-minded ones. It is true that the question produces diverse responses. It is true as well that the question is a prism. As Becker shows in his reflections on the contributions (Chapter 9), it is possible to see the practices of social science in new ways through this prism. The issue of cases touches basic questions in how we, as social scientists, produce results and seem to know what we know. The essays in this collection emanate from the use of this prism in diverse realms of social scientific practice.

In many respects "What is a case?" is a conversation that for us has no real beginning or end. But we also feel that in some respects it has been a missing conversation in the social sciences, because all too often the "case" is a basic, taken-for-granted feature of social science research. It is important to examine taken-for-granted features because they limit our understanding and vision both of social life and of social science. In this sense, "What is a case?" is one question among many others (e.g., "What is a population?" or "What is a variable?") waiting for serious attention. We hope that our project has given this needed conversation new life and that this collection will stimulate new efforts both to answer "What is a case?" and to ask other basic questions about taken-for-granted elements of social science research.

References

Abbott, Andrew, and Alexander Hrycak (1990). "Measuring Resemblance in Sequence Data." *American Journal of Sociology* 96:144–85.

Feagin, Joe R., Anthony M. Orum, and Gideon Sjoberg (1991). *A Case for the Case Study.* Chapel Hill: University of North Carolina Press.

Gubrium, Jaber F., and James A. Holstein (1990). *What Is Family?* Mountain View, CA: Mayfield Publishing Co.

Harper, Douglas (1987). *Working Knowledge: Skill and Community in a Small Shop.* Chicago: University of Chicago Press.

Lieberson, Stanley (1985). *Making It Count: The Improvement of Social Research and Theory.* Berkeley: University of California Press.

Mansbridge, Jane (1986). *Why We Lost the ERA.* Chicago: University of Chicago Press.

Moore, Barrington, Jr. (1966). *Social Origins of Dictatorship and Democracy: Lord and Peasant in the Making of the Modern World.* Boston: Beacon Press.

Nichols, Elizabeth (1986). "Skocpol and Revolution: Comparative Analysis Versus Historical Conjuncture." *Comparative Social Research* 9:163–86.

Platt, Jennifer (1984). "The *Affluent Worker* Revisited," pp. 179–98 in C. Bell and H. Roberts (eds.), *Social Researching: Politics, Problems, Practice*. London: Routledge & Kegan Paul.

Ragin, Charles C. (1987). *The Comparative Method: Moving Beyond Qualitative and Quantitative Strategies*. Berkeley: University of California Press.

(1991). "Introduction: the Problem of Balancing Discourse on Cases and Variables in Comparative Social Research," pp. 1–8 in Charles C. Ragin (ed.), *Issues and Alternatives in Comparative Social Research*. Leiden: E. J. Brill.

Sjoberg, Gideon, Norma Williams, Ted R. Vaughan, and Andrée Sjoberg (1991). "The Case Approach in Social Research: Basic Methodological Issues," pp. 27–79 in Joe R. Feagin, Anthony M. Orum, and Gideon Sjoberg (eds.), *A Case for the Case Study*. Chapel Hill: University of North Carolina Press.

Skocpol, Theda (1986). "Analyzing Configurations in History: A Rejoinder to Nichols." *Comparative Social Research* 9:187–94.

Vaughan, Diane (1986). *Uncoupling: Turning Points in Intimate Relationships*. Oxford: Oxford University Press.

Wallerstein, Immanuel (1974). *The Modern World System: Capitalist Agriculture and the Origins of the European World Economy in the Sixteenth Century*. New York: Academic Press.

Walton, John (1991). *Western Times and Water Wars: State, Culture, and Rebellion in California*. Berkeley: University of California Press.

Wieviorka, Michel (1988). *Sociétés et terrorisme*. Paris: Fayard.

Part I
Critiques of conventional practices

1

Cases of cases . . . of cases

JENNIFER PLATT

This chapter's broad concern is with the ways cases are used in practice to build arguments, and how this relates to conventional methodological imperatives. The ways cases are chosen, analyzed, amalgamated, generalized, and presented are all part of their use in argument. It is assumed that an argument is designed to reach a conclusion which the reader (and the writer) will find convincing. It is thus always relevant to consider the intended audience, and the use of cases may be treated as part of a work's rhetoric.[1] This essay follows the implied themes or questions through a series of examples, chosen to provide diversity along relevant dimensions. The more specific issues raised emerge from close consideration of what is done in the books analyzed.[2] In the light of what is found, the ends are pulled together into some general ideas.

We look first at some works which are in relatively obvious senses case studies, whether or not their authors described them as such.

The Jack-Roller

In *The Jack-Roller* (1930) Shaw gives extremely intensive data on just one individual, a juvenile delinquent; it presents his life history written by himself, as well as a variety of material about him from other sources. The individual it studies is not well known or historically significant; it is clear that he is quite like a lot of other young men at the same time and place. This implies senses in which he can be taken as a case *of* something, and Shaw clearly intends him as a case of a young delinquent. It is interesting, however, that he is also a case in a quite different sense: a case for treatment, a problem – and one on whom, in consequence, a lot of material has already been compiled by caseworkers and others employed by various social agencies. (The instance thus unites two features of the interwar "case-study method," one definitional and the other merely empirically very common: rich qualitative data, and

21

the use by sociologists of data collected by social workers.) Such agencies are by necessity, however large the numbers they process, forced to concern themselves with particular individuals, since they are responsible for their treatment.

Shaw's book is also notable in a quite different way for its use of a single case. The case of "Stanley" was only one of 200 similar case studies which Shaw had, and he also had a program of quantitative research on delinquency. Shaw declares that the purpose of publishing this study was to "illustrate the value of the 'own story' in the study and treatment of the delinquent child" (1930:1). Thus the case is one of a treatment, or of a method of eliciting data needed for treatment purposes, as much as of a person. As Becker points out in his introduction to the 1966 paperback edition, in its original time and place it was part of a larger program which gave it a context of other sorts of data, and so needs to be understood as such. Some of the relevant data were in other studies of the Chicago area, carried out by other researchers. Shaw himself, justifying the use of life-history data, says that they "afford a basis for the formulation of hypotheses with reference to the causal factors involved. . . . The validity of these hypotheses may in turn be tested by the comparative study of other detailed case histories and by formal methods of statistical analysis" (1930:19). Insofar as that use is the one envisaged, the functions performed by the case cannot be seen within the covers of Shaw's book, but only by looking at the wider program.

In another sense, too, the book was part of a wider program, a program of social reform. Bennett (1981) has argued convincingly that life histories of juvenile delinquents have been produced under social circumstances where reformers needed them to address particular constituencies. Life histories make delinquents visible to middle-class potential volunteers and philanthropists, undermine transcendental or physical theories of delinquency, and persuade readers who are already interested but not professionals in the field. Shaw's life histories served to recruit supporters for the Chicago Area Project in which he was a central figure.

The Family Encounters the Depression

One of the most sophisticated instances of deliberate use of "case-study method" is *The Family Encounters the Depression* (Angell 1936). Angell's data were documents solicited from students at his university whose families had suffered a loss of at least 25% of their income as a result of the Depression. Loss of income in the Depression was chosen as a case of an external factor impinging upon social groups of a given kind whose adjustment to it could be studied. Although each document was written by one member, the "case'" was the family described, which was characterized as a unit. Angell explicitly stated that "our series of cases is not in any sense a representative sample, even of the families of college students" (1936:264), and that this does not matter, because the aim is analytic rather than enumerative induction. This "seeks to isolate distinctive types, each of which has its characteristic mode of adjustment, so that when one finds a family of a certain sort, one can predict how it will adjust" (1936:7). However, the number of cases serves a qualitative function, if not a quantitative one: "A good many families have to be studied in order to be sure to find at least one example each of the important types. If possible, it is desirable to have corroborative examples of each one in addition" (1936:7).

This is a very interesting strategy, but it has some obvious difficulties. If there are "distinctive types," a single case different from the others so far found will suffice to exemplify a type; it is not clear, though, why it should be taken for granted that all families of any one type will adjust in the same way, unless the mode of adjustment is built into its definition. The reference to "corroborative examples" is in this context puzzling, since it is not clear what they would be for; this sounds like an inconsistent trace of a quite different set of intellectual assumptions. Secondly, the need to study a number of families inevitably raises the question of how one knows when one has studied enough; that line of questioning seems to lead inexorably to the suggestion that one would be wise to maximize diversity in the cases used, and that drawing all of them from students at one university is not, prima facie, very likely to achieve that.

The description so far gives very little indication of the style of the book, which was probably written as it was partly because a general nonprofessional readership was expected. Most of the methodological discussion is in an appendix, and there Angell describes how he struggled to make sense of the data, trying out different variables to define types until he had found ones which seemed to him to deal satisfactorily with every case. There is no formal operationalization of the variables – and the nature of the material, even though Angell did give his students quite detailed instructions, is diverse enough to mean that that would have been very hard to achieve. The main body of the text does not reflect these struggles, or show anything of the process of induction. Most of it consists of lengthy descriptive quotations from the family accounts, arranged in chapters each of which corresponds to one cell in the typology. For purposes of presentation, thus, the case material is arranged as though it were illustrative of the theoretical scheme; it is not clear whether it is intended as example or ostensive definition, or display of data as evidence.

The absence of any systematic method of getting from individual cases to conclusions means that the conviction of the reader that the conclusion is appropriate must depend either on her own implicit analysis of the cases or on trust in Angell. The latter seems more likely to me, though other readers may find it easier than I do to see a clear fit to general ideas in the great mass of detail presented. To the extent that trust in Angell is crucial, the appeal overtly made is not to authority but to the difficulties he experienced and his sense of their eventual resolution. However, the fact that he is an established professor, refers to a professional literature which he has contributed to and which appears not to have resolved the intellectual problems at issue, and has a sophisticated methodological discussion, presumably adds to his authority and hence to the weight to be attached to his eventual satisfaction. Important, too, is the claim that in the end *every* case has been accounted for; surely a theoretical schema which can achieve that must be valid? I imagine anyone would agree that a theoretical schema which could achieve that when applied to a reasonably varied range of cases would be very promising.

However, there is an obvious difficulty in addition to the one implied earlier about unambiguous operationalization: in principle, there could be more than one theory which fits all the cases.[3] Here it is hard to avoid the issue of qualitative representativeness or range of the particular cases studied since, prima facie, good fit to a more diverse set of cases is harder to achieve (cf. Polya 1968). We may note that Angell originally intended his 50 cases as only an "exploratory" study, to be followed up by a much larger one (1936:271). The larger number of cases was meant to allow for "verification and more detailed analysis" (1936:300), and would presumably have met this point; he concludes, however, that "it is doubtful whether a larger sample would yield enough additional knowledge to justify the effort and expense" (1936:301), though without spelling out the reasons.

The requirement that every case should be accounted for puts the maximum emphasis not on the individuality of each, since it is assumed that they will in practice fall into a relatively small number of types, but on the unimportance of numbers of cases to theoretical explanation. Analytical induction leaves no room for excuses about other variables, or claims which rest only on the proportion of variance accounted for.[4] It is striking that the types Angell eventually arrived at were defined in terms of two variables, each with values effectively high, medium, or low; this is a convergence with quantitative styles which heralded the disappearance of "case-study method" as a recognized alternative approach. The typological strategy has much in common with that which Lazarsfeld developed. The case defined as a point of intersection of variables both retains and loses its meaning as a unique historical individual. Abbott's distinction (Chapter 2) between starting from variables and constructing "cases" from main effects, and taking cases in their complexity and then simplifying them down to key variables, is very relevant here.

A final feature to note about the book is that Angell chose the substantive topic for its methodological interest, to fit the needs of methodological ideas he had previously developed. In that sense it is a case of the *method*. As it happens it started as a case of case-study method and then, because he discovered analytical induction in the course of the work, became (also) one of analytical induction.

Patterns of Culture

Ruth Benedict's *Patterns of Culture* (1935) is an entirely different kind of qualitative study. She examines three societies chosen for their marked differences from each other; whole societies and their cultures are her cases. After an initial chapter in which a large number of instances, in this case cultural traits rather than whole societies, are mentioned in order to demonstrate the extremely wide range of possible human diversity, she treats each of her main cases separately. Her aim is to show that each culture has an internal consistency based on underlying principles. The cases are not analyzed in order to test this hypothesis, nor is it presented as a conclusion reached as a result of examining them; rather, it is taken from the start as a point already established, sufficiently so that no citations or systematic data will need to be given to support it. It is probably intended that it should be accepted on authority, the authority (legitimately?) claimed by an experienced professional anthropologist writing a book aimed at nonprofessionals. The book is meta-anthropology, offering an interpretive account of data collected by others. The approval of the interpretation by these others is invoked to lend further authority to the account (1935:v), and to that extent the weight of the profession generally is put behind it. The interpretation approved is, however, that of the data on the separate cases rather than that of the thesis of the book as a whole.

The cases presented have been chosen for a reason additional to their differences from each other. Benedict argues that it is easier to demonstrate the general point by looking at simpler societies; socially differentiated

Western societies are too complex for it to be easy enough in the present state of knowledge to identify their unifying principles. Nonetheless, she (1935:39) asserts that "this does not mean that the facts and processes we can discover in this way are limited in their application to primitive civilizations. . . . The understanding we need of our own cultural processes can most economically be arrived at by a detour. . . ."

This confident assertion is to some extent undermined when, toward the end of the book, Benedict (1935:161) says that "of course" not all cultures are equally integrated, and indeed some may be characterized by lack of integration. If this is accepted, her initial logic of using cases of integrated simple societies to throw light on more complex ones no longer holds. Now, however, her emphasis seems to have moved elsewhere, to the desirability of passing judgment objectively on the dominant traits of our own society and to the extent of fit between personality and culture. The argument on the latter is that personality is highly malleable culturally, but not totally so; cultures thus create deviance if they do not provide roles which allow for the full range of nonmalleability in the personalities of their members.

To support this conclusion, what would ideally be required is cases which do and do not provide room for diversity of personality type, and this she appears not to have. However, it emerges at this point with special clarity that there is a latent comparison case in the research design, and it is that of contemporary American society. This is seen, on the basis of *Middletown* (Lynd and Lynd 1929) and members' general knowledge, as not providing sufficient room for diversity. The peroration draws the moral of the desirability of avoiding extremes and of being tolerant of both individual and cultural differences.

In order to reach this point she has managed the task – somewhat awkward in principle – of both presenting very alien social patterns as natural and understandable in their context, and therefore not to be criticized from our cultural perspective, and invoking value judgments about certain patterns as "psychopathic." (Perhaps it is assumed that psychiatric categories may be taken to transcend cultural relativity.) Retrospectively, at least, although her earlier language had already given us many signals, we now see her cases as chosen at least in part for the evaluative responses she has to them, or anticipates in her readers: the Pueblo Indians are Good, and the Dobu and Kwakiutl in their different ways Bad. The book as a whole thus uses allegory in Clifford's sense (Clifford and Marcus 1986). The particular ways in which they are good or bad enable her to make, whether by contrast or by analogy, the points she wishes to make about American society. It does not seem accidental that the Pueblo case is treated first and in most detail, because to focus attention at once on a case which is both strange and Good is a rhetorical strategy which puts the reader in the right frame of mind for the total argument.

Street Corner Society

A very different instance of qualitative, case-study research is that old methodological favorite *Street Corner Society* (Whyte 1943). Whyte focuses in detail on two gangs, and moves outward from them to their local social context. Both in the gangs and in their social context considerable detail is given about particular individuals. His initial interest, at that stage very vaguely defined, had been in their area as a slum area; by the end of the book he is reaching conclusions about the area as a whole, though now as a complex and articulated social structure. His cases, thus, could be taken to be all of the individuals, the gangs, and Cornerville as a community. Indeed, one might add the local political machine or network to that list. Episodes, whether individual like Long John's nightmares or communal like the celebration of the feast days of the patron saints, could also be regarded as among the cases studied.

The research strategy followed can hardly be related to a clear initial hypothesis or research question, since there wasn't one, except perhaps of a very vague descriptive kind. In this instance there is a particularly sharp disjunction between the way the research was approached and the way the findings are eventually presented. Cornerville was chosen more or less accidentally as the area in which to conduct the research. The book starts with material about the two gangs, whose stories are introduced as showing the range of careers which Cornerville can offer its young men (but Whyte says its people) and explaining how individuals come to follow different routes (1943:xviii). Whyte says that "the general pattern of life is important, but it can be constructed only through observation of the individuals whose actions make up that pattern" (1943:xix). He will start with the little guys, move up to the big shots, then look at the structure as a whole. There follows a rich account, both historical and analytical, of what he learned about the gangs.

Although one learns a lot about the individuals, and the text is easy to read as just a set of stories, Whyte is consistent in presenting anecdotes as exemplifying more general points about the social structure. Some of the general points he makes are backed by more or less explicit quantification, if only of the order of the understood claim that he made a lot of observations and so must have a good impression of what goes on. These have a different evidential status from those which rest on particular anecdotes, like that of Long John's nightmares and their cure, where the episode is taken as a sign of the more general factor seen as giving rise to it. To the extent that the point is not also supported more quantitatively, the process of inference by which it is reached is not one which rests on the informal sampling logic of the others. We may perhaps take it, too, that Whyte's ability to produce a number of anecdotes with telling details performs the function of inspiring trust that he has indeed really been there and learned a lot, and so supports the implicitly quantitative part of the logic.

The order in which the cases which represent the parts of the structure are presented could be taken to be just the order in which Whyte learned about them. However, insofar as one general message of the book is that Cornerville is a society in its own right, which should not be seen simply as deviant, to put small groups of friends moving in their own social world first, and the gangsters and politicians who are known to and viewed unfavorably by the larger society last, is an effective strategy. This helps to show the familiar stereotypically deviant as containing strange and not unattractive conformities.

Related issues are raised by the "sampling" aspect of his choice of cases on which to make observations. He addresses this directly in the appendix (1943:322–3), describing how he came to realize that he was not writing a community study like *Middletown* (Lynd and Lynd 1929), which was written as about people in general in that community. He was dealing with particular individuals and groups, but decided that he could say something significant about the whole of Cornerville on that basis "if I saw individuals and groups in terms of their positions in the social structure. I must also assume that, whatever the individual and group differences were, there were basic similarities to be found. Thus I would not have to study every corner gang. . . . A study of one corner gang was not enough, to be sure, but if an examination of several more showed up the uniformities that I expected to find, then this part of the task became manageable" (1943:323).

His methodological position thus rests clearly on what might be described either as a theoretical assumption or as an empirical generalization; Whyte does not describe the intellectual route by which he arrived at it. In effect his cases, individuals or groups, are treated as units in the social structure, and it is taken that within that structure there is sufficient uniformity for systematic sampling to be unnecessary. The existence of the structure is, however, inferred from observation of the individuals and groups. They are taken to represent its operations in a qualitative sense, rather than the quantitative one implied by usual sampling strategies. In addition, the individuals are in effect used as informants about units not directly observed, so that Whyte gains more general impressions of the community, and can check his tentative ideas, indirectly; this again implies an assumption about the sufficient, if not the formal, representativeness of the data available. Whyte could be said to have observed the structure as directly as one ever can observe a structure, and in that sense his observational and his theoretical units are the same even if he did not observe the whole of it. The logic by which he gets from observed to unobserved cases is that a structure of the kind which his cases fit and constitute could persist only if the unstudied cases also fit it, and would constrain them to do so.

Street Corner Society is especially interesting because, since the publication in its second edition of the famous methodological appendix, it has become a case of participant observation; indeed, not just a case but an exemplar. It is arguable that, retrospectively, the prime case studied has become, for many readers, that of Whyte: it is his Bildungsroman (as well as the buddy story of Bill and Doc). One way, and a rhetorically very effective way, of reaching a conclusion and taking the reader with you to that conclusion is to tell the story of how you arrived there yourself. This almost certainly entails showing that you were initially wrong or were surprised by what you discovered. This is a very different strategy from the "scientific" one of concealing human agency in the production of the findings, and starting with a hypothesis which has been confirmed.

Boys in White

The final "qualitative"' study to be looked at is *Boys in White* (Becker et al. 1961), also of special interest because of its methodological self-consciousness. This self-consciousness was particularly concerned with the adequacy of the evidence provided by participant observation to support general conclusions about the group studied, with special – though not sole – reference to the question of how much evidence there is. When general statements are made in the book, therefore, they are likely to be supported by figures [e.g., "our field notes yield 87 instances of use of the perspective" (Becker et al. 1961:309)]. The data presented include many such instances; they also include some descriptions of the behavior observed in particular episodes, and lengthy quotations from conversation with the medical students studied. But what are the cases?

The study was conducted in one medical school, but it was not a study of the school as such, either in the sense that the researchers had a special interest in the University of Kansas Medical School or in the sense that they tried to study every aspect of it; their interest was in the effect of medical school on students, and they concentrated on the students' experience. The University of Kansas Medical School was, thus, used as a case of a medical school. Some attention is given to the question of its representativeness, and some remarks are made about ways in which it is likely to differ from other medical schools, but the chapter in which this is done concludes: "We write in the conviction that the way in which these young men develop their perspectives on their present and future is, in its essentials, like that in which other medical students develop theirs" (1961:63). No justification for this conviction is offered at that point, but the rest of the book makes it clear that it rests on rational theoretical grounds rather than on ideas about sampling. The major causes seen as producing the patterns of behavior observed in Kansas are ones seen as inhering in the nature of what it is to be a medical student faced with a body of potential knowledge larger than there is any realistic prospect of learning during the course. The rational argument, about the naturalness of certain responses to environmental pressure, is also to some extent backed up by the empirical one that quite different groups (mostly industrial workers) have been found to react in analogous ways when faced with similar situations. The University of Kansas Medical School is, thus, the place where the study was done rather than the case studied.

Social units intermediate in size between the individual and the whole school are discussed. These units are the year-groups, seen as developing collective perspectives which follow from the interaction between students' initial perspectives and their shared experiences, and the fraternities which were seen to structure daily social interaction. It is hard to see these as cases, except perhaps when comparisons are made between different fraternities in terms of their recruitment and its consequences for social integration, and that is done only to account for differences between individuals in the course of the process by which the collective perspective emerges.

Were individual medical students the cases studied? Obviously they were in the sense that most of the observations were made of them. Moreover they are given names, some of the names recur, and some of their personal situations are described in detail. However, the same individuals are not followed through as Doc or Long John is in *Street Corner Society*; indeed, the authors deliberately concentrated on what the students had in common rather than what distinguished them (1961: 22). Nor, on the other hand, are numbers of individuals having a given characteristic often added up. This follows from the unusual sampling strategy adopted.

The researchers did not, as in most participant observation studies, attach themselves to one particular group of students and observe them as they passed through the institution. Instead, they had short periods of observation of each of the year-groups of students in a variety of situations and at different points over the year. In a real sense, therefore, the sample was one of points of time in the medical-school career more than it was one of individuals. (It thus assumes what Abbott in Chapter 2 calls a stage or career theory of the process of becoming a doctor.) It is not easy to translate that into the language of cases, unless "case" becomes more or less synonymous with "observation." Insofar as the main things that are counted to reach conclusions are the available observations on a particular topic, it makes sense for it to become so. Some statements are, indeed, made by the authors which support such a description. For instance, the foregoing quotation about the 87 instances observed is immediately followed: "Considering that we saw only a few students at a time, it is clear that the actual number of incidents occurring which we were not able to observe must have been much greater" (Becker et al. 1961:309). Thus, although the authors recognize the existence of a variety of social units, none of these theoretical and empirical entities appear to *constitute* the cases which are used in their data, although they provide the material and are referred to in the cases.

We may still sensibly ask how it is that the cases are used to reach the conclusions. The authors say that they started the research with open minds about design, in the sense that they did not have hypotheses, instruments of data collection, or analytic procedures specified in advance, and that their conception of the research problem changed over the course of the work, though they did have some more general theoretical and methodological commitments. What in the book is the main research problem "became our central focus only when we were engaged in the final analysis of our materials" (1961:17). The introductory chapter of the book, however, as is conventional, sets the intellectual scene in a way which leads up to and incorporates that central focus, which is used as the key principle of organization for all the other chapters. These chapters follow the students through the chronological sequence of years in medical school, although we are told that the researchers chose to observe the clinical years first although they come later in the sequence. Thus it is absolutely clear that the results are presented in an order which does not recapitulate the writers' experience. The "cases" used only became cases of what they are used as cases of retrospectively (cf. Walton, Chapter 5). But within chapters, as well as the book as a whole, broad interpretations tend to be presented first. One of the reasons why these seem particularly persuasive is that they tend to treat what happens empirically as commonsensical, rational, following logically from structural features of the situation. For instance: "The environment . . . forces on students certain choices of perspective and suggests others" (1961:80). "They must still decide what is important and worth remembering" (1961:221). "Students' views of patients draw heavily . . . on student culture. . . . To the degree that this is so, it supports our view that medical students' behavior can best be understood by seeing them primarily as *students*" (1961:314).

Each of these statements is made at the *beginning* of a chapter which then provides evidence to support it. It is, of course, a valuable social-scientific achievement to understand and explain a social situation so thoroughly that you can make its outcomes and your theories about them look self-evident. One of the ways this is done, however, involves an element of circularity. Placing a general proposition first, as if it could already be taken as given, makes the data presented next look like confirmation of an idea already to some extent established, and guarantees that the items offered will be interpreted as instances of the proposition rather than as evidence which might have led in other directions, or have been grouped under other heads. The authors say (1961:22) that they revised their provisional generalizations if negative cases arose, and sought data relevant to their emerging interpretations, and to that extent cannot be accused of the classic mistake of "testing" hypotheses on the same data from which they were derived. The reader, however, is not offered the intermediate interpretations and the negative cases – and if she were, one might suggest that the authors were shirking the analysis of their data.

Rhetorically, thus, one is offered a logically ambiguous relation between evidence on the cases studied and conclusions. When, toward the end of the book, a proposition so general as to be plainly applicable to many situations not studied is offered ["Values operate and influence behavior in situations in which they seem to the actor to be relevant" (1961:431)], we are surely not meant to see it as derived directly and solely from the data of this study. I take it that it is implicitly drawing on other cases, perhaps drawn from general social experience or "common sense" as much as from social-scientific sources.

It might well be thought that most of the complexities in the use of cases which we have suggested in the qualitative studies so far examined would not arise in more standard quantitative studies, especially those based on surveys with conventional samples. Let us see if this is so.

The People's Choice

We start with a classic survey, Lazarsfeld, Berelson, and Gaudet's *The People's Choice* (1944). This is a panel study of the presidential election campaign of 1940. It was carried out in Erie County, Ohio. A systematic sample of the county's population was drawn, and within this there were stratified representative subsamples of which one constituted the panel and three the control groups with which it was compared. The panel was interviewed seven times over the campaign period, and each of the control groups was interviewed only once after the initial occasion. The prime function of the control groups was to allow any effects on the panel of repeated interviewing to be identified; however, data on them were sometimes also used to give a larger sample size on some key questions.

Three kinds of cases can immediately be identified in this research design: the county, the campaign, and the individual. Lazarsfeld and associates make it clear that the particular county and campaign were not of interest in themselves; what they were concerned with was the conditions influencing people's decisions to vote as they did. Reasons are given for the choice of Erie County: "it was small enough to permit close supervision of the interviewers . . . it was relatively free from sectional peculiarities . . . it had deviated very little from the national voting trends . . . it is not unlikely that Erie County was as representative of the northern and western sections of the country[5] as any similarly small area could be" (1944:3). These reasons take it for granted that one had to choose a county or similar small area, and explain why that particular one could be seen as a reasonable choice. But why did one have to?

Two quite different sorts of answers can be suggested, and it is not clear from the book which one is intended. The first answer would be that it was a basic component of the research design to use the social context, characterized as it could not be from one individual's questionnaire responses, to explain voting behaviour. The material available is indeed sometimes used in that way, but no statement of intention to do so is made in the description of the research plan; Glock (1988:34) says, however, that a community base was chosen to ensure that respondents had access to the same newspapers and radio stations. That goes well with the initial presumption that voters would change their minds a lot during the campaign, which would put explanatory weight on campaign events. In practice there was not much change, so less transient factors had to bulk larger in explanation.

The second answer would be that to confine interviewing to one small geographical area is much cheaper; at the time of the study the national survey organizations of today, with their permanent field staffs, did not exist, and practical sampling strategies of a kind that would enable them to be fruitfully used had hardly been developed. To the extent that the first answer is the right one, the county is a case of a social area, and its weak claims to representativeness are not very important since the object is not to predict the distribution of votes but to show how voting decisions are formed. (Note the interesting similarity to the logic of Angell's lack of concern about the quantitative representativeness of his cases.) To the extent that the second answer is the right one, the county is not a "case" in the design at all, but an intellectual accident.

The individuals in the sample were cases of voters, and for most of the time they are treated as interchangeable units whose answers can be added and percentaged. We may distinguish between two different kinds of account given of the aggregates thus constituted: one retains their identity as aggregates, the other treats them as if they were meaningful social groups. As an example of the latter, take the heading of Chart 27 (Lazarsfeld et al. 1944:78), which says: "Those who read and listen to campaign materials more than average . . . end up with a higher degree of interest than those with exposure below average." What the chart actually shows is that among those with exposure above average 21% showed great interest, whereas only 8% did among those with exposure below average. What these data literally show is, thus, that more of those with higher exposure end up with greater interest, not that all of them do as the heading appears to say. What is going on in the heading is a sort of shorthand,[6] which leads to the imputation of the characteristics of some members of (what may be) an arbitrary aggregate created by the research to the aggregate as a whole; it would make substantive sense to do this only if the aggregate were a real social group, in which the characteristics of some members could meaningfully be regarded as somehow characterizing other members who do not themselves possess them. This is a form of the ecological fallacy, since we are given no reason to believe that in this case it is a real social group. On other occasions the authors seem painstakingly to avoid this fallacy; I direct attention to it because it is so common, not because of its salience in *The People's Choice*.

The issue is worth further exploration, since one would expect there to be a close relation between the units implied by theorizing and those used as cases in the data collected. For much of the analysis in *The People's Choice*, all variables are equal: a factor measured in the research, treated as characterizing the individual. Sometimes this has rather odd consequences, as when, in the section on cross-pressures, the voter's own attitudes or past decisions are treated methodologically as though they were the same sort of thing as his socioeconomic status (SES) or the political preferences of his friends (1944:56–69). (This is, in effect, a way of working with variables instead of cases while still at least appearing to retain some of the caseness of cases.) How they are intended to be regarded theoretically is not always clear in the discussion. Part of the problem is that some of the factors could easily operate in more than one way. SES, for instance, could affect the vote through the voter's unmediated perception of his objective interests, or through the social pressure from associates to which it exposes him. Each idea appears at some points in the text, not always with any direct evidence that the interpretation used is justified[7] or is consistent with the argument at other points. The Catholic church is, however, treated as a real social group with a collective history (1944:23). (No issues appear to have been salient in that election to which the content of Catholic beliefs was relevant, though in more recent elections that has not always been so.)

Broadly, however, by the end of the book the emphasis has shifted decisively to the idea that personal influence in small groups of direct associates is crucial. The study remains empirically, though, one of a sample of individuals, so that group effects can be studied only through their reports of experience in groups, and of personal characteristics which are then grouped by the researchers. This indicates a key problem of design, which Lazarsfeld and his associates were to pursue in subsequent work (described in the Preface to the third edition of the book). Among this work is Coleman, Katz, and Menzel's *Medical Innovation* (1966), which has a sample precisely structured to deal with the problem, as it could be because by then the issue had been theorized and the practical survey experience had cumulated. The problem addressed is that of the spread of a medical innovation. The sample chosen was of doctors in four areas, the target was to interview all the doctors in those areas in relevant specialties, and the doctors interviewed were asked to name their close medical associates – who it was highly likely would also have been included in the sample. Thus it was clear that the data directly available were about real social relations (if not necessarily groups) rather than demographic aggregates. The cases, however, remained individual doctors rather than medical networks, although the networks found are salient in the interpretations.

Another issue which arises in relation to the question of whether groups are real is that of deviant cases and their significance. If groups are real it may be presumed that methodologically deviant individual cases are less likely to occur, but if they do occur their substantive significance is probably not great because group factors are likely to override individual ones. If groups are not real, however, and the research is distinguishing mere aggregates, individuals need to be accounted for, and perhaps classified in terms of other variables which

place them in more homogeneous aggregates. Deviant cases by definition merit special attention, although they may not always receive it.
The People's Choice often, but not always, gives them that attention. The
category of people exposed to cross-pressures is in part a collection of
deviant cases of different kinds, since for at least some of the variables
used to define cross-pressure it was being in a minority in relation to
others rated the same on it which constituted the "cross-pressure." The
interest of the book's treatment of this is that it does not focus on
explaining how people came to be in that minority, but treats this as a
new variable with which to explain voting behavior. Methodological
deviant cases are thus redefined as substantively deviant in theoretically relevant ways.

Before leaving *The People's Choice* we should note that, like *Street
Corner Society*, it can also be seen as providing a case of a method, here
the panel study. The panel technique is introduced in it as a new
method, although not one whose application is in itself the object of the
study. The method bulks large in the prefaces to the second and third
edition, and on the back cover of the paperback of the third edition. The
book was also used, as were many of the projects with which he was
associated, as a case in Lazarsfeld's program of codification and improvement of research methods. As time goes by, the election of 1940
retreats further into history, and later works have carried the analysis of
opinion formation and voting behavior further, but the book continues
to be used as an exemplar of the panel study, and so increasingly takes
on, in the eyes of its users, the status of that kind of case. At the same
time, of course, it also becomes a report of historical data, and can be
used as such by researchers interested in its period or in long-term
changes. As part of this process it may also, as Walton (Chapter 5)
points out in relation to his instance, become seen as a case of something else; the new historical context shifts the theoretical terms of
reference.

The relation between the units used in theory and the cases used in
method seems sufficiently interesting to justify further attention. I have,
therefore, chosen two further cases to look at which seem likely to add
useful examples to our collection because they are surveys in the area of
class. The Marxian intellectual tradition is clear that classes are real
groups; mainstream United States sociology has often used the term
"class'" to mean little more than status aggregate; mainstream British
sociology before the 1970s tended to use the term to refer to what were
seen as constituting something very like "status groups" in the strict
Weberian sense, and traces of that tendency still remain despite more
recent developments. (It is possible that these theoretical differences

reflect real differences in national social structure, but we shall not pursue that line of thought.)

Social Mobility and Class Structure in Modern Britain

John H. Goldthorpe's *Social Mobility and Class Structure in Modern Britain* (1980) raises a range of issues about the choice and use of cases. Two different declared interests guide it; one is a strictly sociological interest in the significance of social mobility in relation to class formation and action, and the other is a normative interest which defines greater social openness of opportunity for the individual as a desirable goal. The survey concentrates on the mobility experience of its sample. The sample is one of individual men in England and Wales (but Scotland is assumed to be broadly similar, and so the data are referred to as on Britain). Women are omitted, but assumed to be indirectly covered as far as class is concerned. The sample was stratified by geographical area. Although no rationale is given for this stratification, it may be assumed that it was done for practical reasons, to cluster the interviews, since no use is made in the text of geographical units. The initial sample of individuals was also used to provide a sample of households and "institutions" of residence, but this was done only to supplement the deficiencies of the Electoral Register as a sampling frame; again these larger social units are not used in the text. It thus remains in practice a direct sample of individual cases, but one which for some purposes is defined as constituting an indirect sample of families and households.

There is an excellent conceptual fit between the sample of individuals and the concern with equality of individual opportunity, but fit is more problematic in relation to the concern with class formation and sociopolitical action. Class structure is operationally defined in terms of the numbers of cases falling into the different categories used to classify individuals, and these categories are, at least proximately, defined in terms of occupation. Crucial to the significance of this are the criteria used to put occupations into the same category. These use both occupational function and employment status, and are designed to "combine occupational categories whose members would appear, in the light of the available evidence, to be typically comparable, on the one hand, in terms of their sources and levels of income and other conditions of employment, their degree of economic security and chances of economic advancement; and, on the other, in their location within the systems of authority and control governing the process of production in which they are engaged, and hence in their degree of autonomy in performing their work tasks and roles" (Goldthorpe 1980:39). (Oddly, the last clause is omitted in the second edition.[8])

It is noteworthy that the initial occupational categories, drawn from the Hope-Goldthorpe scale (Goldthorpe and Hope 1974), were combined to produce these "class" categories in ways which ignored their *order* in it; the list of classes is, thus, intended to be clearly distinct conceptually from a scale ranking occupational prestige or "general desirability." It follows that movement between categories in the scale may not always be appropriately described as "upward" or "downward," and for this reason it is referred to as such only when the movement is into or out of Classes I and II (Goldthorpe 1980:42). Here it is clear that there is a tension between the interests in opportunity for social mobility and in class formation, since the former implies hierarchy.

It will be noted that the criteria used for grouping occupations in the same class are ones which refer to the basis for objective interests. In terms, thus, of the potential for sociopolitical action, those interests are as much individual as collective and thus do not in themselves point clearly to collective action, though circumstances might be such that the solutions to individual problems are collective ones. There is nothing in the operational definition which refers to the possible communal aspects of classes.

The book's general discussion treats the demographic homogeneity of its classes, in terms of current members' social origins, as of key importance; thus the "working class" (Classes VI and VII in the scheme) is seen as having a high and increasing potential for class formation and action because of its high level of self-recruitment. ("Class formation" here of course implies a different sense of "class" from that in the operational definition of the occupational groups.) It may be presumed that a lot is taken to follow from the combination of shared interest and demographic homogeneity, and in the detailed discussion of class formation communal and status-group aspects are referred to; the main data, however, have not defined the cases in such a way that any direct measures of these theoretical ideas can be used. Data have been collected on social ties across "class" lines, and good use is made of them in discussing class formation, but they do not feed back into the operational definitions of the groupings used. (The data, however, can be and are used to demonstrate that the empirical ground for some other theoretical approaches is shaky.) It is suggested that characteristic class attitudes and behavior should be sought among long-term members rather than newcomers (Goldthorpe 1980:172); this implies that the "characteristic" may not be quantitatively typical, and throws doubt on the social meaningfulness of the categories used when this could be so.

The "class" (occupational) structure found is treated as a social reality at the group level in that it is taken as a given, within which individual mobility patterns and chances may be discussed; that is, the possibility that any features of the observed outcome might be the *product* of the distribution of individual or subgroup causes is not considered. This goes with the questionable assumption, almost universal in mobility studies, that opportunities available can be taken as completely measured by opportunities actually taken. Thus there is a tension at the heart of the book between theorizing which is in part concerned with real social groups, and a choice of cases which focuses on individuals. This leaves it highly ambiguous how far classes should be regarded as among the book's cases. I think it is not unfair to say that, excellent as the book is, they are so theoretically but not operationally. Whether it is possible to use classes-as-real-social-groups as operational cases without running into at least equally serious difficulties is not obvious. This raises general questions about the operational treatment of groups, which will later be discussed further.

The exclusion of women from the sample, and class analysis more generally, has been much discussed and criticized – and stoutly defended (Goldthorpe 1983, 1984; Stanworth 1984; Heath and Britten 1984). It would not be appropriate to review the general arguments here, but some of the implications for the use of cases will be considered. It was pointed out earlier that women's exclusion was justified in terms which implied that the cases studied should be considered as family households rather than individuals. There are some obvious difficulties about this. For instance, we do not know which of the men have wider households associated with them, or for those who do what their size and composition are; we know nothing about any households with no men; even if we are not interested in the occupational experience of half the population, there is something odd about defining the structure within which the other half is stable or mobile only in terms of the occupations held by that half. (The high degree of gender segregation by occupation makes this more odd, not less; if women were randomly distributed, their omission would not affect the overall pattern.) As far as the substantive theorizing is concerned, the omission of women implies that the social location, individual opportunities, and propensity for collective action by men are unaffected by the occupational characteristics of their partners; those are contested assumptions.

Goldthorpe's study could also be taken to be one of the case of Britain. It could certainly be used as such by others, and he has subsequently been active in comparative work. In this book, though, it is not used in that way. Comparisons with other countries are not much attended to; that is because the central comparison is with a social ideal, that of equality of opportunity, rather than with other social realities (cf. Ragin 1987:4).

Classes

My second instance in the field of class is E. O. Wright's *Classes* (1985), chosen as an explicitly Marxist work. Wright recognizes and discusses the problem of bringing survey data to bear on theoretical ideas which are concerned with large social groups and movements and have traditionally been used on historical data. He argues (1985:142) that individual-level variables can, nonetheless, be used because if the macrolevel factors are really important they must have microlevel consequences.[9] From the point of view of macrotheory this might be seen as using microdata as an indirect measure, or indicator, of the variables of real concern. To the extent that this is so, the empirical cases are not the study's theoretical cases. However, whether or not that is a correct statement of the matter depends on the nature of the theoretical link seen between individual and group: Is a class conceived of as an aggregate of people with the same interests, an emergent social reality whose nature depends upon potentially varying social relations among individuals, or an underlying or overriding social reality which determines individual behavior rather than being its product? The difficulty of expressing some of these ideas in operational rather than metaphorical terms may indicate problems inherent in them.[10]

A crucial feature of Wright's theory is his idea of the existence of contradictory class locations. Since the contradiction is internal to the position of the individual, it is not clear what should be predicted at the level of the individual. In general principle, a clash of two conflicting forces could be resolved in a variety of ways: one defeats the other; they cancel each other out ("cross-pressures"?); the outcome is the average of their separate effects; or a qualitatively new condition is created. In his comparison of the explanatory value of his conceptual scheme with that of Poulantzas, Wright (1985:137) manages to avoid this issue by specifying only that members of contested categories should be "more like" members of the category they were placed in than its alternative with respect to the class-relevant issues considered. We may note that this follows the traditional U.S. practice of treating classes as aggregates of individuals.

Wright provides a number of tables which adjudicate between his and Poulantzas's class definitions. The hypotheses they test take the form: "The difference between groups A and B will be significantly more than that between groups B and C." Most of these tables compare average values for classes defined in the two ways. The use of averages seems to imply a range of possible values within each class, rather than the internal homogeneity and external discontinuity one might have expected. Curiously, this is not an instance, either, of the use of a rate to characterize a group which one might expect of someone committed to a theory which emphasizes the reality of groups, but a use which refers one back to the individual characteristics of the group's members. Deviant cases are discussed only in the sense of raising the possibility that other variables might also be relevant. Once again there is an ambiguity about the status of the cases.

Finally, Wright uses cases of another kind: he compares Sweden and the USA. What he is concerned with is the relationship between class structure and class consciousness. Sweden and the USA are taken as examples of strongly contrasted capitalist societies, the logic being that a pattern which is present in both must indeed represent a significant underlying factor when they are so different. In that sense two cases of capitalist societies at opposite ends of the spectrum are taken, by an a fortiori rather than a sampling argument, to represent the rest. However, the differences between them are used as well as the similarities, this time to support the argument that the historical specificity of a society affects the way a common underlying force is expressed. In that sense they are merely two cases which happen to be different, rather than making any claim to represent.

Discussion

We are now ready to review the issues our concrete examples have raised, and to indicate some patterns in the ways cases can figure in sociological arguments.

First, it is evident that the kind of case a whole work is may change over time. The author has an initial intention, more or less clearly formulated; as the research is carried out, unexpected findings and new ideas develop; after it is completed, it may come to be used (by the author or others) for other purposes. A study of a case of a slum becomes an exemplary case of participant observation. There is, of course, no reason at all why the same work should not be a case of more than one thing; probably the commonest coexisting identities represent the substantive empirical topic (gangs), a more general theoretical category (small groups), and a methodological category.

Second, there are issues of sampling and design. The cases to be studied are, or should be, chosen for particular intellectual purposes.

The logic of choice has typically been discussed only on a very narrow front in works on method. As far as sampling is concerned, the only theoretical concern has been that the sample should be representative of a population. For design, as distinct from sampling, the logical beauty of experimental design has drawn attention away from other possibilities. [Glaser and Strauss's conception (1967) of theoretical sampling is a shining exception to this generalization.] In the short list of books examined here, several other kinds of possibilities have emerged. Wright chooses two countries to compare because they are polar types within a broader category, and assumes that where they are similar they can be taken to represent all the other members of that category. Benedict chooses three societies, very different from each other, to illustrate a generalization treated as already established, and chooses "simple" ones because the general point is easier to see in them. Angell takes a convenience sample of individuals, with no claims to representativeness of any population, because his theoretical position assumes the uniformity of nature within types and he is not trying to count the prevalence of the types. Whyte looks at a few gangs and assumes that they form part of a larger social structure which ensures that other such units within it must be essentially the same. Shaw presents a single case with the implicit claim that it is ordinary, rather than typical, and deals with the question of numbers in other studies.

In each of these instances the author has made what seemed a reasonable assumption, about what could be taken as already known, which provided grounds for excluding some cases which would have been needed for the internal composition of the "sample" to replicate that of the population; she was also not concerned with making numerical estimates of population values. There is, of course, room for discussion about whether their "reasonable assumptions" were, or remain, sufficiently well grounded to build an argument on them. What grounds are needed is not absolute, but depends on what the argument is.

The cases on which data are directly collected may be used to represent others in a variety of ways which do not involve any logic of sampling. It is very common for larger social groups than the family to be taken as in some sense represented by individuals, especially in surveys, where the individual attribute becomes a variable which stands for the larger group. Thus the Catholics who happen to come up in the sample represent the Catholic church, the property owners represent the bourgeoisie, and so on. Whether this seems odd depends on the theoretical assumptions made. Angell takes his students to "represent" their families in a quite different sense; the data collected from the students are intended to be about their families as units, not themselves as individuals. More interestingly, Goldthorpe takes men to "represent" their womenfolk in the analysis of class and mobility because he thinks the women are different, not because they are the same; conceptually, the men are representing their family households because their position is assumed to dominate them. Harper argues (Chapter 6) that in ethnographic work a single case may represent a group – but that it is only after much initial study that a case which is representative can be identified. (Interestingly, the two individual cases he mentions sound as if the senses in which they are taken to be "representative" might differ, with his tramp buddy seen as typical, while Willie epitomizes more than he typifies. Both, however, could also be taken to embody what are seen as essential features of the situation less aptly represented by other actual participants. This has something in common with Wieviorka's exemplary or paradigmatic cases; see Chapter 7.)

These instances open up a range of senses of representation; we discuss three briefly. Although Goldthorpe uses a sampling logic to justify his practice, it could equally be seen in terms of a quite different logic. There is a long tradition outside sociology of treating particular individuals or groups (monarchs, priesthoods, the proletariat) as in some special sense containing the essence of a situation; in substantive theorizing this would go with such ideas as hegemony, center (as opposed to periphery), or the great society. Another intellectual tradition deals in signs and symbols, and then cases represent that which they signify or symbolize; in the more mundane tradition of sociological method, this might be partially translated into the idea of the index or indicator. Finally, there is the rhetorical device of the synecdoche, a part taken to stand for the whole: "[T]he elegance obtains through the appropriate management of the synecdoche, in which the consciousness of a managed partiality carries the implication . . . that a surplus of meaning inheres in the connections that have been established" (Cook 1988:220). In using this, one may or may not be doing the research itself as well as its presentation.

When Mrs. Thatcher famously said "There is no such thing as society" she was indicating a serious methodological problem for sociologists: How can we operationalize the idea of a social group if it is not adequately described by the sum of the characteristics of its members? As we have shown in relation to some of the works studied, there can easily be a discrepancy between the units or cases directly studied and those theorized, both on sampling issues and in the way the data are analyzed. Whenever the proportion of individuals having a characteristic is treated as characterizing other individuals in the same category, the assumption is implied – though seldom justified – that that category defines a real group, not just an aggregate; it follows that deviant cases do not need to be accounted for, because in a sense they already have been. Where real groups of any size are concerned, it is much easier to deal with those which are formally organized. Glock, Ringer, and Babbie's study of the Episcopal church sampled parishioners clustered by parish, rectors of sampled parishes, and bishops (Glock 1988:35); it is a lot harder to approach a class with the same logic, though it would certainly be interesting to try. Where groups have collective representations, in the Durkheimian sense, those may be studied, but there can still be problems about the meaning of imputing them to individual members. These are perhaps less with groups, such as nation states, in which membership is formal and compulsory. Gallie's comparative study (1978) of France and England provides a good example of the use of national history as a group characteristic.

As with so many subjects, Lazarsfeld and his associates (who include Glock) have offered some valuable ideas, which link methodological with theoretical concerns. They distinguish between aggregative characteristics (which are the sum of individual characteristics) and global characteristics, which apply to the collective as a whole (Lazarsfeld, Pasanella, and Rosenberg 1972:219–37), and point out that collectivities may be characterized by properties which are analytical (based on data about each member), structural (found by performing some operation on data about the relations of members), or again global (based on data not about individual members).

Whether one starts from explicit theoretical assumptions or develops interpretations by working with empirical data, the kind of case it is appropriate to use depends upon such distinctions. Individuals as cases are needed to establish aggregative properties, while only larger social units will do as cases where global properties are concerned. (However, this issue may be blurred when one observes that data may be collected on units which are not those used in the analysis; global properties might, for instance, be inferred from observations of individuals.) Even these distinctions, however, do not take us as far as we might wish in distinguishing groups from aggregates in the choice of cases. Where a group is not formally organized, there may be no a priori choice which will help. It is my impression that in class analysis, at least, there is such an established body of theory that data are seldom used to test the validity of its conceptions; to start empirically is condemned as atheoretical, and empirically deviant cases are likely to be accounted for as, for instance, showing false consciousness.

Most of our instances use individuals as cases. Most of them also, however, use other units such as the gang, community, or society, even if only one of them appears in the study's main data. We note the distinction between happening to do a study in one place and using the place as a case in the study. Whyte and Wright use Cornerville and Sweden/USA as cases, and Lazarsfeld and associates' use of Erie County is ambiguous or intermediate; Goldthorpe does not use Britain as a case, nor do Becker and associates use the University of Kansas Medical School as one. Using the locus of the study as a case implies reaching conclusions about it as a supra-individual social unit (cf. Wieviorka, Chapter 7).

Cases outside the data collected may play an important role in the argument. Sometimes these are simply cases on which someone else has already collected the data, which can be referred to. As it happens none of our instances provides very clear examples of this, though perhaps Benedict's assumption that the internal uniformity of cultures generally can be taken as given will do, even though she does not refer to specific data to support it. More interesting is her use of the USA, where, although she refers to *Middletown*, it is clear that she is not relying on it so much as on assumed general knowledge of her own society. In a rather similar way Goldthorpe uses a case not in his data – though this time it is utopian rather than dystopian – in order to bring out their characteristics. His case, however, is a hypothetical rather than a real one.

So far we have been concerned with cases as they appear in the macrostructure of arguments; we turn now to look briefly at microstructure. The microstructure of purely quantitative studies is likely to be rather simple: cases are things to be added up and manipulated mathematically. All cases are equal. However, much of the time it is not cases that are being added and manipulated; the working units are variables, treated as though they had an autonomous existence (cf. Abbott, Chapter 2). Well, perhaps for all practical purposes they do. Whether or not they do is an empirical question, the answer to which might vary in different circumstances. They do if we can describe, explain, or predict as we wish to when cases are treated merely as the point of intersection of variables. If we cannot, perhaps we need to return to the case as an integral whole bearing a history. However, the variables used in straight quantitative research do sometimes carry a history, and Goldthorpe's data on social mobility provide an excellent example of this.

When cases are used qualitatively, they can perform a variety of functions. The simplest of these is the example, which can be used in a mainly quantitative study. In *The People's Choice*, a detailed history of one man's fluctuating voting intentions is given to show the complexity of the movement which could take place during the campaign. Closely related to the example is the ostensive definition, which shows what is meant by pointing to an instance. If the intention in introducing a particular case is not explicitly stated, it may not be clear, and this may blur the logic of the argument. I suggested earlier that this happened in *The Family Encounters the Depression*, when quite lengthy accounts of particular families were presented under theoretical headings; they could be read as ostensive definition, with the implication that the analytical work was done elsewhere (outside the text), or as data, in which case they are unanalyzed, and so the reader is in effect being asked either to do the analytical work or to assent to Angell's judgment. In *Social Mobility and Class Structure in Modern Britain*, one chapter, concerned with the nature of the experience of social mobility, uses life histories written by a subsample of respondents. [That choice seems to have been made for practical reasons to do with the training of the field force available; a semistructured interview would have been preferred (Goldthorpe 1980:217–8).] Goldthorpe would probably have liked to analyze them quantitatively, but that was scarcely practicable; some general propositions are built up, and in effect qualitative presentation of examples is used to bridge the gaps. It is concluded that, although only 38% of those in the sample actually returned life histories, their accounts and the interpretations of them are unlikely to be so unrepresentative that they are misleading (1980:247). The segregation of all the book's "qualitative" data into one chapter (near the end) on one topic creates a marked disjunction between "the facts" and men's experience of them, which, although somewhat accidental in its origins, says something about the book's intellectual style.[11] Had Goldthorpe wished to reinforce his macrolevel conclusions with the presentation of individualized cases through the book he could have found ways of doing so, but he chose not to.

In *Street Corner Society*, individuals, gangs and episodes are presented as cases, but despite a superficially anecdotal style, they are making general points. The general points are not, however, usually made by quantitative accumulation of reported cases. The cases are the outward and visible signs of inferred social-structural principles, and we may assume – though we are not told – that those actually presented were chosen from the much larger number Whyte had at his disposal because they were seen as either typical or crucial. In *Boys in White* we do not need to make such an assumption because we *are* told, as a general statement on method if not at every relevant point in the text, and that changes the significance of the cases deployed even when they have not been counted. *Boys in White* follows a sampling logic in its microstructure, giving us the evidence, where Whyte tends to give us something more like his conclusions from the evidence with some illustrative examples. Thus essentially similar cases in the text perform functions which vary with their context.

This stylistic point directs attention to a more general one, that of the relationship between what the researcher has done and what is presented to the reader. No writer presents all his raw data (though Angell comes surprisingly near to it) and every detail of how they were processed; strategies of selection and summary are used. The conventional introductory chapter or appendix gives information on the methods which are applied through the rest of the work. The conclusions reached are assumed to apply to and/or follow from the cases studied. The book as written, however, comes after the conclusions have been reached, and is written in knowledge of them. A book can be written as a voyage of discovery,[12] though few of them are, and then one gets the Bildungs-roman with the author as case, or perhaps – though this is not represented among my examples – the detective story, "The Case of the Mysterious Anomaly" [cf. Clifford and Marcus (1986) on typical plots in anthropological writing]. The mistakes, surprises, and changes of plan tend more often to be concealed or reserved for the appendix or the separate autobiographical statement, and we may end up with something more like "The Case of the Researcher Who Knew Too Much." This leads to ambiguity, of the kind we have noted in several of our instances, about whether the cases displayed in the text are acting as data in themselves, or merely as illustrations of points based on larger numbers of cases not directly displayed. Mason (1989:133) suggests that in philosophical writing metaphors may work as a compressed and accessible way of communicating the essence of a complex argument, and this idea could easily be extended to cover cases in sociology. To the extent that the reader finds the cases displayed convincing, this distinction may be of little practical importance. One may suspect that there can be reasons other than the weight of the evidence directly provided for finding them convincing. For instance, cases that one can recognize in one's own experience, or which are ideologically congenial, carry a ready-made conviction with them. Edmondson (1984) has discussed such issues so extensively that the points will not be developed further here.

Once one recognizes the possibility that the reader may be required to bring her own cases to the argument, it is also evident that she may do so even if the author does not implicitly expect it, and so the same work may have different meanings for different readers. Radway (1984) has demonstrated this point beautifully for the reading of romances by literary critics and by the romances' normal readers. As far as I am aware no one has yet done comparable work on sociological readers, although citation studies (e.g., Platt 1984) may provide hints in that direction by showing the contexts in which works are referred to by different writers.

For the cases within the study, there is the question of what they should be taken to be cases of, and this depends on the focus of interest and the theoretical framework as much as on the nature of the case in itself. Stanley, the "jack roller," could have been offered as a case of a child of Polish immigrants to Chicago, but it is as a case of a delinquent that he appears. Erie County could have been offered as a case of a midwestern community and its political life, but instead data on its inhabitants are used as cases of voters in a political campaign. In both instances, sufficient data were available to define the terms of reference in another way. *Street Corner Society* offers cases of several different social units, and also theorizes them in such a way that their potential as cases of "small group" or "social structure" is brought out. Such potential is in principle equally present in any empirical study, but authors vary in the extent to which they overtly theorize it themselves. Others may very well theorize it for them, or for their own purposes [e.g., Homans's *The Human Group* (1951)], and indeed it is assumed that at the level of the intellectual community of sociology and its division of labor this will routinely happen. From this point of view it is accidental whether or not the author does it, except that the assumptions made are likely to steer others in the use they make of the work.

I hope to have shown that analysis of the ways cases are used is a valuable tool, and that there are many interesting uses seldom discussed in conventional texts on method. A thorough analysis in terms of cases must consider (at least) the following: the kind of case the whole work is and can be used as; the cases the work is about, theoretically; the cases the work has data on, and the cases the work does not have direct data on which these are taken to represent; the cases the work presents data on, and the relation between them and those it has but does not present data on; the cases the work uses in its argument without having collected, or possibly even providing, data on them. The issue of the relation between these kinds of cases and the adequacy of the argument to reach its conclusion is an important one; it involves matters of rhetoric as well as logic, and of substantive theory as well as abstract method.

Coda

Etymologically, a coda is a tail. This essay will now swallow its own tail, in a meta-analysis of a meta-analysis.

The reader is likely to have noticed, as the author has, that she is using cases to discuss the use of cases. How are these cases used, and what does this tell us about the validity of its arguments? This essay has been written to show its general ideas emerging from particular cases, and this truthfully reflects how the thinking was done – though that tells us nothing about the merits of its conclusions. It could equally have been written to present its material the other way round, with the cases appearing merely as examples to illustrate the general ideas.

The books used were chosen on a mixture of criteria. First, I felt it necessary to include some which self-consciously located themselves within the traditional category "case-study method," as well as some more recent works which had something in common with it in their qualitative style. Second, it was necessary to include some relatively conventional large-scale quantitative works. From the many which could have been chosen, I selected ones which raised issues I wanted to explore about the nature of the units used as cases and their relation to theorizing; two of them came from the area of stratification in order to permit comparison of the consequences of different theoretical assumptions. Third, I wanted to ensure that whole societies were represented among the cases used in the instances studied. Finally, only well-known books were chosen, so that descriptive material could be kept to a minimum in the text since I could rely on the audience bringing a body of background knowledge to bear. My characterizations are often not documented, but the reader is implicitly or explicitly referred to publicly available data (the books) if documentation is wanted. I cannot be sure, however, that all my cases will be as well known to my readers as they are to me. (Noting before I met him the familiarity of the cases used as examples by another contributor to this symposium, I inferred that he was of the same generation as myself, and a check of the American Sociological Association membership list confirmed my inference. Each generation has its own exemplars, which tend to recur as "cases" in their writings.) Although all my points are certainly not new, I hope that some of them have succeeded in making the familiar strange. Points would not seem worth making if they were wholly familiar, and to that extent the particular cases deployed in the argument have been selected for their potential to bring to it some element of novelty; one needs a background of familiarity for novelty to appear, and that is an additional reason for choosing familiar works.

It is clear that although my choices had reasons, conceptually better choices might have been made. However, these better choices could have been made only retrospectively, since they would have represented the variables I found analytically useful in examining the cases from which I started.

No claim can be, or is, made that the books studied are representative, but no conclusion is reached which would make such a claim relevant. The object of the study has been to identify possibilities in the use of cases, and to consider their implications for analytical and evaluative methodology. It is very probable that there are other possibilities besides those identified here. If I, or someone else, could compile an exhaustive list, that would be a valuable contribution, although an empirically exhaustive list at one point in time could always become incomplete as new uses were created. This essay's aim, however, is the more modest one of suggesting useful questions rather than giving all the answers. For such an aim the particular choice of cases is not important, so long as they do indeed suggest some useful questions.[13] However, "useful" might reasonably be taken to connote (among other things) "fairly widely applicable." I hope that the questions I have raised are indeed such, but I have not provided the reader with any systematic data on that point. I have implicitly assumed that systematic data are unnecessary when we all know, from our general life experience as sociologists, that design and sampling choices of certain kinds have to be made, that individual cases are commonly added up to reach conclusions about groups, that short or long vignettes of people or episodes are often presented, and so on ("and so on" implies that I can rely on you to extend my partial list from shared knowledge).

Sometimes I have used characteristics of the whole books as my cases, but more often I have taken chapters or episodes, or methodological practices abstracted from their context or substantive content. To the extent that the argument is not about whole works as integral cases, this seems legitimate, though it might always be possible for a critic to suggest that something relevant and important has been lost by abstraction. Where a book examined later in the text exemplifies a point already made, this has been mentioned fleetingly or not at all, because the accumulation of a few more cases of the same pattern would not affect the argument. The books used are dealt with almost exactly in historical order, though there is also a qualitative/quantitative distinction. This reflects my original hope to see something significant in the sequence of historical development. In the event, I did not, in part because I was not happy to attach historical meaning to a sequence not chosen for its representativeness. I do not like the qualitative/quantitative division, which in general I regard as an unhelpful one, but making it followed from the decision to start from what were commonly regarded as case studies and then to go on to works not normally looked at in that way.

It is unfortunate, however, that the combination of these decisions could give the impression that I think in terms of historical development from qualitative to quantitative. To avoid that it would have been good to have included a pre–World War II quantitative study; had I done so, however, its lack of modern statistical sophistication might have made it easier for the reader to impute anything revealed about its use of cases to that cause, and so to reject the applicability of the points made to contemporary work.

References

Angell, Robert C. (1936). *The Family Encounters the Depression*. Reprinted Gloucester, MA: Peter Smith, 1965.

Barton, Allen (1955). "The Concept of Property-Space in Social Research," pp. 40–53 in Paul F. Lazarsfeld and Morris Rosenberg (eds.), *The Language of Social Research*. Glencoe, IL: Free Press.

Becker, Howard S., Blanche Greer, Everett C. Hughes, and Anselm L. Strauss (1961). *Boys in White: Student Culture in Medical School*. Chicago: University of Chicago Press.

Benedict, Ruth (1935). *Patterns of Culture*. Reprinted London: Routledge & Kegan Paul, 1961.

Bennett, James (1981). *Oral History and Delinquency*. Chicago: University of Chicago Press.

Burke, Kenneth (1952). *A Grammar of Motives*. New York: Prentice Hall.

Clifford, James, and George E. Marcus (eds.) (1986). *Writing Culture*. Berkeley: University of California Press.

Coleman, James S., Elihu Katz, and Herbert Menzel (1966). *Medical Innovation: A Diffusion Study*. New York: Bobbs-Merrill.

Cook, Albert (1988). *History/Writing*. Cambridge University Press.

Crompton, Rosemary (1990). "Goldthorpe and Marxist Theories of Historical Development," pp. 95–109 in J. Clark, C. Modgil, and S. Modgil (eds.), *John H. Goldthorpe: Consensus and Controversy*. London: Falmer Press.

Edmondson, Ricca (1984). *Rhetoric in Sociology*. London: Macmillan.

Gallie, Duncan (1978). *In Search of the New Working Class*. Cambridge University Press.

Glaser, Barney G., and Anselm L. Strauss (1967). *The Discovery of Grounded Theory: Strategies for Qualitative Research*. London: Weidenfeld & Nicholson.

Glock, Charles Y. (1988). "Reflections on Doing Survey Research," pp. 31–59 in Hubert J. O'Gorman (ed.), *Surveying Social Life*. Middletown, CT: Wesleyan University Press.

Goldthorpe, John H. (1980). *Social Mobility and Class Structure in Modern Britain*. Oxford: Oxford University Press.

  (1983). "Women and Class Analysis: In Defence of the Conventional View," *Sociology* 17:465–88.

  (1984). "Women and Class Analysis: A Reply to the Replies," *Sociology* 18: 491–9.

Goldthorpe, John H., and Keith Hope (1974). *The Social Grading of Occupations.* Oxford: Clarendon Press.

Heath, Anthony, and Nicky Britten (1984). "Women's Jobs Do Make a Difference: A Reply to Goldthorpe," *Sociology* 18:475–90.

Homans, George C. (1951). *The Human Group.* London: Routledge & Kegan Paul.

Lazarsfeld, Paul F., Bernard Berelson, and Hazel Gaudet (1944). *The People's Choice.* Reprinted (paperback) New York: Columbia University Press, 1968.

Lazarsfeld, Paul F., Ann K. Pasanella, and Morris Rosenberg (eds.) (1972). *Continuities in the Language of Social Research.* New York: Free Press.

Lynd, Robert S., and Helen M. Lynd (1929). *Middletown: A Study in Contemporary American Culture.* New York: Harcourt, Brace.

Mason, Jeff (1989). *Philosophical Rhetoric.* London: Routledge.

Platt, Jennifer (1984). "The *Affluent Worker* Revisited," pp. 179–98 in Colin Bell and Helen Roberts (eds.), *Social Researching: Politics, Problems, Practice.* London: Routledge & Kegan Paul.

   (1987). "The SSRC Restudy of Angell's Cases from *The Family Encounters the Depression*," mimeograph, University of Sussex.

Polya, George (1968). *Patterns of Plausible Inference.* Princeton, NJ: Princeton University Press.

Radway, Janice A. (1984). *Reading the Romance.* Chapel Hill: University of North Carolina Press.

Ragin, Charles C. (1987). *The Comparative Method: Moving Beyond Qualitative and Quantitative Strategies.* Berkeley: University of California Press.

Shaw, Clifford R. (1930). *The Jack-Roller.* Reprinted Chicago: University of Chicago Press, 1966.

Stanworth, Michelle (1984). "Women and Class Analysis: A Reply to Goldthorpe," *Sociology* 18:159–70.

Whyte, William F. (1943). *Street Corner Society: The Social Structure of an Italian Slum.* Reprinted Chicago: University of Chicago Press, 1955.

Wright, Erik O. (1985). *Classes.* London: Verso.

   (1989). "Reflections on *Classes*," pp. 49–77 in Erik O. Wright (ed.), *The Debate on Classes.* London: Verso.

2

What do cases do? Some notes on activity in sociological analysis[1]

ANDREW ABBOTT

This chapter addresses three issues. It first asks what happens to the actions of "cases" in standard quantitative methods, showing that they lose their complexity and their narrative order. It then considers work that takes those things seriously, particularly historical case studies, examining how case complexity and case action function in such studies. It closes with a consideration of how to generalize about complexity and narrative order across cases. As this summary makes clear, a central message of this essay is that we must disentangle the population-versus-case distinction from the analysis-versus-narrative one.

I am using "case" here in the sense of "instance." Instances can be of two kinds. First, a particular entity may be an instance (case) of a population. Here, we have "case" as single-element subset; the population is some set of social objects (persons, companies), and the cases are its members. But a particular entity may also be an instance (case) of a conceptual class. Here, we have "case" as exemplar; the conceptual class has some property (e.g., it is a structural type like bureaucracy), and the cases exemplify that property. Clearly these are different definitions with very different implications. As we shall see later, some sociologists assume that there are social objects that are not inherently "conceptual," while others do not.[2]

By asking what cases do, I am assuming that the case is an agent. This idea is somewhat foreign to some sociological traditions. We don't generally think of the cases in the General Social Survey as agents with intentions and histories. But it is precisely my intent to begin with the question of what such cases "do" in the Weberian (etc.) sense of social action. What kinds of activities do they undertake? What do they try to accomplish? What kinds of agents are they?

What do cases do in standard positivist articles?

A simple way to ascertain what cases do in standard empirical sociological studies is to open the latest *American Journal of Sociology* (November 1989 as of this writing) and analyze some articles in detail. I will here consider the first three. My procedure is simple. I find all the narrative sentences, the sentences whose predicates are activities or parts of the social process. [See Danto (1985) for a technical definition of narrative sentences.] I then consider who are the subjects of these sentences, what kinds of activities are involved, and how the predicates are related to causality. I also consider when in the argument narrative sentences are likely to appear and how cases are (implicitly) construed by the authors.

The usual disclaimers apply. I am not attacking or debunking the particular authors involved. Their work's appearance in such a journal warrants its acceptance as disciplinarily proper and representative. And I am not trying to debunk the whole style of work involved. I merely wish to discover something about its "case" assumptions. I have used quotations extensively, since the exact locutions employed are of central importance. A thing may be said several ways; but it is precisely in the choice of one of those ways that assumptions about cases are most clear.[3]

In the first paper, Charles Halaby and David Weakliem (1989) are investigating the relation between worker control and attachment to the firm. Their "cases" are workers. (Cases in this kind of literature are usually called "units of analysis," a term with considerably different connotations – of equivalence among individuals and of the ' pre-eminence of analytic categories – than those of "case.") Halaby and Weakliem investigate several hypotheses, and it is in these hypothesis discussions that we first find narrative sentences.

The first hypothesis argues that worker control dignifies work.

This may be evidenced empirically in the transformation that increasing control effects in the significance of work. In the absence of control, work is a mere instrumental activity, a means of subsistence: the worker works to produce wares. But with increasing control the work itself becomes a terminal value that is invested with significance in its own right as an expression of self. For reasons not always made clear . . . the value assigned to the work itself carries over into the employment relation, resulting in higher attachment. [1989:553–4]

Note that "the worker works [only in order] to produce wares" is the only sentence in which cases act. Elsewhere, variables do the acting. In "the work itself becomes a terminal value," "the value . . . carries over into the employment relation," and "the transformation that increasing control effects in the significance of work," variables are the subjects of the clauses. Presumably these are variable-based descriptions of psychic processes that take place "in the heads of the cases." Still, the variables, not the cases, do the acting here.

Halaby and Weakliem next propose the hypothesis that excessive supervision violates cultural norms.

[Theorists] argue that supervisory practices that limit workers' independence and control of their work violate the "independence norm in American culture" and therefore result in dissatisfaction and turnover. [1989:554]

Here, the variables are directly personified as agents: "[P]ractices . . . violate the . . . norm . . . and result . . . ." We have moved away from the simple causal language ("becomes," "carries over," "effects") of hypothesis 1 to a more active vocabulary ("violates"). Again, this is presumably a psychic shorthand, yet there is no case agency even at the psychic level. The worker doesn't think about these things; the things themselves directly act in his or her psyche. The personality is merely the setting in which the causes act, not itself an agent acting (e.g., reflecting) on them.

The final major hypothesis is the authors' new theoretical contribution, what they call a "match quality" hypothesis, emphasizing the fit between innate worker characteristics and job characteristics.

Control of task-related job activities gives a worker the freedom to employ his skills and abilities more fully and thereby achieve more fully the maximum level of productivity commensurate with his productive resources. This means that the potential gains in productivity that might accompany a job change will tend to be low for autonomous workers. Such workers will therefore arrive at pessimistic estimates of the potential wage returns to job change and will exhibit higher levels of attachment to the current employers. [1989:554]

Now this is different. In the preexisting theories, which are discussed first, we get extremely analytic statements couched in terms of variables. The "stories" (the psychic reflections of individual workers) that lie behind these variables' relations are left totally implicit. But here in the authors' own, new hypothesis, we start to see singular workers more clearly. They are reasoning and reflecting, and their reflections lead through a process that implies a particular relation between the variables studied (that is, a positive relation between worker control measures and job attachment measures). To justify that entailed relation between variables requires the creation of a plausible narrative about particular cases. Under such-and-such conditions, a worker of such-and-such a type will think so-and-so and hence act in such-and-such a way.

In the discussion, we find the same sort of division. On the one hand, we find some pseudo-narrative statements that are actually simple descriptions of the correlations.

... it is clear, then, that workers who experience a high degree of control over their work activities are significantly more optimistic about their chances of eliciting reward-equivalent offers from other employers, with their attachment to the current jobs suffering accordingly. [1989:576]

Since the variables are responses to sentences of the "I think that . . ." type, they can readily be transformed into such pseudo–descriptive statements. The worker need not be seen here as acting or thinking, but merely as the locale for the variables' doing their thing. There is no real action, for even though the workers "experience" a high degree of control, they merely "are" significantly more optimistic.

But we also have the following:

It should be noted that these results assume that worker control and match quality are causally prior to the intrinsic value of work. . . . Social theory largely ignores the possibility that workers may choose autonomous jobs and high-quality matches based on their prior orientation to work as an instrumental or terminal value. Indeed, it could be argued that regardless of a worker's prior orientation, it is only through the actual exercise of control and the full use of his productive capacities that the worker realizes self-actualization and the work has intrinsic value. [1989:577]

This passage proposes an "alternative story," and here again, as we move away from the standard or the expected, we get actual worker activity, in this case choice of jobs.[4] The proposed narrative undermines the prior "causal story" of the variables (as opposed to the actual stories of the workers); the variables won't be entailed this way if the new narrative holds. And therefore a model with "other arrows" has to be tested. This second model is rejected because it gives some theoretically implausible results on one relation, which the original model does not.

It is important to note the role here of the alternative narrative. For any particular set of causal variable relations to hold, all agents (cases) must follow only one story. As Blau and Duncan (1967:167) admitted, with commendable embarrassment, to estimate the regression coefficients that supposedly measure the effects of causes one has to assume that the causal model is exactly the same for every case, something that is obviously untrue. Now two different narratives may entail the same set of variable relations. But if they do, analysts will seek other entailed variables to distinguish them. The ideal, that is, is a one-to-one relation between narratives and entailed-variable models. But in that case "causality" effectively means narration; the notion that the two really differ (that variables are entailed by a narrative, rather than representing it) is a fiction. Even the move to variables as actors doesn't really get us away from narration, for every narrative with cases as actors entails a set of relations among variables (a narrative with variables as actors). Challenges to those relations arise when alternative case narratives entail alternative variable relations. The level of case narrative, paradoxically, is a necessary evil for these (as for other) authors, even though most activity in this study takes place at the level of variables, where things are considerably more tidy.[5]

The authors then find a major and unexpected direct negative effect of control on attachment and must decide what to do about it. Now my prediction, from the implicit theory I have been developing, is that that would entail a move to direct narrative work. Here is the passage:

> [decision-making and problem-solving skills accumulated by autonomous workers] may give autonomous workers a competitive advantage over their less autonomous counterparts in the search for mobility gains. With match quality held fixed, autonomous workers would have more incentive to be oriented toward mobility, with their attachment suffering accordingly. [1989:582]

Note that the description remains a narrative of variables. But we are starting to see the workers as individuals with actual incentives and hence potentiality for action. What follows completes the transition:

> . . . it would not be surprising if a receptiveness to change expressed itself as a heightened orientation to job mobility among autonomous workers. Such workers might realize that their productivity depends less on the identities of their employers and more on access to the means of production coupled with unfettered exercise of their skills. This would promote "attachment to skill" (e.g., profession, craft, etc.) insofar as such workers might not much care for whom they work as long as they have the opportunity to employ their productive resources . . . . [1989:583]

Here we start with variables as actors ("receptiveness . . . expressed itself as a heightened orientation") and then move into a several-step real narrative, with real actors, even though their acts are mere reflections about the real activity of changing jobs. Note that the reality of narrative is undermined by the subjunctive verbs; the authors are worried because such an alternative narrative has unmeasured steps. They are really happy only with very simple case action or direct "action" by variables.

In summary, most narrative sentences here have variables as subjects; it is when a variable "does something" narratively that the authors think themselves to be speaking most directly of causality. For anything unexpected, however, the level of real (case) narrativity rises, both in the number of steps in the narrative chain and in the replacement of variables as subjects by workers themselves. Finally, methodological restrictions allow only one narrative, which must cover the stories of all the cases, although the search for alternative variables betokens a covert assumption that causality is logically dependent on narration. We should recall that the realist metaphysics implicit in treating variables (universals) as agents was last taken seriously in the age of Aquinas. Of course, the official position of sociological positivism on variables is a nominalist one, but in this quite typical paper the "best" causal sentences are clearly realist ones in which variables act.

So cases do rather little here. What are their characteristics besides weak agency? They are made uniform by virtue of their following identical narratives. They are made enduring and fixed by the models, which treat them as such in all ways except those "varying" in the model. The rhetoric inevitably implicit in an individual study means that their only significant qualities are those defined by their relevance to that study's dependent variable – attachment. The cases are thus not complex entities whose character is simplified in this model, but characterless entities "complexified" by the variables that assign properties to them. To the extent that cases do emerge and act, they follow a very simple rational calculation scheme whose parameters are set by the actual realities of their situation. All the action lies in the parameters; the cases, even when they are reflecting workers, simply register the rational calculator's obvious decision among varying incentives.

We can test this analysis by applying it to the next paper, Eliza Pavalko's (1989) examination of interstate variation in the adoption of workmen's compensation. Pavalko's piece has the additional merit of invoking another of the standard methods of positivism, event-history methods. Perhaps this technique, whose name promises a focus on events and history, will deal more graciously with the activities of cases. Another interesting variation is that the cases are states, rather than biological individuals; we must thus encounter the hydra of methodological individualism.

The author begins by discussing prior case studies, early analyses of policy adoption that generally followed the case method. She then gives us a justification for moving beyond these.

Analyses of the actors and interests involved in the adoption of workmen's compensation have indicated some of the pressures for adoption. But this most visible level of politics cannot show underlying aspects of the political process that "shape the agenda of politics and the relative priority of issues and solutions" (Offe 1984, p. 159). To address this underlying level we need to shift our focus from individual actors to macroindicators that shaped politicians' perceptions of the need for workmen's compensation, the range of possible decisions and the consequences of their action or inaction. [1989:593]

Immediately, then, we get a defense of the emergent macrolevel against the methodological individualists, who attribute all activity to biological individuals, although in this case perhaps allowing for individual interest groups. Note that the shift is as much from the material to the cultural as from micro to macro; the macro (material) indicators are important for their cultural effects (i.e., on perception). That the move from microlevel to macrolevel involves such information issues directly recalls the Halaby and Weakliem "cases," who, in their limited role as actors, made rationally reflective decisions *only within the bounds of their information*. Here, too, individuals are presumed to be straightforward rational calculators. And since all types of individuals exist in most states (legislators, businessmen, etc.), there should be no difference in policy adoption unless their knowledge varies across states. Since that knowledge is in turn largely shaped by the "real" environment, variables driving real differences in that real environment (i.e., variables at the state, emergent level) have causal priority in the system. The justification for treating the states as cases, that is, involves the simplifying assumption of a rational-action paradigm for individual actors. (In fact, the author will ultimately move to such a model for states.[6])

Pavalko's first hypothesis concerns business interests.

The employer's liability system was a problem for employers, particularly those in big business, because of high cost and unpredictability of long court battles. [1989:598]

This variable gets no narrative justification at all. It is simply presented as an implied condition for action. Since actor *a* has interest *x*, actor *a* will do act *y*. Costly, unpredictable court battles will make big business want workmen's compensation, and hence workmen's compensation will appear. Of course, there may be intervening steps, but the underlying notion is that even at the state level, it suffices to provide a one-step implicit justificatory narrative based on rational-action assumptions. Virtually all the other variables get the same sort of treatment. A short, simple phrase establishing that a certain actor had certain interests or faced certain conditions is coupled with the assumption that actors will act on their interests, and together they produce a one-step narrative running from condition to action via interest. There are about a dozen variables so proposed.

Only one longer story is told. On my theory, that will prove to be, first, the author's and, second, the one that gets empirically supported. The predictions are correct. On page 599, we get a much more complicated narrative, too long to quote, which goes basically as follows. (I give it in exact order, which, as can be seen, is not proper chronological order.)

1. Workmen's compensation meant that guilt didn't need to be established.

2. Which meant that changes in the labor process that increased both productivity and accidents could be rationalized as "inevitable outcomes of progress."
3. Legislators were interested in increasing productivity because their jobs depended on it.
4. Poor management of labor/management relations could result in low productivity.
4a. Court disputes on accidents are an indicator of bad relations.
5. Workmen's compensation, because of 1 and 2, could solve 4 and 4a.
6. Hence workmen's compensation arrives.

After the empirical material, this story is again recounted, in proper narrative order this time (pp. 608–9). It is the chief subject of the paper's conclusions.

Overall the narrative sentences in Pavalko's paper are quite similar to those in Halaby and Weakliem's. Most of them reduce activity to a one-step rational-action model. Except for those in the last, complex story, none allows contingency over several steps or between variables or events. Even in the last story, everything dovetails to produce one result; there are no real accidents or contingencies. Nor do any of these narratives really involve actors with substantial complexity. The individual-level actors become rational-action ciphers for their interests. The corporate-level actors – the states – are (like the "cases" of Halaby and Weakliem) characterless things. We don't have Iowa or Illinois or Idaho; we have states whose only properties are the values of "main effects" input to the method of partial likelihood. The cases' only significant qualities are those hypothesized to bear on workmen's compensation in this model. Furthermore, these qualities act in isolation from one another and without regard to narrative sequence. And finally, the level of narrativity again rises for the unexpected and the authorial.

There is one new aspect to the relation of case and narrative here, however. It has to do with how many cases there really are. In the body of the paper, we lose sight of the fact – clear in the opening discussion of a couple of cases (states) – that in fact we have simply 48 stories here. Estimating the parameters using standard partial-likelihood methods pretends that what we really have is 369 cases. (Each state appears once for each year in which it lacks a compensation law as well as once for the year in which it acquires one.) All of these are seen as independent realizations of a stochastic process. Now to the historian there are only 48 stories at the group level, although obviously there are many more at the individual level. Those 48 stories are very complex ones; that is really the problem. But in the paper the 48 complex, chained narratives are made to seem like 369 independent, one-step narratives and the "causal" steps in those 369 stories all become one-step rational-action stories (as in Halaby and Weakliem). This occurs because the methods disregard the connections between the actually connected narrative steps that are documented in the historians' case studies. "Case," therefore, has a very different sense here than in a case study of workmen's compensation in, say, Massachusetts. To say that "Massachusetts is a case . . ." raises one set of issues in both types of study. But Pavalko treats "Massachusetts in 1913" as a case independent of "Massachusetts in 1912." Not only spatial but also temporal lines distinguish cases.[7]

Narratives in these standard positivist articles contrast very strongly with those in William Bridges and Robert Nelson's article (1989) on gender inequality in hierarchical pay systems, the third article in the November 1989 *American Journal of Sociology*. Here the authors analyze a single "case" (the State of Washington civil-service system). They apply quantitative methods to a universe of individual "cases" *within* that case, but only to establish that a baseline pay model doesn't work because of gender inequalities. The actual explanation of those inequalities occurs in narratives.

The narratives explaining gender inequalities are highly complex, featuring varying actors with varying interests, varying pasts, and varying motives. Not only do agents have the simple rational motivations of the other articles [as does the union, the American Federation of State, County, and Municipal Employees (AFSCME), for example] but also they act on the basis of custom (the finance departments) and bias (numerous groups throughout the system). Bridges and Nelson view the whole system as too large to narrate or describe fully, but as having consistent results (gender inequality in pay) because of various systematically interlocked contingencies. For example, AFSCME lobbies in a particular way and opposes all splinter groups (and therefore specifically female splinter groups) because they contest its turf. But this in turn moves active "equity concerns" into the splinter groups, which feel they can't cooperate with agency heads, who tend, for historical reasons, to be male and hence problematic for the female splinter groups. This leaves AFSCME negotiating most of the other issues, including male pay grievances (because only the female ones are likely to be taken to the more vocal female splinter groups). Since AFSCME, again for various historical reasons, happens to negotiate pretty well and tends to succeed in getting raises when it is active, these raises therefore tend to be disproportionately for men.

In this article, then, we have narrativity and complexity. As before, but much less apologetically, they are introduced to account for results inexplicable in standard models, here the "administered efficiency" model for salary determination. Narrative allows interaction of attributes to take causal priority. It is not the variables of union success, union opposition to competitors, and percent male in major power positions that determine, as main effects, the pay inequalities in a system. Rather it is the interaction of an AFSCME that is both successful and anti-splinter and agency heads that tend to be male. Particular interactions, not independent variables, determine the course of social narratives.

What then do cases do in standard positivist analysis? For the most part, they do little. Narrative sentences usually have variables as subjects. For anything unexpected and for the authorial hypothesis, the level of narrativity rises in various ways. When cases do do something, it is generally conceived as a simple rational calculation. All particularity lies in the parameters of calculation. Since only the parameters change, there are no complex narratives; narratives are always one-step decisions. There are no real contingencies or forkings in the road. There is simply the high road of the variables and the rest – which is error.

Furthermore, cases themselves are largely undifferentiated and uniform, since in most models they all have to follow the same narrative, which is couched as a narrative of acting variables, not of acting individuals. Cases are characterless; they have no qualities other than those hypothesized to determine the dependent variable, and even those qualities act in isolation from one another. The case is constructed, built up parsimoniously out of main effects, rather than deconstructed by simplifying its complexity.

The single-case narrative

In a way, it is hardly surprising that cases can't do much and that they all act alike within this analytic world. In fact, we generally think that only individual case studies can really "be narrative" and that only population studies can really "be analytic." Let us consider, then, what cases do and how they are individualized in single-case studies where narrative *is* involved. Having done that, we will then be ready to see whether there are multicase approaches that can preserve some of the desirable properties that cases have in single-case studies.[8]

The first step of the single-case narrative is delimiting the case itself, what historiographers have called the "central subject problem" (Hull 1975). There are many varieties of central subjects in historical case studies, for subjects need not be social actors or groups. They can be events (World War I), social groups (the Oneida Community), or even states of affairs (the structure of politics on the accession of George III). The crucial difficulty (a subject of much historiographical conflict) lies in drawing boundaries around the central subject given the continuous character of the social manifold. Note how this difficulty is avoided by the population/analytic approach, which tends to work with populations where cases are unambiguously distinct (biological individuals, states) and to feel uncomfortable with populations where they are not (classes, pressure groups).

Once the case is delimited, the unity of the "case" (as social actor, for example) is held to require that case attributes take their meaning from the "case context." Thus, if 40% of psychiatrists are members of the APA, then the meaning, that is, the narrative potential (which, as we have seen, in the positivist approach actually determines the causal power), of that occurrence arises from whether that is a big or small number for psychiatrists, given the past and given their other kinds of organizational life and activities. The meaning of this 40% *does not* arise from the fact that it is less than the 60% of lawyers in the ABA or the 75% of doctors in the AMA, and so forth, as in the population/analytic approach cited earlier, where attributes are independently defined (cf. Abell 1987:chap. 2). The two approaches thus differ sharply in their reading of the ontological status of cases as social entities. The single-case-narrative view is that cases may be deconstructed; they start off whole and get simplified. The population/analytic view is that they start out with mere existence, to which properties are added.

The two views also differ in that the case/narrative approach allows the "case" to be transformed in fundamental ways. Unlike Pavalko, a historian of welfare policy in Massachusetts might be quite interested in the implications of legislative turnover for workmen's compensation. Not only such microtransformation is allowed, but also transformation in essence: from death to life or life to death, from one unit to two, from two cases to one to two split along some new line. That is, case narratives can mix demographic and (variable-type) analytic happenings in ways forbidden by the case concept implicit in the population/analytic studies discussed earlier. There, caseness has to do with endurance and thingness; appearance, disappearance, combination, and transformation are problematic and must be treated as censoring, group disappearance, or some other makeshift. (This reinforces the tendency in such methods to emphasize "irreducible" things like biological individuals as cases.) Thus, in population/analytic approaches demographic and causal explanations can be and are explicitly separated, as by Stinchcombe (1968), and with hypertrophy of methods within each, there results a real problem when they must be combined. Yet within the case/narrative approach transformation in attributes can be so extreme that a case which began as an instance of one category may complete a study as an instance of another; a state can become a nation, a craft can become a profession, and so on.

Thus the ontology of cases differs sharply in population/analytic and case/narrative approaches. The former requires rigidly delimitable cases, assigns them properties with trans-case meanings, builds cases on the foundation of simple existence, and refuses all fundamental transformations. The latter, by contrast, assumes cases will have fuzzy boundaries, takes all properties to have case-specific meanings, analyzes by simplifying presumably complex cases, and allows, even focuses on, case transformation. These differences in the ontology of cases are further magnified by the handling of narrative, by saying what it is that cases do. Describing what the case does or endures is what philosophers of history call the colligation problem. It has several subparts. [See Abbott (1984) for an extended discussion and references.]

The first is identifying the events involved. Events, like concepts in more familiar methods, are hypotheticals. Every historian considers dozens of indicating occurrences when deciding whether a given event has taken place. It is one thing to say that ten medical schools have been founded and another to say that the medical profession is deeply concerned about professional education. It is one thing to describe the courses of ten battles, and quite another to identify the turning of the tide in a war. Moreover, these hypothetical events have varying duration and visibility. Interest in professional ethics codes, for example, spread much more rapidly than did interest in professional education, and thus "took less time" as an event. The drive for professional education was a long one and, moreover, was "happening" long before it managed to bear fruit in improved schools. Note the presumption, analogous to that about cases, that events are complex. Events are defined by a whole constellation of attributes and properties. The transformations discussed earlier are excellent examples of such complex events. Cases may thus do or endure a wide variety of things, each of which may be seen as an event arising either in agency (what they do) or in structure (what they endure).

These events must then be arranged in a plot that sets them in the loose causal order that we generally regard as explanatory. For Pavalko's workmen's compensation adoptions, this means finding out the crucial steps in the coming of the policy, finding out who had what kinds of agency with respect to each, what were the critical decisions and their consequences, and who made them, where, how, and with whose help. The coming of the policy is then seen as a sequence of major turning points [events or "kernels" in Barthes's terms; see Chatman (1978)] and sets of situational consequences flowing from those events. An example closely comparable to Pavalko's paper comes from Sutherland's paper (1950) on the adoption of sexual psychopath laws by the various states. There, the kernels are (1) a state of fear, partly national and partly induced by spectacular local events, (2) anxious, agitated activity by diverse groups, and (3) appointment of a committee, often dominated by psychiatrists, which usually produces a sexual-psychopath law. What matters to Sutherland are the contingencies that push a state along this path or turn a state off it, not general variables that may or may not have importance depending on how far the process has gone.

By contrast, in the population/analytic approach, plot has a different definition and a different role. If we represent each case at each time by a point in a variable space, finding the plot is a matter of connecting the dots of time$_1$, time$_2$, etc. This plot is basically continuous. To be sure, population/analytic methods must in practice treat the measures in each case's story – the measures of having control and being attached and seeking alternate employment for Halaby and Weakliem's workers – as discrete, because they are measured only occasionally. But they are in causal theory continuously measurable. (This contrasts directly with the case/narrative assumption of finite duration, which would treat these "measures" at time t as "events." In such methods, no variable need be observed at all times; maybe the worker sometimes doesn't care about control or attachment!) There are many questions about similarities among these continuous tracks (narrative plots) that cannot be addressed by linear transformation models (with their continuity assumptions), because such similarities can be found only by looking "along the tracks" for similarities. It is striking that the population/analytic model does not perform this search for resemblance in "plot," in the case/narrative sense, but rather assumes (because it has to) an identical plot at an abstract level, that of the effect parameters. The parameters are implicitly justified by referring all the cases to a single isomorphic plot at the level of case narrative. The result is thus a peculiar bootstrapping, in which the theoretical dominance of the narrative plot is conceded, but its variety must be homogenized because the variables "plot" can admit only one narrative plot.[9]

The move from population/analytic approach to case/narrative approach is thus a move first to a new way of regarding cases – as fuzzy realities with autonomously defined complex properties – and a move second to seeing cases as engaged in a perpetual dialogue with their environment, a dialogue of action and constraint that we call plot.

The idea that we ought to think about social processes in terms of complex cases going through plots has its own problems, however.

There are three principal ones. The first is that plots intersect. A given event has many immediate antecendents, each of which has many immediate antecedents, and conversely a given event has many consequents, each of which has many consequents. One can write studies considering all the antecedents of a given event, a genre illustrated by Fay's (1966) celebrated analysis of the origins of World War I, and one can equally write studies considering the descendants of an event, as in Keynes's (1920) discussion of that war's economic consequences. But of course these causes and consequences lie in the genealogies of other events as well – just as one's grandparents have other grandchildren and one's grandchildren other grandparents. The plots of the case/narrative approach must assume away this network character of historical causality.

Another problem with plot is its ontological status as a social reality. Hayden White (1973) has argued that there are really only four kinds of historical plots:

1. Tragedy (everyone tries to be reasonable, but gets in a muddle anyway), a genre illustrated by Tocqueville on the French Revolution.
2. Comedy (everyone is awful, but things turn out all right in the end), a genre illustrated by von Ranke's historical writings.
3. Romance (light emerges from darkness), a genre illustrated by Michelet.
4. Irony (things always get worse, and the historian's writing about them won't help anyway), a genre illustrated by Burkhardt's writings.

White's paradigm is a little overdone, but still has important implications. Certainly sociologists are by now quite used to heavily emplotted (because heavily politicized) narrative theories; the labeling theory of deviance and the Marxist theory of class conflict are examples. We should thus be seriously worried about whether plot is ever anything other than an analyst's dream, is ever really there in the social process.

A related problem is the implicit assumption that subsections of the social process have beginnings, middles, and ends, rather than simple endless middles. Why is Muncie in 1895 a beginning? What happens when *Middletown in Transition* is written, redefining *Middletown* (in the 1920s) as not a middle, but rather a beginning? Are there really ends? Of course, World War II comes to an end, but do its consequences? Now clearly, individuals can have finite life courses, as do some social entities. So, as in the population/analytic approach, there are some pressures here for studying biological individuals and other definite, finite social entities. But with other kinds of entities, like nations and commercial organizations, the issue of plot as having beginning, middle, and end – the issue usually called periodization – is a major problem.[10]

It is hardly fair to ask what cases do in population/analytic methods without asking the inverse question of what becomes of analytic concerns in case/narrative approaches: How in fact do narratives explain? In a curious way the answer to this question doesn't much matter, for narrative is where positivists turn when reasoning in variables fails, and of course a particular narrative is what is rejected if an entailed set of variable relationships is implausible or incorrect. But still, in practice, variables are what matter in the positivist approach. The question remains of how explanation works in the case/narrative approach, where we don't have the facile language of variables to help us ask questions about causality.

This problem has supported a celebrated literature in the philosophy of history. There are three basic models for "historical" explanation. The first is the covering-law model of Carl Hempel (1942). Historians, on this argument, use social science "laws" that cover a given case in order to further understand that particular case. Popper (1950:448) argued to the contrary that all social covering laws are trivial (the classic example being that people do what they are interested in doing), an argument he would undoubtedly apply to the interest-action law implicit in the first two studies discussed earlier. He ultimately came to believe that the covering-law model was worthless because all the real explanatory action was in the side conditions specifying which covering laws hold, i.e., what the case is a case of. (Cf. Walton's argument presented in Chapter 5.)

The covering-law model has the further conspicuous disadvantage that historians themselves usually reject it. A more congenial model is the "understanding" model of Collingwood (1946), Dray (1957), and many others, which deals to some extent with Popper's issue of side conditions. According to Collingwood, the historian aims to get inside a historical figure's own justification of action, to understand what was "reasonable" given that figure's tastes and conditions. [The reasonable is not necessarily the rational, although one might make rationality one version of reasonability, as Stinchcombe (1990) recently argued.] The Collingwood position is thus a broadened version of current rational-choice theory; the historian figures out "what it made sense for the actor to do," given the actor's beliefs, knowledge, and psychology. This view has been seen by recent philosophers of history as an extreme "idealist" one, given to dangerous subjectivism, and at present it is probably the most philosophically discredited view of historical explanation, precisely because of our difficulty in reconstructing past dispositions. It is thus quite paradoxical that this view is also at the heart of such narrative as we do see in analytic/positivist sociology. The two approaches differ only in how one finds the "context of decision": by intuition/ reconstruction (in Collingwoodian history) or by positivist measure (in the articles analyzed here). It is also worth noting that while Colling-wood's view is discredited among philosophers of history, the kinds of explanations it defends are used daily by historians.

The third principal view of narrative explanation is the "followabil-ity" view of W. B. Gallie (1968). Like Collingwood's constructionism, this view attempts to describe how narrative history actually works. On this argument narrative is itself explanatory by virtue of truth, consis-tent chronology, and a coherent central subject. Narrative is held to combine things that are determined by general laws with things that are contingent, producing a plausible, because followable, story. This no-tion of combination is much looser than the formalities of the covering-law model, but still leaves a place for general determinism that is missing in the Collingwoodian position.

The case/narrative approach to explanation thus differs from the population/analytic one in important ways. It ignores "variables" (in its language, "types of events") when they aren't narratively important, whereas population/analytic approaches must always treat all included variables as equally salient (although perhaps differing in coefficient). This means that case/narrative explanation follows the causal action. Rather than assuming universal or constant relevance, it explains only "what needs to be explained" and lets the rest of things slide along in background. This selective attention goes along with an emphasis on contingency. Things happen because of constellations of factors, not because of a few fundamental effects acting independently.[11] And the roving focus of the case/narrative approach has another distinct advan-tage over the population/analytic approach. It need make no assump-tion that all causes lie on the same analytical level (as in standard sociological models). Tiny events (assassinations) can have a big effect.

Sociological narratives

Not all narratives, however, concern only one case. Quite the contrary. Often we think that many cases follow similar narratives. A distinguished sociological tradition has considered this issue of universal narratives. Robert Park and a generation of his students developed a concept of "natural history" that generalized developmental narratives for gangs, marriages, revolutions, and occupational careers. Park's whole conception of social life was decidedly in terms of events. In his introduction to Lyford Edwards's *Natural History of Revolution* (1927), Park wrote:

[That there are tactics of revolutions] presupposes the existence of something typical and generic in these movements – something that can be described in general terms. It presupposes in short the existence of materials for a scientific account of revolution since science – natural science – in the long run is little more than a description in conceptual terms of the processes by which events take place, together with explanations which permit events to be predicted and controlled. . . . Like industrial crises, revolutions, when they do occur, tend to describe in their evolution a characteristic cycle of change. . . . What remains to be done is to reduce this revolutionary cycle not merely to a conceptual but to a temporal sequence, one in which the series of changes through which every revolutionary movement tends to pass are so determined and accurately described that they can be measured in temporal units. [Edwards 1927:x, xiii]

Thus, Park saw causal analysis as secondary to description, and saw description as narrative in its fundamental approach.

Among the strongest works of the natural-history tradition were narrative studies of single cases, notably Clifford Shaw's celebrated studies of Stanley the jack roller (Shaw 1930) and Sidney the delinquent (Shaw 1931). Yet these great cases had less impact in upholding narrative analysis in sociology than one might have expected. In the first place, both Shaw and later commentators emphasized the rich detail of the data more than its narrative character per se. Second, although Shaw did argue that the meaning of current events tended to be dictated by past sequences of events, he in fact saw this process as less contingent than directed. In both his great cases, the fundamental image was one of convergence toward a personality type that sustained the delinquency activities. He quoted W. I. Thomas on this subject:

It appears that behavior traits and their totality as represented by the personality are the outcome of a series of definitions of situations with resulting reactions and their fixation in a body of attitudes or psychological sets. [Shaw 1930:13, citing Thomas 1925]

Shaw's purpose was

to show that the habits, attitudes, and philosophy of life underlying these criminal acts were built up gradually through the successive social experiences of the offender over a period of years. [One should see delinquency] not as an isolated act, but in its relation to the mental and physical condition of the offender, the whole sequence of events in his life and the social and cultural situations in which his delinquent behavior occurred. [Shaw 1931:xiii]

Delinquency studies took this "convergent" narrative form automatically, for they were concerned only with individuals who ended up at a particular point and with the paths that brought them to that point. The convergence narrative was one they shared with, for example, the great Freudian case narratives, by which they were indeed somewhat influenced. Only many years later did others become interested in what became of Stanley later on, that is, in the whole of the narrative of his life (Snodgrass 1982).

Other writers in the Park tradition more explicitly emphasized the narrative approach. Park himself set forth the famous "race-relations cycle" in a 1926 paper. Edwards's *Natural History of Revolution* appeared in 1927, as did Mowrer's *Family Disorganization* and Thrasher's *The Gang*. All three used "natural history" to refer explicitly to an expected order or pattern of events. For Park's colleague Ernest W. Burgess, however, "natural history" meant less a specific narrative or pattern of particular events than the general notion that biological and ecological metaphors effectively oriented the investigator (Burgess 1925). Hence in his work, as in much of the work derived from the Chicago Area Project, there was a sense of temporality, even of "succession," but a greater reluctance to identify a specific set of events in a specific pattern or patterns. Reckless's *Vice in Chicago* (1933) was a prototype of this looser view of natural history, which was also illustrated in the magisterial *Juvenile Delinquency and Urban Areas* of Shaw and McKay (1942). A number of works, particularly Cressey's *Taxi-Dance Hall* (1932), but also Mowrer's and Thrasher's books, combined both Park's detailed-sequence model for one aspect of their topic with Burgess's looser "successional" approach for another.

Even in Thrasher, Mowrer, Edwards, and Cressey the image of narrative was fairly loose. First, early stages were often defined in a deliberately vague way. For Edwards, for example, there were "preliminary" and then "advanced" symptoms of unrest: mobility and rising expectations among the former, new intellectual allegiances and "oppression psychosis" among the latter. None of these was absolutely necessary, nor did they necessarily come in a particular order. Mowrer's early stages were "loss of respect" and "pattern of life tension," and he explicitly regarded each as a summary of subordinate sequences of events. Thrasher regarded a spontaneous play-group as becoming a gang when it began "to excite disapproval and opposition," but did not say whose the disapproval was or what its specific objects were. Park's own "assimilation" and "accommodation" were of course more abstract still.

Second, unlike Shaw with his convergence plots, the natural historians tended to see their "plots" as diverging. Thrasher ended up with five kinds of gangs arising in various ways, as well as numerous routes off the main track throughout the process (spontaneous disintegration, etc.). Many of Cressey's taxi-dancers dropped out without becoming recruited to the cyclical process of degradation he outlined. Mowrer argued that the same overall process of events obtained for marriages whether they culminated in organization or in disorganization.

This did not mean, of course, a surrender of the narrative approach, nor a denial of its utility. Rather, Park and his students recognized the complexities of social narratives and adjusted for them by avoiding a simple and rigid sequence theory. Subsequent writers in this line have followed the same approach. Probably the strongest single line of "natural historians" surviving after World War II were the students of occupations taught by Everett Hughes, himself a student of both Park and Burgess. Oswald Hall, Howard Becker, Rue Bucher, and others continued to apply natural-history metaphors for decades. Usually, as in Bucher and Strauss's influential 1961 paper on professions, the image was Burgess's looser one of a competitive ecology. In Hall's equally influential 1949 paper on medicine, however, the image was again one of stages, loosely defined in the manner of Thrasher, Mowrer, and Edwards. Articles taking these natural-history approaches to occupations have continued to the present (e.g., Bucher 1988) and currently are central in the social-problems literature (Spector and Kitsuse 1987).

In a way it is clear why the narrative image survived best in the study of occupations. In the study of revolutions, its chief rival was the unique case history, which could retain immensely more detail. Indeed, when Skocpol wrote her comparative analysis of revolutions in 1979, Edwards was still a relevant reference, so little comparative work had been done since (Skocpol 1979:37). In the study of the family and of delinquency, by contrast, the immense number of cases meant that the chief competitor was aggregate, global analysis. Already in the 1920s, in studies of the family, for example, there were two schools. The "interactional" approach was founded on Meadean social psychology and rested on Burgess-type ecological analysis of differing rates. The "social-change" approach looked at overall social developments and related these to societywide variables (Komarovsky and Waller 1945; Nimkoff 1948). The latter approach, under the leadership of William Ogburn and others, was to mature in the 1930s as the "social-trends" approach and to dominate social research generally. In such an approach, there was only one narrative – that of the whole society – and so comparative narrative disappeared as a problem. That occupations survived as an island of natural-history methods reflects the object of study itself. Too many for an exhaustive set of case studies, too few and too ill-defined for aggregate or global analysis, occupations nonetheless showed fertile and complex historical developments that required some form of temporal theorizing.

The problem, in one sense, with the Chicago narrative approach at its best – exemplified by Cressey, Mowrer, or Thrasher – was that it retained so much information about individuals, about narratives, about groups. One way to reduce that complexity was to cut the narratives into pieces and investigate the "causal power" of each step. In studies of delinquency and race relations that is clearly what happened. The individual steps in the early Chicago narratives ultimately became the little plausibility stories justifying the analysis of this or that variable. These steps, that is, led to the rhetoric of analysis so clearly demonstrated in the opening section of this essay. Lyman's 1968 paper on the race-relations cycle urged precisely this dissection of a "theory" into a set of "models," and Aldrich's later review of ecological succession (1975) recognized (there was no longer a real need to urge) the same thing. This was not a rapid process, for clearly generations of writers survived to whom the variable-based analyses were supplements to the underlying narrative masterpieces. But it began in the Ogburn social-trends era. Blumer wrote the first of several critiques of the concept of "a variable" in 1931, and clearly wrote it from a narrative standpoint.

Multicase narratives

This brief history of the fate of universal-narrative models in sociology serves to introduce my closing discussion. We are often interested in universal narratives, that is, in narratives we expect to observe, with minor variation, across a number of cases. As we have seen, the single-case approach permits narrative to function in a fluid and powerful way. By contrast, narrative functions virtually formalistically in most multicase positivist work, even though there, too, narrative is seen as the final, ultimate source of explanation. But I have implied throughout that we must disentangle these dichotomies. The difference between population and case approaches is not the same as the difference between analytic and narrative approaches. Hence we must consider the issue of multiple-case *narratives*, which can also be regarded as the issue of demonstrating common narratives across many cases or as the issue of what to do when one's "cases" are narratives. The Chicago writers dealt with all of these questions, but failed to articulate narrative study with the emerging forms of analysis one can loosely call "causal." [For a history of the latter, see Bernert (1983).] It is that articulation – or in some cases the formal reasons for the lack of it – that I am seeking to outline in this essay.

The Chicago work shows that there is no inherent reason why narratives can be given only for single cases, and indeed they are particularly important for analyzing small numbers of cases (Stinchcombe 1978). There is a simple reason for this. When a universe consists of thousands of cases, we are generally happy to separate the case-study literature and the population/analytic literature – Halaby and Weakliem's workers versus, say, Michael Burawoy's (1979). But where the universe is smaller, as in Pavalko's 48 states, we are considerably less willing to make the sharp separation, in part because we are likely to have single-case studies of a substantial fraction of the universe. In such situations, population/analytic approaches seem to reject too much important information. Their discussions seem thin and insubstantial beside the vibrant richness of the narrative case studies. And since cases are fewer, it seems that population-level analysts ought to retain more of the relevant information. But strangely the constraints of methods (in particular of degrees of freedom) mean that the smaller the number of cases, the less the information quantitative methods can work with. The relation between the case-study and population approaches thus becomes most difficult in this middle range.[12]

Among the important information rejected by population/analytic approaches is the narrative sequence of events in the various cases. With appropriate methods, however, one can study this sequence and see whether universal narratives appear across cases. It is absolutely central to realize that we can become concerned about narrative without becoming concerned about all the other simplifying assumptions made in the population/analytic approach. Thus we need not question the assumption that cases are not related to each other in some sort of structure (in which case diffusion, constraint, and dominance might determine things we otherwise attribute to the independent variables) or the assumption that case attributes have unique and distinguishable meanings (otherwise the complexity and ambiguity of each case and its properties requires hermeneutic methods). These, too, are fundamental simplifying assumptions in positivism, and, in what follows, I am going to continue making them. That is, I will deal with one problematic assumption of standard approaches but not the others. The networks literature – which deals with the structure assumption just given – does much the same thing for the structure assumption.[13]

There are different types of universal narratives, which can be ranked from strictly to loosely specified. At the highly specified end of the continuum are stage theories, where we believe in a common sequence of unique events. We may expect some deviations from it, but generally anticipate an autonomous, steady pattern. Familiar examples include developmental psychological theories (Piaget), developmental models of economies (Rostow), and, within sociology, theories of collective behavior (Smelser), family life cycle (Glick), professionalization (Wilensky), dialectical materialism (Marx), and comparative revolutions (Skocpol). Much of the literature on stage theories has focused on telling the stages apart – this was a major problem with Rostow – but the idea of stage theories is well established in social science.

A second, less well specified form of universal narrative occurs in what I shall call career theories. Career theories emphasize the interaction of causes, the mixture of structure and determination, the dialectic of necessary and sufficient causality. Here there is less expectation of regular patterns, although such patterns are still to some extent evident. Events often repeat, durations are unpredictable, opportunity shapes history. Also, agency here plays a larger role. Examples are job histories (White, Spilerman) and processes of labeling for deviants (Scheff, Goffman). Perhaps because there are more cases available (the universes are larger), this area has seen extensive formal modeling, although most of it has disaggregated careers into individual transitions. [For an elegant example combining many approaches, see Faulkner (1983).]

The most indeterminate of narrative models are models I shall call interactionist. They are indeterminate partly because they emphasize structure; even more than in careers, patterned relations shape the developments of the future. Yet paradoxically they are also indeterminate because they emphasize interactants' agency, their ability to reshape, often through cultural redefinition, not only the future of a narrative, but its past as well. Some interactionist models emphasize the structure, the field of relations. Examples are the early interactionist analysis of cities (Park, Burgess), more general models of human ecology (Hawley), world-systems theory (Wallerstein), and my own work on the professions. In these structural models, the actual telling of stories is avoided. Rather, authors analyze the structure's ability to favor some kinds of stories and prevent others, the parameters that shape stories within it. Individual stories of cases are told, but largely to illustrate possible patterns. There is little expectation that such stories are characteristic except in illustrating possible patterns, since a fundamental premise of these models is that the various intrastructural narratives are not independent. These models provide not universal narratives themselves, but universal constraining frameworks for narratives.

There are also views of interaction that lack this emphasis on structural constraint. These emphasize the independent agency of interactants, their ability to twist and turn not only the interaction but also the rules governing those moves and their pattern. This is the basic stuff of classic symbolic interactionism and of Goffmanian interaction, formalized in work on conversational analysis. The focus on rules (e.g., for turn-taking) allows the analysts to escape the problem that possible narratives ramify endlessly through the free will of actors.

From a conceptual and methodological point of view, the stricter forms are the easiest types of universal narratives to analyze. Stage or developmental theories hold that a given set of events tends to happen in one of a number of common orders. As I have noted, this issue particularly arises in situations where there is much detailed knowledge of the individual cases, as opposed to those in which cases number in the thousands and are not known in detail. Professions are a good example. If we are interested in characteristic orders of professionalization – from licensing to association to school to journal to ethics code – there are anywhere from 20 to 100 cases, depending on our definitions. There are vast amounts of data on each case (since virtually all are objects of case studies), including exact dates of these and many other events occurring to all of them. Depending on one's assumptions about the relation between causality and the passage of time, there is a variety of directly applicable techniques. One can apply scaling methods to consider order of unique events, which I have done, for example, in studying the development of local American medical communities (Abbott in press). The cases are cities and towns, and the stories are the order in which various professionalizing events occur. And one can apply fancier techniques – the optimal matching/alignment methods of DNA research – to examine direct sequence resemblance in narratives where events repeat. I have done this with stories about the adoption of welfare programs in twenty developed welfare states [Pavalko's issue on a national scale; see Abbott and DeViney (1991)]. Here the cases are nations and the events are the coming of workmen's compensation, pensions, and other major welfare programs. I have also done it with job histories of eighteenth-century German musicians, where the events are holding one of 35 types of jobs in a given year (Abbott and Hrycak 1990). As these elliptical examples make clear, the move from single-case narrative to multicase narrative involves lots of assumptions about cases, plots, events, and their measurement. But it does retain the ability of cases to do something.[14]

In many ways the stage-theory case is straightforward. It is much more challenging to develop narratives for the general "career" type of narrative. Here the assumption of a relatively plotlike development is unjustified because the narrative can take sudden, "interactive" turns under the impact of external constraints or indeed of other narratives. In methodology, this issue raises the difficulty of models for mutual constraint, models in which stories of the different cases aren't independent. There is a small literature on this problem, starting with Harrison White's *Chains of Opportunity* (1970).

But the more difficult problem is not methodological, but conceptual. The conflation of narrative with single-case analysis has hidden from us the importance of building conceptual models for narrative steps. In the single-case narrative, each step need only be told; it need not be conceived as a version of a more generic type of event. I have discussed elsewhere (Abbott 1984) certain issues of conceptualization of events in multicase narrative research. These concern aggregating occurrences into conceptual events (as discussed earlier) and measuring the latter with the former. But those issues concern a very low level of generality. The more important problem in conceptualizing multicase narratives comes at the general level. We need generic models for types of causality and for "narrative steps." This issue is unfamiliar in the population/analytic techniques, for there causal steps need little conceptualization. They are loosely attached to ideal-typical narratives, but are themselves seen as unproblematic. "Worker control causes worker attachment" has its scientific ring precisely because the real problems of conceptualization are hidden in the implicit narrative. But with multicase narrative models these problems come out into the open. [For an interesting example, see McPhee (1963:184–234).]

The issue of generic types of links in social causal chains was raised many years ago by Arthur Stinchcombe (1968). Stinchcombe laid out a series of causal processes that produce sequential patterns: functional, demographic, and historicist. These are one-step causal patterns that produce characteristic social sequences when iterated over the long term. The functional one, for example, produces sequences where departures from some equilibrium continually alternate with reestablishments of that equilibrium. Historicism produces sequences converging and stabilizing on a level. One notes other kinds of generic sequences – oscillating ones produced by "harmonic" causal links (Kroeber on fashion) and schismogenetic ones produced by "conflict exacerbating" links (Marx on class conflict).

At a somewhat less general level, any conceptual distinction produces a set of potential generic narrative links at a somewhat less general level. Thus, if we are interested in the relation between social structure and culture, Berger and Luckmann (1967) give useful names for narrative links in which the bonds of the two break down in certain ways. The process by which social structures lose their grounding in culture and develop an autonomous, continuing, often routine character, Berger and Luckmann call institutionalization. An "institutionalization link" in a narrative is thus one in which the chief event is a loosening of these bonds. Conversely, the process of reforging those bonds, they (and many others) call legitimation, and such individual narrative steps might be considered legitimation links. The general hypothesis of authors like Weber and Troeltsch is that links of these two kinds tend to follow one another in long cycles rather than short ones, and that shorter cycles are often associated with ruptures in social structure. It may, of course, be that institutionalization is ultimately more certain if it alternates occasionally with (re)legitimation. But the central point is that consistent names might help formulate important hypotheses about patterned narrative changes in social and cultural structure. With terms like these, we can establish generic "plots" to investigate across many cases.

If one considers the micro/macrocharacter of these social and cultural systems, one can create further terminology for generic types of narrative links. Links embodying macroshifts in cultural systems can be called paradigm or style shifts. Links in which microsocial structures align to produce macroshifts can be called collective-action links, and so on. The point of developing these terms is that hypotheses like, for example, Diana Crane's (1972) about changes in science could usefully be cast into the same terminology as, say, White and White's work on *Canvases and Careers* (1965). Rather than reducing these rich studies to justifications for a set of variables in population/analytic studies, we can encode their conclusions as predicting certain kinds of plots for stylistic or scientific changes across cases. Many hypotheses we have investigated with ill-fitting population/analytic methods could better be phrased as narrative models of this kind, allowing for agency and action among cases and for the unity of each case's history.

It follows from my earlier discussion of Pavalko's article that a very valuable set of concepts for generic links would deal with the issues of micro/macrorelations tout court. I shall call these "entity-process" links and close with a brief discussion of them. (Cf. Diane Vaughan's argument in Chapter 8 of this volume.)

The simplest entity processes are familiar from demography, the processes of birth and death. With "irreducible" actors like biological individuals, these tend to be nonproblematic; with emergents like occupations or pressure groups, birth and death are difficult in both conceptualization and measurement. Among other important entity processes are merger and division – again processes that are easily labeled, but not so easily modeled. All four of these processes are centrally important events in narratives of social processes, and, for emergents, at least, all four require far more careful conceptualization than is presently available.

Another fundamental entity process is microtransformation – transformation of the microlevel of an emergent group with or without transformation of its macroidentity or macroproperties. A first type of microtransformation is turnover, which can happen through migration and replacement, through a restructuring of member life cycle in the group, or through new sources of recruitment, bringing new individuals with fundamentally different attributes into a group. All of this can occur with or without any formal change in macroproperties like a group's self-definition or ideologies.

A second version of microtransformation is internal metamorphosis, the change of member properties without turnover. This can happen through aging, collective action, or other processes in which the emergent properties of the group may (or sometimes may not) sharply change simply because of internal changes (often *common* changes) among members. Finally, microtransformation may occur through microstructural change. The internal arrangements of a group may change in ways that may affect its aggregate properties and its recruitment patterns. Internal hierarchies may lead to internal divisions. Or internal reorganization may fundamentally transform the acting character of a group.

Still another entity process is macrotransformation, fundamental change of the emergent entity without concurrent microchange. A first version of macrotransformation concerns change in basic properties of the emergent without constituent change. Occupational characteristics can change rapidly even though members don't change through turnover and other processes. In such cases macrotransformation may change the underlying meaning of the occupation for the individuals involved. A more subtle macrotransformation occurs when change in macroattributes occurs *without* affecting what we might call the "structural meaning" of the variables. The professions provide an excellent example. No nineteenth-century professional would regard any American professional of the late twentieth century as "a professional." The modern professional relies too much on others, works too often in congregate situations and too often for other people, advertises like a common tradesman, and so on. Yet the late-twentieth-century professional occupies much the same *relative* place in today's labor force as did the nineteenth-century professional in yesterday's. Professionals still hold pride of place. The content of that pride is different, but its structural meaning remains the same. This kind of macrotransformation, which we might call structural isomorphism, is common in temporal studies.

This discussion brings me less to the end of this essay than into the beginning of another. To develop a serious catalogue of "narrative steps" that sociologists consider so often as to need standardized names for them is a substantial project. I have indicated some of the directions here, building on earlier work (Abbott 1983). But the logical foundations of the effort lie in issues of case. It is because population/analytic approaches deal so poorly with the activity and ontology of cases that we tend to turn to single-case narratives. Only by analyzing single-case narrative in detail can we discover the aspects of narration and caseness that make it so attractive. But my contention here has been that we can and should disentangle the population/case distinction from the analytic/narrative one. By doing so, we may be able to construct new forms of population-level studies based on narrative, forms that retain some of the attention to case activity and case complexity that we find so enticing in the single-case-narrative approach, but that at the same time allow us to create narrative generalizations across cases.

Some readers of this essay see this as a daunting task. They question, too, who might be the audience for it. I think the "impossibility" stems from unfamiliarity. We have all grown accustomed to think in either the causality-variables-population-analytic way or the plot-events-case-narrative way. We have a hard time imagining what it means to generalize narrative, although, as I have said, our sociological ancestors were quite comfortable with it. So I think the impossibility will go away after we've tried narrative generalization a bit and found out what it can do.

This means being pretty simpleminded at first. We can't have complex and subtle analyses until we've had some stumbling and preliminary ones. But there are – and here is the answer to the audience question – many sociologists interested in typical narrative patterns. The life-course theorists want to find out if there are life patterns. The stress analysts want to know if particular sequences lead to stress. The organization theorists want to know if particular patterns lead to successful innovations.[15]

Beyond these lies a broader, policy-minded audience that is presently under the complete sway of population/analytic methods. Regression coefficients now establish the parameters of public policy by providing both liberals and conservatives with "scientific" evidence of who is doing how well and how badly and what "causal forces" lie behind those outcomes. Political figures believe that if we change the parameters or increase people's levels of certain variables, then outcomes will change in some desirable way. If reality actually happens in stories, there is no reason why this should happen.

A social science expressed in terms of typical stories would provide far better access for policy intervention than the present social science of variables. (Cf. Wieviorka's paper, Chapter 7 in this volume.) Anybody who knew the typical stories of organizations under great external and internal stress would never have believed that breaking up AT&T would result in a highly profitable firm and a cheaper overall phone service. But policymakers saw economists' equations proving that profit equaled so many parts research plus so many parts resources plus so many parts market competition and so on. No one bothered to ask whether one could tell a real story that led from AT&T as of 1983 to the vision they had in mind. In fact there wasn't one. And so the phone bills that were to get cheaper got both more expensive and less comprehensible, the research laboratory that was to invent wonderful new devices was dismantled, and the firm achieves its current (short-run) profits by laying off the very scientists who policymakers thought were the foundation of the future. AT&T's major new venture is in credit cards. The population/analytic approach is precisely the social science that said this would not happen. But it all makes great narrative sense.

References

Abbott, Andrew (1983). "Sequences of Social Events." *Historical Methods* 16:129–47.

(1984). "Event Sequence and Event Duration." *Historical Methods* 17:192–204.

(1988). "Transcending General Linear Reality." *Sociological Theory* 6:169–86.

(1990). "Conceptions of Time and Events in Social Science Methods." *Historical Methods* 23:140–50.

(1991). "The Order of Professionalization." *Work and Occupations* 18:355–84.

Abbott, Andrew, and Stanley DeViney (in press). "The Welfare State as Transnational Event." *Social Science History*.

Abbott, Andrew, and Alexander Hrycak (1990). "Measuring Resemblance in Sequence Data." *American Journal of Sociology* 96:144–85.

Abell, Peter (1987). *The Syntax of Social Life*. Oxford: Oxford University Press.

Aldrich, Howard (1975). "Ecological Succession in Racially Changing Neighborhoods." *Urban Affairs Quarterly* 10:327–48.

Allison, Paul (1982). "Discrete-Time Methods for the Analysis of Event Histories," pp. 61–98 in Samuel Leinhardt (ed.), *Sociological Methodology, 1982*. San Francisco: Jossey-Bass.

Berger, Peter and Thomas Luckmann (1967). *The Social Construction of Reality*. New York: Doubleday.

Bernert, C. (1983). "The Career of Causal Analysis in American Sociology." *British Journal of Sociology* 34:230–54.

Blau, Peter B., and Otis D. Duncan (1967). *The American Occupational Structure*. New York: Free Press.

Blumer, Herbert (1931). "Science without Concepts." *American Journal of Sociology* 36:515–33.

Bridges, William P., and Robert L. Nelson (1989). "Markets in Hierarchies." *American Journal of Sociology* 95:616–58.

Bucher, Rue (1988). "On the Natural History of Health Care Occupations." *Work and Occupations* 15:131–47.

Bucher, Rue, and Anselm Strauss (1961). "Professions in Process." *American Journal of Sociology* 66:325–34.

Burawoy, Michael (1979). *Manufacturing Consent*. Chicago: University of Chicago Press.

Burgess, Ernest W. (1925). "The Growth of the City," pp. 47–62 in R. E. Park, E. W. Burgess, and R. D. McKenzie (eds.), *The City.* Chicago: University of Chicago Press.

Chatman, Seymour (1978). *Story and Discourse.* Ithaca: Cornell University Press.

Collingwood, Robin G. (1946). *The Idea of History.* Oxford: Oxford University Press.

Crane, Diana (1972). *Invisible Colleges.* Chicago: University of Chicago Press.

Cressey, Paul G. (1932). *The Taxi-Dance Hall.* Chicago: University of Chicago Press.

Danto, Arthur C. (1985). *Narration and Knowledge.* New York: Columbia University Press.

Dray, William (1957). *Laws and Explanation in History.* Oxford: Oxford University Press.

Edwards, Lyford P. (1927). *The Natural History of Revolution.* Chicago: University of Chicago Press.

Faulkner, Robert (1983). *Music on Demand.* New Brunswick NJ: Transaction.

Fay, Sidney B. (1966). *The Origins of the World War.* New York: Free Press.

Gallie, W. B. (1968). *Philosophy and the Historical Understanding.* New York: Schocken.

Halaby, Charles N., and David L. Weakliem (1989). "Worker Control and Attachment to the Firm." *American Journal of Sociology* 95:549–91.

Hall, Oswald (1949). "Types of Medical Careers." *American Journal of Sociology* 55:243–53.

Hempel, Carl G. (1942). "The Function of General Laws in History." *Journal of Philosophy* 39:35–48.

Hull, David L. (1975). "Central Subjects and Historical Narratives." *History and Theory* 14:253–74.

Kennedy, Peter (1985). *A Guide to Econometrics.* Cambridge, MA: MIT Press.

Keynes, John M. (1920). *The Economic Consequences of the Peace.* New York: Harcourt Brace.

Komarovsky, Mirra, and Willard Waller (1945). "Studies of the Family." *American Journal of Sociology* 50:443–51.

Lyman, Stanford M. (1968). "The Race Relations Cycle of Robert E. Park." *Pacific Sociological Review* 11:16–22.

McPhee, William (1963). *Formal Theories of Mass Behavior.* New York: Free Press.

Mortensen, Dale (1988). "Wages, Separation, and Job Tenure." *Journal of Labor Economics* 6:445–71.

Mowrer, Ernest R. (1927). *Family Disorganization.* Chicago: University of Chicago Press.

Neyman, Jerzy (1935). "Complex Experiments." *Journal of the Royal Statistical Association* [Suppl.] 2:235–42.

Nimkoff, Meyer F. (1948). "Trends of Family Research." *American Journal of Sociology* 53:477–82.

Pavalko, Eliza K. (1989). "State Timing of Policy Adoption." *American Journal of Sociology* 95:592–615.

Popper, Karl (1950). *The Open Society and Its Enemies.* Princeton, NJ: Princeton University Press.

Reckless, Walter C. (1933). *Vice in Chicago.* Chicago: University of Chicago Press.

Shaw, Clifford (1930). *The Jack-Roller.* Chicago: University of Chicago Press.

(1931). *The Natural History of a Delinquent Career.* Chicago: University of Chicago Press.

Shaw, Clifford, and Henry D. McKay (1942). *Juvenile Delinquency and Urban Areas.* Chicago: University of Chicago Press.

Skocpol, Theda (1979). *States and Social Revolutions: A Comparative Analysis of France, Russia, and China.* Cambridge University Press.

Snodgrass, Jon (1982). *The Jack-Roller at Seventy.* Lexington, MA: D. C. Heath.

Spector, Malcolm, and John Kitsuse (1987). *Constructing Social Problems.* New York: Aldine de Gruyter.

Stinchcombe, Arthur (1968). *Constructing Social Theories.* New York: Harcourt Brace Jovanovitch.

(1978). *Theoretical Methods in Social History.* New York: Academic.

(1990). "Reason and Rationality," pp. 285–317 in Karen Cook and Margaret Levi (eds.), *The Limits of Rationality.* Chicago: University of Chicago Press.

Sutherland, Edwin H. (1950). "The Diffusion of Sexual Psychopath Laws." *American Journal of Sociology* 56:142–48.

Thomas, William I. (1925). "The Problem of Personality in the Urban Environment," pp. 30–9 in *Publications of the American Sociological Society: Papers and Proceedings of the Twentieth Annual Meeting.*

Thrasher, Frederic M. (1927). *The Gang.* Chicago: University of Chicago Press.

White, Hayden (1973). *Metahistory.* Baltimore: Johns Hopkins University Press.

White, Harrison C. (1970). *Chains of Opportunity.* Cambridge, MA: Harvard University Press.

White, Harrison C., and Cynthia White (1965). *Canvases and Careers.* New York: Wiley.

3
Cases are for identity, for explanation, or for control[1]

HARRISON C. WHITE

Before we take action or assess actions, the world gets split into manageable chunks, in the form of strands of personal ties or gradients of geography or whatever. This is an everyday fact of perception, as well as an element in what standard stories evolve for common use. From shamans to lawyers, we have evolved specialists in how to do the splitting.

For social scientists, too, it is a crucial commitment, which deserves recurrent examination. Choice of the kind of partition, as well as of particular boundaries, is all too easily taken for granted. Yet the aptness of measurement and modeling schemes, and thus proper training in methodology, will depend on this choice. We may obsess about numerical details of sampling and miss how important is the initial and perhaps unspoken split.

Partition into case studies is one basic option in social analysis. Another basic option is partition into "profiles," such as size distributions, which may be, for example, of persons or of organizations or of cities, perhaps of some subset with particular attributes (e.g., Tuck 1965; Zipf 1949). Size distributions reflect order through sheer counts, whereas, as we shall see, a case study takes a single count and opens it up, with attention to context.

Three species of case studies will be argued. These species are distinguished with respect to purpose, context, and effects. Practices of professionals and other worldly specialists give us initial leads, and we can try to answer questions about these practices. Why, in this country at a certain period, did the use of the "case method" in training of professionals became so prominent that it has an entry in *Webster's Dictionary*?[2] How should case studies be designed?

Worldly cases

Among Webster's many definitions of "case," the most suggestive is the grammatical one: "a form taken by a noun, pronoun, or adjective to show its relation to neighboring words; any such relation whether expressed by inflection or otherwise." Any definition of case studies should build in an awareness of the relational purport of cases.

Since "case" is a term with much significance in human affairs, its usages have always spawned conflicts, as today among professions' practices (Abbott 1988) or among approaches to international studies (Ashley 1980). These are struggles over uses of case studies in constituting practices of all sorts (e.g., Allison 1971). Scholarly issues about case studies both reflect and are impacted by worldly affairs.

Scope. The range in scope of case studies within social science has to be smaller than we might like. We build case studies mostly for a middling range of size, and a narrow range of recent time, and we do so at social levels below an elite. But we can get leads for bolder ventures: from, say, William the Conqueror's Domesday book (Stenton 1965),[3] or Lenin's early analysis from Russian county social statistics of peasant social formations (1962–70:vol. I).[4] Revolutionary change comes from, as well as breeds, case studies of novel scope.

We also can get leads from observing the microphenomenology of everyday life, as, for example, Goffman did (1955; 1963; 1967; 1971; 1974). A smile on a person is an exact analogy to a grammatical case on a word. A fever in a person is imperfect as analogy, however: "fever" invokes general physical environment as well as specific social locale, whereas a smile is a relation to selected others – not, it is true, in specific network terms but at least in neighborhood. Smiles get used in larger institutional patterns; so do cases. Both are used relationally and usually by intention.

But a middling range, such as can be observed in the practices of guilds and professions, is more germane to normal social science. Long before the codification of social science, middling systems for framing cases had evolved in usage and become socially embodied in particular institutions. That is, as case usages were negotiated and reflected in language – medical or legal or mercantile or whatever – they were also becoming embedded into and nested with larger and larger coteries of specialists for overseeing and even enforcing the framings of and admissions to status as cases, and to formulation in studies. Cases matter; there is nothing innocent in how they are framed.

Religion, law, politics. One can expect to find particular institutions claiming to "own" distinctive styles of case study. We can use "religion," "law," and "politics" as tentative labels by institutional realm for species of case study.[5] Religion establishes "the case for each Us being Us." Durkheim (1915) pointed out how religion, in origin, was a matter of defining identity, as for a particular tribal band with its totem. "Identity" carries its usual social-psychological connotations of a self-aware entity capable of generating social action, which is to say action not programmed as fixed repertoire of instinctual or learned response. Without identity there can be no intention.

Yet there must be an underside or interior of this identity, a dual aspect which also should be made explicit. Each "I" must be an "us," for only the interlocking of us-constituents can generate the energy and uniqueness made manifest as "I."[6] This means that identity also establishes equivalence, an equivalence of the constituents through their disciplined togetherness. Paradox is part of establishing identity, as is best captured by case study which itself breeds further case study.

Gottwald's massive tome (1979) is a sociological dissection of establishing "the case for an Us." Gottwald traces the complex formation of Israel as an identity. In so doing, he is at the same time giving an account of the Old Testament as institutionalized study of "the case," which is to say sacred history. The Bible exhibits again and again how case study accommodates paradox through arrogating a uniqueness of identity to itself. Revolutionary change is involved and will recur. The papal revolution of Gregory VII founded the Catholic church in today's sense (Berman 1983:part I) largely from his case study of the early papacy (Barraclough 1968).[7] And this revolutionary identity set the scene for the explosion into personal identities which was the Reformation, marked by personal confessions as case studies.

The case study establishing identity need not have an explicitly religious aura. Enormously scaled down, the yearbook of a high school's senior class is in the same idiom. Another example is a market survey which undergirds the entry of a new firm.

Now go on to the second species. In any social formation, "law" is a label for the process by which institutions tidy up messes into cases. Law tells contentious parties how, and about what, it is they have been wrangling. This might be a feud dignified through genealogical reckoning, or pushing and shoving become a case of water rights or grazing custom. Law in so doing has to create and invoke explanations. This is carried to further depths and generality in legal codes and perhaps grows into the enterprise of philosophy. At the other extreme, legal explanations are prefigured in homely explanations to ease family squabbles.

Thus this idiom, under whatever label it is given, is eclectic. As a species it is a matter of explaining away and so must yield spreads of cases whose study is to yield sets of stories able to accommodate, ex post, whatever has happened. Explanations are accountings just like those offered by CPAs. Such explanations interpret satisfactorily both because they stay within a prescribed frame and because they always fit the facts, which in a sense they create.

"Politics" is the third label, applied to social fixing to maintain control. Here is a third species of case study. In politics, cases come up here, there, everywhere. A case is taken up not in its own right but only as it fits into a feedback loop of fixing and control.

Politics is analogous to engineering, which seeks to fix and gain control of the physical. But engineering interventions may also break up social arrangements which had remained robust through endless purely social incidents.[8] Politics then can fix up such disarrangements resulting from engineering and other physical incidents. And yet politics may simultaneously further crack open the arrangements. Politics may exacerbate as well as smooth.

Politics neither propounds explanations nor focuses identity, as do case studies from the first two species. Case studies in politics are ad hoc around a flexible meta-goal of fixing for control. Above all, political case studies are concerned with timing and timeliness. Not surprisingly, they disdain unique truths, on the one hand, and they disdain consistent frames for stories, on the other hand.

Ambiguity from words and examples used is bound to obscure these distinctions among the three species. And actual usages in worldly affairs will mix and match these three options for partitioning into cases these three species of studies. Such mixing will occur both by policy and for expediency and advantage. Three examples:

The Catholic church sensibly imbeds its identity/doctrine in the legal-philosophical dress of Thomism draped around Aristotelian surveys of cases.[9]

The criminal law of a region wraps itself in a regal mantle coming out of a wholly different logic of "the case" that sustains the identity of a sacred locality, a religion, or a nation.

Political fixing uses case surveys as explanatory grist in argumentation for control, as Mr. Gorbachev demonstrated for several years.

The most ambiguous of the three terms for case species is "law." Law is the institution best established and so the one which has been elaborated in the most directions. In our day the directions include statute and common law, not to mention civil, judicial, and administrative law. In any social formation,[10] legal studies tend toward the eclectic consideration of mixed circumstances through sets of cases. These sets of cases neither amount to nor exclude a claim at "the truth." These sets neither afford nor exclude real purchase on fixing for control. On the one side, early medieval law offered a mix that came closest to what I am calling the religious rubric.[11] And on the other side, some forms of arbitration and mediation (e.g., cf. Bloom 1981) approach pure political engineering; they approach the use of case study as fixing for control.

Three species in science

Social scientific case studies also can be put into three species of case studies, which follow the same lines that had already been institutionalized in religious and legal and political-engineering forms, which latter today all use case studies from social science. Each "invisible college" of social science (Crane 1972) will tend toward its own mix from the three species. And thereby each of the recognized disciplines, the established academic departments, will evolve a distinctive second-order mix for itself.

Let us turn for further guidance to existing surveys of case studies in social science. The one by the political scientist Lijphart (1971) is representative. He distinguishes four basic methods of establishing general empirical propositions. Two, comparative case studies and statistical, he has as similar except in the fewness of cases in the former. Combine these two and equate them to case sets as handled in the law. Lijphart has the familiar solo case study as another basic method, but we can equate it with politics as engineering, with the use of a case study in fixing for control.

Lijphart's last method is the experimental method. This should correspond to establishing "the case," of establishing identity, as by genealogy or religion or locality. Can this mapping be justified?

Experiment yields identity. Here "experiment" means the original version from natural science. Such experiments have literal controls in physical space-time process. In contrast, the "experimental design" of statistical terminology is best assimilated to comparative studies/statistics.

The central point is that no single experiment means anything at all by itself. Examine the actual practice of science[12] and you will learn that even the particular laboratory engages in endless variations and trials during "an experiment." Indeed all sorts of contortions intervene before a laboratory finally comes up with experimental runs which may be believable and which thus are to be reported. The actual practice of experiment requires an intense concern with what is to be thrown out.

Any runs can be reported meaningfully *only* to an ongoing "school" of experimental work of that particular sort. No one else is prepared either to receive or to dispute the runs. Experiments must mesh into a nested depth of interpretations which are layered socially as well as culturally.

The actual experimental method is a highly embedded one. It is multiply layered in procedure as well as in social context and interpretive structure. Experiment is directed to establishing "the truth," which amounts to finding and fixing an identity, or interlocking set of identities, in a region of phenomena. And so experiment can be a guide to features of the search for identity in general: it triggers recognition that intense concern for what is thrown out characterizes any search for identity.

Identity is also and simultaneously the equation of distinct concrete instances as being truly equivalent. Associated with experiments are models, which test, and which are the frames for the identities being constructed. A "law" in the natural sciences belongs with the experimental method. Scientific law does not belong with law in society, for scientific experiment is a definitive case statement of singular "truth."

Michel Wieviorka's account, Chapter 7 in this volume, of an imaginative and interactive study of terrorists, and their presumed followers, represents this first, multiply layered, species in social science. So do Douglas Harper's two presentations in this volume (Chapter 6), on tramps as fruit pickers and on a Yankee country tinkerer as center of a farming community. For a still broader canvas, I cite a thesis by Brubaker (1990) for the complex embedding of identity as citizenship into and at several scales of context, historical, ethnic, and geographical.

Explaining. A useful litmus test for the second species, explaining, is the use of the term "variable." In social science the concept of variable, being derived from physical space, does not sit easy. It seems an awkward borrowing in hopes that some analytic power will rub off from natural science. The term "variable" is mostly used in this second species, that is, in comparative/statistical case studies, because there the clarity and stability imputed to environment lend credence to use of variables. Tied with the term "variable" is the term "cause," which is yet another awkward borrowing. The coefficients which are reputed to measure causes among variables – path coefficients and the like – may exhibit no stability at all. Valid identification of some stable underlying structure, one robust enough to support cause constructs, is a great challenge.[13]

Comparative study of cases should not, however, be seen as the exclusive domain of the quantitative approach. The disjunction between qualitative and quantitative is pernicious for the serious study of social action, in its complex embeddings and mutuality. John Walton's study of a California water war, described in Chapter 5 of this volume, is a model of qualitative comparison.

On the surface, Walton's account is straight historical. In his first pass, Walton could locate no comparable cases, which was itself a notable accomplishment in comparative logic. Rather than fall back on an idiosyncratic identity study, he persevered to find a striking parallel in foresters' struggles against the Black Acts in the England of the 1720s. More significant than the populist coloring suggested, since it was already prominent in the California record, is the analytic insight which Walton gains about emergence of regional incorporation.

Lieberson, in Chapter 4 of this volume, demonstrates pitfalls in such interpretations derived from few cases, but such interpretations will remain a prime source of new social science theory. And, more importantly, explanatory case studies are constitutive of the idea worlds with which actors construct and reconstruct their perceived realities. The social reality which Lieberson wants to explain exists only because of and through explanatory case studies – billions of them – being carried out all the time and almost always on the base of a few cases. By social science conventions, just bits and pieces of the relatively few case studies by social science are even available to be used in ordinary life.

Local mutual agreements yield the stories which are the folk deposit of cases. Some of these agreements evolve into sets of story lines agreed across a community or a local language-population. Jennifer Platt aptly remarks in Chapter 1: "Case study is the substance of things hoped for, the evidence of things not seen."[14]

Control by crisis interdict. A crisis is a construct through which to seek and engender control. This construct both presumes and induces some case study, in fact the third species of case study, a species centered around interdict, which itself is focused around timing. Crisis is never "owned" by any one party to the process. Timing is important as the intersection between the mutually contingent character of social action by distinct actors and the evanescence of information in the flows being canvased.

Codeword Barbarossa, by a political scientist (Whaley 1973), is a model study of one of the most focused of modern crises, Hitler's invasion of

Soviet Russia. Whaley asks how it was that nearly total surprise was achieved. A myriad of interacting maneuvers over flows of intelligence, spurious as well as observable, provide the centerpiece (chap. 3–5) of his study. There is a whole genre of related "security" studies of states. Betts provides both a general survey (1982), in which he is bold enough to analyze future surprise attacks (chap. 6–9), and a survey of nuclear-attack threats specifically (1987).

Sociological study contributes a parallel from surprise attack in business. Eccles and Crane (1988:chap. 1) use as their lead example First Boston's construction of the deal which resulted in the takeover of Union Carbide. They provide analysis in terms of changing network relations which could be transformed to Betts's case. The historical Cuff (1973), like Eccles and Crane, probes beneath the surface while still focusing on the timings of feints and moves in a case study of control and crisis. His topic is the evolution of the War Industries Board, under the ostensible headship of Bernard Baruch, as the organizational field for the crisis of mobilizing American industry at entry into World War I. His account also cries out for specification in network terms.

Explicit social science theorizing of "crisis" began with Marx and has recently been assessed by Habermas (1975:chap. 1) as a development of classical dramaturgy[15] via Parsonian action theory. Habermas is actually talking about a cross between the first species of case study, focused on identity, and this third species, focused on control: "A social-scientifically appropriate crisis concept must grasp the connection between system integration (specific steering performances of systems with capacity to maintain their boundaries) and social integration (of life worlds that are symbolically structured). The problem is to demonstrate their interconnection" (1975:4). It may, however, prove a mistake to so conflate studies of control with those of identity, which studies are signaled respectively by concern with timing and concern with what is thrown out.

Ambiguity from mixings of words and social usages does obscure the distinctions among the three species for social science just as it did for social institutions. For example, the term "control" is abused by its use in so-called experimental design or other statistical multivariate analysis. All scientific fields commonly hedge their bets: For example, the new field of chemical engineering in the 1920s claimed to have "the truth" (manufacture through continuous-flow processes) amidst its astonishing ability to establish control in any mess of glops. The way chemical engineering did this was soon imitated in the 1930s by the emergent social science of polling via sample survey. And particular studies nearly always meld different purposes. For example, Brubaker, in the study cited earlier, contrasts French with German conceptions and practices, but this comparison is strictly in the service of establishing their respective practices of identity formation.

There is, in other words, a mix-and-match of usages, but the three rubrics still can work as analytic distinctions.

Study design as action

The design of case studies should depend on mission. Prefigure, explain, interdict: these are proposed as three possible basic missions. Study design and selection of cases do and should relate to one and another of these three possibilities, implicitly or explicitly.

Prefigure? Begin with "the case" as species, whether it be experiment or some other base of a search for identity. Cause is being sought, but indeed cause is in some sense being imposed. This first species of case study is not really about prediction in the ordinary sense, not at all. The whole point is to limit the environment so much as to elicit the required, the correct response, which is to say the identity. Prefiguring is what the first species accomplishes.

Wallerstein's surveys (1974, 1980) of states, using world-systems theory, and Levi-Strauss's surveys (1969) of classificatory kinship systems both exemplify the first species, even though each manifestly uses comparative studies. A better-focused exemplar of the same approach is a recent identification of Japanese uniqueness against a comparative canvas of other nations' stratification postures (Ishida, Goldthorpe and Erikson 1991). These authors induce the distinctive identity of Japan, seen in social-class terms, as not stemming from some generic cultural traits but rather as stemming from the unique sequence in which modern class positions made themselves available to existing groupings, lower middle class and peasant, which themselves were within the European range.

On a smaller scale, the interdigitated set of surveys of the International Typographical Union by Lipset, Trow, and Coleman (1956) combine to establish identity for this congeries of organizations, but even more for printing as an occupation. On a still smaller and briefer scale, Whyte's participant-observation study (1943) of a youth gang induces a similar nesting of crosscutting identities. The gang itself is an identity prefigured in many minds for ethnic slum youth, but Doc and other characters in Whyte's scene are as much joint constructions of identity as pre-given persons. There is much rumination by the gang regarding how each is prefigured, rumination after the facts of emergences. Blythe's characterization (1979) of aging is yet another exemplar of this first species, "the case" study which is eliciting and building identity. Blythe is uncovering how aging cohorts and a village are identities that are both in construction, interactively, through ruminations presented as prefigurings.

Explaining away? The law, and comparative/statistical studies more generally, are about explanation. They aim for spread and balance in accountings. Their task is to provide sets of stories through which most happenings can be explained away, explained simultaneously from different points of view.[16] It is to that end that the law and such studies discern valuations, many and diverse, behind the social phenomena.

Explainings away are diverse not just to accommodate differing locations of actors but also because, unlike for an identity study, a main outcome is to disperse responses rather than have them possibly cohere into joint projects. Explanations soothe. On a microscale such studies are known as "cooling the mark out" (Goffman) with plausible ex post account. Inane projections of the future scene are a distinctive sign of this second species.[17]

Eckstein (1975; cf. Dogan and Pelassy 1984) offers a useful menu of comparative surveys of large social units. His own purpose is to argue for the solo case study, which he treats as an adumbrated survey, a nifty way to probe the plausibility of a theory. The traditional distinctions he makes, as of the solo case as narrative and clinical, in opposition to the comparative as analytic and experimental, cross the present ones. These distinctions arguably are not as useful: Eckstein is not paying attention to the social pressures engendering, and the social outcomes which accommodate, case studies. These are the very pressures and accommodations that channel case studies into three distinct species.

Davis and Smith (1988) and Page and Shapiro (1991) inventory large numbers of surveys of individuals, each on its face a comparative study. But Page and Shapiro are trying to draw out a general truth about the rationality of collective public opinion, so that their book is an identity study – one which makes use of all sorts of evidence. Davis, like Eckstein, is after not a single theme or truth but rather a balanced assessment of all sorts of regularities. Davis, like Eckstein, is seeking to establish explanations. Explanations are like projections, although the former are made after the fact and the latter are made before the fact, and each avoids establishing identity or setting up interdict.

Interdict? In the wings of any appearance by "cases" must be "environment." Perhaps the first and most basic cases are localities. The implications of inside the boundary versus the rest, which is to say the environment, are omnipresent. Many social scientists indeed make the environment the key player of their case studies (e.g., Lawrence and Lorsch 1967; Pfeffer and Salancik 1978). The concern of the third species of case study is to interdict, which is exactly to play upon all environments rather than be acted upon by some single environment.

Intervention takes the active mode toward environment. Fixing-for-control studies, the third species of case, thus have an entirely different relation to "environment": Rather than seeking a stable environment (second species) or a neutered environment (first species), a political engineer is endlessly changing and renegotiating and restructuring what might be environment, and with particular emphasis on time boundaries.[18] Turf fights among professions and professionals (Abbott 1988) can be translated into who does and should define environments of cases, which is in part a matter of who is in the best position to interdict and gain rewards thereof. Social scientists as professionals are uneasy about being labeled as political engineers and may mislabel their case studies that in fact do interdict.

Bailey's monograph (1984) is an excellent source of material on interdict studies. Bailey was himself a player among the many social scientists in government positions all scrambling to have hands in the New York City fiscal crisis of the 1970s. Interdicts, multiple interdicts by "private" and state sources, were the themes of their studies. Bailey in his studies spots the importance of timing and the uses made of confusion over "goals." A parallel study (Alford 1975) on New York's health-care crisis, though painstaking, is misled. The author is on the outside of the scene of interdicts, here recurrent as well as massive interdicts, and he aims for explanation, which implies goals and criteria of orderliness and openness.

A similar contrast on a much vaster scale can be drawn between a historian's account (Kuhn 1970) of the Taiping rebellion and Hsiao's study (1960) of imperial governance in that era. Kuhn captures the interactive, time-sensitive nature of the maze of gentry efforts to fix up the breaks in their social dikes, as they confronted, with precious little help from a decayed state, a bizarre missionary sect. Hsiao reports, on the other hand, only the overall architecture of control as promulgated, and he only tut-tuts about local anomalies: Hsiao aims for an identity case study, as indeed did the imperial officials he draws upon. On the surface, Kuhn's is a comparative survey of reactions by localities, and accordingly Kuhn's could be accounted a comparative/statistical case study. But Kuhn is after not just the contingent dynamics within a locality but how control effort just here plays off outcome or model of control just there, just then. Taken as a whole, Kuhn's is a classic study of interlocking interdict efforts; it is, put in engineering terms, a study of fix-it control.

The same author can get right one interdict case study, for example, Schwartz (1976) on struggles of a Southern postbellum populist movement, only to flop back in later work into a comparative and uncontingent mode of analysis for what is an interdict situation: Mintz and Schwartz (1985) argue from mere architecture of director interlock to bankers' putting the arm on industry in the "merger and acquisition era."

There is bite to the speciation. If you want to understand control, you should not turn to the comparative/statistical case study, which explains so nicely – which, to be precise, explains away so nicely. Achieving some control is a reality of social process in its own social timings which disdains and cuts across exactly the sets of stories, the smooth explanations for multiple actors, that constitute the bulk of workaday conversation and social science.

Environment as nested perspectives

This line of argument requires and presupposes the interdigitation of three orders of perspectives: those of actors as well as perspectives of institutions and of social sciences. Each order of perspective influences the other two. And in each shows up the same trifurcate outline in species of case study.

From generations into persons. Sets of persons can be traced in group biographies which turn mere cohorts into generations. For example, Doug McAdam (1988) builds from a group portrait of rights activists, retrospective to 1964, toward a more general definition of the 1960s counterculture generation in the United States. In the same recent American context, another sociologist, Stephen Cornell (1988), traces the emergence not just of a generation but of a whole people, native Americans. Hundreds of tribes heretofore utterly distinct and different in their own perspectives begin to become a people, though not as yet with as binding an impact as Gottwald traced for an earlier formation of a people.

A famous negative example is Halevy's account (1974) of a generation that did *not* happen. Halevy traces the local notables who were handed national power "on a platter" in the bemused, comic-opera

France of 1830, only to let it fall away. Not just identity, but explanation and indeed also traces of interdiction[19] are shown in accounts like these, which really must be tapestries of case studies.

Persons emerge from generations as much as generations emerge from persons. For that matter, both must always be emerging with and from localities too. Layered realities are built up, in which codified interpretations of existing realities become aspects of new realities. This is part of what Abbott argues, in his critique in Chapter 2 of this volume, is being elided by the usual quantitative study in sociology. With nary a count in sight, the poet Blythe (1969, 1979) has much of general moment to tell us about aging and generations from his continuing case studies of individuals nested in his continuing case study of a village.

The sociologist Griswold (1986) has shown how to turn such layering into a positive tool of social analysis. She surveys the resurrections, over the course of 400 years, of two genres of Renaissance play. "Revenge tragedies" and "city comedies," she argues, resonate with problems of, and so are revived in, just certain times and climes. Revival of a genre is resurrection of a generation.

Persons. Persons as wholes come late in any ontogeny of cases. For example, many of those studies of the second species which are about individuals concern themselves not with persons but with various limited projections of persons, projections as mere bipeds or as residents or whatever. Even the autobiography is aimed at others than the subject. Biography itself comes late, biography is postclassical (Chesnut 1986).

Person as biography, whether social scientific or worldly, can be any species of case study. Biography as prototype or hero is the study of identity, once removed; it is the first species. More often, biography contributes to the stock of stories in explanations. And biography may be a weapon of interdiction in struggles for control.

It follows that a given historical personage may change over time and according to biographical purpose. Church (1976) details this for Louis XIV. He begins with the humanist perspective of Voltaire[20] and continues through the social science lens of the Annales school.[21] Church shows at each step how the interpretation reflected and was used in ongoing political struggles across France and also within French academia.

Although biography can be an important example of the first species, of identity studies, biography also presupposes larger identities as contexts, as environment for individuals.[22] Modern lives often are construed as evolving intersections of organizations, in short, as careers, and all lives presuppose early family contexts. These subtle nestings in context which are requisite in biography seem best developed in literature, indeed in novels as a specifically modern genre. But some social scientists also have shown mastery of it – for example, Erik Erickson (1958).

Style. The design of case studies, both worldly and scientific, is habitual in part. Ostensible rationale, such as some principle of optimization, is a weak guide to designs. Species of case study can, after all, be distinguished just because design reflects institutional forms. Case studies come in all sorts of cultural depth, and even the simplest case has cultural facets not capturable by my discrimination into three species.

Institutions as well as persons are quite literally constituted out of case studies, but as woven into story sets and folded into someone's histories. More depth and subtlety are required, some sorts of perspectives that cut across and go beyond species. Use the term "style" for these sorts of perspective.

Particular actors of all sorts and sizes are doing and using case studies. They have all sorts of purposes, so that the studies, even when rudimentary, may combine all three analytic species. Individuals mostly use species "without benefit of clergy," so to speak – without the benefit of formal theology, law, political engineering, or their descendant social sciences. The style of a study not only mixes species but also reflects all three orders of perspective distinguished earlier, of persons, institutions, and social sciences. Style is an intersection of design-for-action with nesting-as-perspective across species of cases. This is true whether in social science or in worldly affairs.

Style cannot be a matter of neat definitions. Style tends to slip by us as individual social scientists. This is so partly because style is not some single stroke but rather an endless nesting of prior choices which frame what we can now see: Such nesting is as true with respect to perception of social life as it is of human beings' perceptions of the physical environment.[23]

Despite all these warnings and provisos, let us chance a sketch of style for each species. Two opposed grammatical constructions characterize the first two species. Caesar's "I came; I saw; I conquered" exemplifies parataxis, the doing away with subordination. This harsh contraposition is a style of presentation fitting for "the case" because its truth goes with abrupt changes and it pushes toward a focus in outcome, toward singular outcome. The Old Testament is used by Auerbach (1953) as an exemplar, in agreement with our earlier labeling of this species as religious.

Opposed to parataxis is hypotaxis, with its reconciliations into flowing prose through subordinations and other artifices of periphrases. Classical Greek and Latin prose, from Aristotle through Cicero, exemplifies this second style. Such unbroken flow of account remains today the aim for law report and statistical survey alike, in their renderings of diverse cases. This style pushes toward multiple and parallel outcomes able to explain away phenomena, explain them away even to diversely situated parties. It is the style for the second species. Riposte and the follow-on is a style contrasting with both the first two. It seems the natural style of presentation for political engineering. From a control case, our third species, comes an interdiction keyed to time.

This conjectured correlation of presentation style to species can be illustrated – dangerous though Jennifer Platt argues that to be – right within this volume (Chapter 1). Platt's own style is surely hypotaxis, and her output indeed consists in generalizations. These qualities are shared by Vaughan's essay (Chapter 8) in her imaginative contrasts among organizational misconduct, which itself is the subjects' own rubric in which to soothe and explain away. One by one, the other essays fall into the style and output for that species which has already been proposed for it in previous sections.

Professional practices in cases

Social scientists can learn from professional practice, as well as the converse. Variation in style and variation in output both should help show how species tie to professional practices, just as both variations can help disentangle species within concrete investigations in social science. Professional pragmatics can encourage social scientists to mix species. Professional examples can point up the complex nesting of studies within frames of reference that themselves resulted from still other lines of studies. Conversely, research can suggest improvements in professional practice.

Take a recent development, the growing uneasiness with conventional statistical dicta about comparative case studies. Scientists Krantz and Briggs (1990) emphasize a distinction between estimates of commonness, the forte of statistics, and estimates of strength or what might be called depth of evidence. They are still wrestling with how to assess the latter, but so far they emphasize collocation of expert judgments – which is in itself a mimicry of good professional practice. While commonness has to do with explaining, with my second species, depth has to do either with establishing identity, scientific law being a special case, or else with interdiction to seek control. This would suggest that expert judgments are less apropos for explanatory studies than they are for the other two species. And perhaps measurement of the timely and contingent would be a valuable extension of the proposals of Krantz and Briggs.

Evolution.   Professions can be traced playing roles in the evolution of all three species of case study. From the religion-theology path emerges a unique, bipartite valuation or polarization applying across the board. This is polarization as good and bad, or pure and impure, or sacred and profane, wherein good specifies identity. A profession splits off and then keeps split with its own identity only through a religious-experimental path such as is mapped by the first species of case study.

Professions evolved in part to deal with the tension between local and general, because, from the earliest precursor forms such as prostitution, they were dealing impersonally and across context, using shiftable values, with what were supposed to be deeply rooted and sacred localities as in genealogy. From this second path, which it is natural to associate with philosophy, comes a set of multiple values, a set within which there can be change and evolution. This is the way of discipline by similarity enforcement, with localities separated just because of and to allow such similarity.

But professionals act to fix relations when they can; they don't just explain away, important though that is. Professionals interdict, professionals offer control, in a contingent and disciplined way. This is the way of fix-it control, control by playing off and manipulation of others who often are seen to be locality-guided.

Training through case studies.   There is no surprise in this general account so far: a profession or the professions can reflect and use mixtures of styles; they mix species of case studies. Let us move on to answer a specific question: What accounts for kinds of training for a profession in a given society? The answer is – since medicine gained some capability and since the law meshed with business practice, both happening in the nineteenth century (Starr 1985; Horwitz 1977) – that training into a profession should be more effective when it engenders capacity to interdict, capacity at fix-it control. Now probe this answer.

The case-study method was introduced at Harvard Law School by its first dean, Christopher Columbus Langdell, in 1870 (Barber 1953). On its face this method could be used, and since has been much used, to survey and compare cases, and even to weave identity accounts out of or as cases. The use of discussion is the key puzzle.

A profession is a complex institution, which needs a continuous rebuilding and reaffirmation of identity for itself and its members (Abbott 1988). Concentric circles of purity model the way this is done (Abbott 1981), and they go with and require training in identity case studies. And to this, discussion seems at best unhelpful.

Turn to graduate schools of business. Purity circles and identity surely are not germane here; business administration is not a profession. And the case method centered on discussion has proved very effective, more central perhaps than in law schools.

A graduate school of business is training for general management, which is to say it is training exactly for fix-it control, for political engineering of a pure sort, for interdiction factored out from the distractions of a professional façade. Discussion is the center of, and the case study in itself just the playing field for, induction to the contingent timing and political confusion of political engineering. That is what general management is.

Strong discussion and debate, on some ground of common cases, is itself the simulacrum of getting control. If this analysis is valid, similar methods of inducing expertise should become evident in electoral politics upon investigation.[24] Perhaps medical schools use a case method of teaching clinical work to the same end – but where the contingencies now are the rapidly changing and chaotic tropes and fugues of patients, rather than the social problematics of professional practice.

Social sciences have also become, in part, professional practices, and we can draw insights for the social sciences too. Consider the argument of Pletsch (1981) that the solo case study (and "culture" as an explanation) is kept for investigations of the Second and Third Worlds, whereas the more prestigious analytic-comparative study is kept for the First World. His inference of bias is surely unfounded. In that era (1950–75) social scientists were thought able to "fix it" and interdict for the Second and Third Worlds, but, I suspect, social scientists were thought to be good, at best, for "explaining away" in First World societies, to have primarily the merely decorative value which rhetoricians had in classical civilization. The solo case study can be the medium of a fix-it-control investigation, whereas the analytic, the comparative/statistical study is for explaining away: Pletsch got the invidious ranking exactly wrong.

Conclusion

Many tasks and puzzles remain. Probes for nepotisms and for antecedents, literal or symbolic, are ubiquitous, so that case studies should not be constrained to discrete enclaves. How can network analysis (Wellman and Berkowitz 1988) be construed in terms of case studies?

Within the social sciences, economics tends to construe as choice situations what sociology calls cases.[25] Why should this be? And does it matter? What is the significance of stochastic models for case studies? (Cf. Padgett 1981, 1990.) On this latter question, the work of Feller (1968) is a mine of riches, as much for worldly practice as for scientific studies.

One problem is that most social science techniques are pale copies of engineering approaches, rather than being specific to social action and to social spaces. Control engineering (Bennett 1979) has developed approaches more general and powerful than any fix-it-control techniques used in social sciences so far. Structural context is important to any serious study, but it can be especially crucial in studying social action, which shapes itself in perceptions and conjectures about context, most especially about other social action as context. The three species which have been discriminated here – both in social science and in institutional practices – amount to first cuts at structural context in this enlarged sense. Even this first cut has brought a sharp moral:

Prediction is myth; its replacement should be a discrimination into prefiguring, projecting, and interdiction.

References

Abbott, Andrew (1981). "Status and Status Strain in the Professions." *American Journal of Sociology* 86: 819–36.
   (1988). *The System of Professions.* Chicago: University of Chicago Press.
Alford, Robert R. (1975). *Health Care Politics.* Chicago: University of Chicago Press.
Allison, Graham T. (1971). *Essence of Decision.* Boston: Little, Brown.
Ashley, Richard K. (1980). *The Political Economy of War and Peace.* London: Pinter.
Auerbach, Erich (1953). *Mimesis: The Representation of Reality in Western Literature.* Princeton, NJ: Princeton University Press.
Bailey, Robert W. (1984). *The Crisis Regime: The MAC, the EFCB and the Political Impact of the New York City Financial Crisis.* Albany, NY: SUNY Press.
Barber, Bernard (1953). "Case Materials and Case Analysis in American Professional Training." Unpublished manuscript, Columbia University.
Barraclough, Geoffrey (1968). *The Medieval Papacy.* New York: Harcourt, Brace & World.
Baxandall, M. (1975). *Painting and Experience in Fifteenth Century Italy.* Oxford: Oxford University Press.
Bennett, S. (1979). *A History of Control Engineering, 1800–1930.* New York: Peter Peregrinus.
Berman, Harold J. (1983). *Law and Revolution: The Formation of the Western Legal Tradition.* Cambridge, MA: Harvard University Press.
Betts, Richard K. (1982). *Surprise Attack.* Washington, DC: Brookings Institution.

(1987). *Nuclear Blackmail and Nuclear Deterrence.* Washington, DC: Brookings Institution.

Bloch, R. Howard (1977). *Medieval French Literature and Law.* Berkeley: University of California Press.

Bloom, David (1981). "Is Arbitration *Really* Compatible with Bargaining?" *Industrial Relations* 20:233–44.

Blythe, Ronald (1969). *Akenfield: Portrait of an English Village.* New York: Pantheon.

(1979). *The View in Winter: Reflections on Old Age.* New York: Harcourt Brace Jovanovich.

Brubaker, William R. (1990). *Citizenship and Nationhood in France and Germany.* Ph.D. dissertation, Department of Sociology, Columbia University.

Bryson, Arthur, and Yu-Chi Ho (1969). *Applied Optimal Control; Optimization, Estimation and Control.* Waltham, MA: Blaisdell.

Caro, Anthony (1974). *The Power Broker: Robert Moses and the Fall of New York.* New York: Knopf.

(1990). *Lyndon Johnson: The Path to Power.* New York: Random House.

Chesnut, Glenn (1986). *The First Christian Histories.* Macon, GA: Mercer University Press.

Church, William F. (1976). *Louis XIV in Historical Thought.* New York: Norton.

Cornell, Stephen (1988). *The Return of the Native: American Indian Political Resurgence.* Oxford: Oxford University Press.

Cozzens, Susan E. (1989). *Social Control and Multiple Discovery in Science: The Opiate Receptor Case.* Albany, NY: SUNY Press.

Crane, Diana (1972). *Invisible Colleges.* Chicago: University of Chicago Press.

Cuff, Robert D. (1973). *The War Industries Board.* Baltimore: Johns Hopkins University Press.

Davis, James A., and Tom W. Smith (1988). *General Social Surveys, 1972–1988: Cumulative Codebook.* Chicago: National Opinion Research Center.

Dogan, Mattei, and Dominique Pelassy (1984). *How to Compare Nations.* Chatham, NJ: Chatham House.

Durkheim, Emile (1915). *The Elementary Forms of the Religious Life,* translated by J. W. Swain. London: Allen & Unwin.

Eccles, Robert G., and Dwight B. Crane (1988). *Doing Deals: Investment Banks at Work.* Boston: Harvard Business School Press.

Eckstein, Harry (1975). "Case Study and Theory in Political Science," Chapter 3 in Fred I. Greenstein and Nelson W. Polsby (eds.), *Handbook of Political Science.* Reading, MA: Addison-Wesley.

Erickson, Erik (1958). *Young Man Luther.* New York: Norton.

Evans, Peter (1977). "Multiple Hierarchies and Organization Control." *Administrative Science Quarterly* 22:364–85.

Fama, Eugene F., and Michael C. Jensen (1983). "Separation of Ownership and Control." *Journal of Law and Economics* 26:301–23.

Feller, William (1968). *An Introduction to Probability Theory and Its Application.* 3rd ed. New York: Wiley.

Fleck, Ludwik (1979). *Genesis and Development of a Scientific Fact,* translated by Fred Bradley and Thaddeus J. Trenn (1935 German text). Chicago: University of Chicago Press.

Gibson, Eleanor J. (1991). *An Odyssey in Learning and Perception.* Cambridge, MA: MIT Press.

Goffman, Erving (1955). "On Face Work." *Psychiatry* 18: 213–31.

(1963). *Behavior in Public Places.* Glencoe, IL: Free Press.

(1967). *Interaction Ritual.* New York: Pantheon.

(1971). *Relations in Public.* New York: Harper.

(1974). *Frame Analysis.* New York: Harper & Row.

Gottwald, Norman K. (1979). *The Tribes of Jahweh: A Sociology of the Religion of Liberated Israel, 1250–1050 B.C.E.* Maryknoll, NY: Orbis Books.

Grether, David M., R. Mark Isaac, and Charles R. Plot (1989). *The Allocation of Scarce Resources: Experimental Economics and the Problem of Allocating Airport Slots.* Boulder, CO: Westview.

Griswold, Wendy (1986). *Renaissance Revivals.* Chicago: University of Chicago Press.

Habermas, Jurgen (1975). *Legitimation Crisis,* translated by T. McCarthy. Boston: Beacon.

Halevy, Daniel (1974). *The End of the Notables,* translated by A. Silvera. Middletown, CT: Wesleyan University Press.

Horwitz, Morton J. (1977). *The Transformation of American Law, 1780–1860.* Cambridge, MA: Harvard University Press.

Hsiao, Kung-chuan (1960). *Rural China; Imperial Control in the Nineteenth Century.* Seattle: University of Washington Press.

Ishida, Hiroshi, John H. Goldthorpe, and Robert Erikson (1991). "Intergenerational Class Mobility in Post-War Japan: Conformity or Peculiarity in Cross-National Perspective?" *American Journal of Sociology* 96:954–92.

Kellett, J. R. (1958). "The Breakdown of Gild and Corporation Control over the Handicraft and Retail Trade in London." *Economic History Review* 10: 381–94.

Knorr-Cetina, Karin, and A. V. Cicourel (eds.) (1981). *Advances in Social Theory and Methodology: Toward an Integration of Micro- and Macro-Sociologies.* London: Routledge & Kegan Paul.

Kotz, David M. (1978). *Bank Control of Large Corporations in the U.S.* Berkeley: University of California Press.

Krantz, David H., and Laura K. Briggs (1990). "Judgments of Frequency and Evidence Strength." Unpublished manuscript, Department of Psychology, Columbia University.

Kreps, David M. (1988). *Notes on the Theory of Choice.* Boulder, CO: Westview.

Kuhn, Philip A. (1970). *Rebellion and its Enemies in Late Imperial China.* Cambridge, MA: Harvard University Press.

Lawrence, Paul, and Jay Lorsch (1967). *Organizations and Environment.* Cambridge, MA: Harvard University Press.

Leach, Edmund R. (1954). *The Political Systems of Highland Burma.* Boston: Beacon.

Leamer, Edward (1978). *Specification Searches: Ad Hoc Inference with Non-experimental Data.* New York: Wiley.

Leifer, Eric M., and Harrison C. White (1986). "Wheeling and Annealing: Federal and Multidivisional Control, " pp. 223–242 in James F. Short (ed.), *The Social Fabric: Issues and Dimensions.* Beverly Hills, CA: Sage.

Leigh, James R. (1987). *Applied Control Theory*, 2nd ed. London: Peter Peregrinus.

Lenin, Vladmir Il'ich. (1962–70). *Collected Works*, 45 vols. Moscow: Foreign Language Publishing House.

Levi-Strauss, Claude (1969). *The Elementary Structures of Kinship*, rev. ed. Boston: Beacon Press.

Lijphart, Arend (1971). "Comparative Politics and the Comparative Method." *American Political Science Review* 65:682–93.

Lipset, Seymour M., Martin A. Trow, and James S. Coleman (1956). *Union Democracy*. Garden City, NY: Doubleday.

McAdam, Douglas (1982). *Political Process and the Development of Black Insurgency*. Chicago: University of Chicago Press.

(1988). *Freedom Summer*. Oxford: Oxford University Press.

Mintz, Beth, and Michael Schwartz (1985). *The Power Structure of American Business*. Chicago: University of Chicago Press.

Nohria, Nitin (1990). "A Quasi-Market in Technology Based Enterprises: The Case of the 128 Venture Group." Unpublished manuscript, Graduate School of Business Administration, Harvard Universit.y.

Padgett, John F. (1981). "Hierarchy and Ecological Control in Federal Budgetary Decision-Making." *American Journal of Sociology* 87:75–129.

(1990). "Plea Bargaining and Prohibition in the Federal Courts: 1908–1934." *Law and Society Review* 24:413–450.

Page, Benjamin I., and Robert L. Shapiro (1991). *The Rational Public*. Chicago: University of Chicago Press.

Patterson, Nerys T. (1981). "Material and Symbolic Exchange in Early Irish Clientship," pp. 54–61 in James E. Doan and C. G. Buttimer (eds.), *Proceedings of the Harvard Celtic Colloquium* (vol. 4).

Pfeffer, Jeffrey, and Gerald Salancik (1978). *The External Control of Organizations*. New York: Harper.

Pletsch, Carl E. (1981). "The Three Worlds, or the Division of Social Scientific Labor, circa 1950–1975." *Comparative Studies in Society and History* 23: 565–90.

Schwartz, Michael (1976). *Radical Protest and Social Structure*. New York: Academic Press.

Simon, Herbert A. (1945). *Administrative Behavior*. New York: Macmillan.

Starr, Paul (1985). *American Medicine*. Cambridge, MA: Harvard University Press.

Stenton, Frank (1965). *The First Century of English Feudalism*. Oxford: Oxford University Press.

Stewman, Shelby, and S. L. Konda (1983). "Careers and Organizational Labor Markets: Demographic Models of Organizational Behavior." *American Journal of Sociology* 88:637–85.

Tuck, Ronald H. (1965). *An Essay on the Economic Theory of Rank*. Oxford: Blackwell.

Udy, Stanley (1970). *Work in Traditional and Modern Society*. Englewood Cliffs, NJ: Prentice-Hall.

Wallerstein, Immanuel (1974, 1980). *The Modern World-System* (vols. I and II). New York: Academic Press.

Wellman, Barry, and S. D. Berkowitz (eds.) (1988). *Social Structures: A Network Approach*. Cambridge University Press.

Whaley, Barton (1973). *Codeword Barbarossa*. Cambridge, MA: MIT Press.

White, Harrison C. (1970). *Chains of Opportunity*. Cambridge, MA: Harvard University Press.

(1991). "Theory for Control in Social Relations by Decoupling Production from Identities among Networks." Unpublished manuscript, Center for the Social Sciences, Columbia University.

(in press). *Identity and Control: A Structural Theory of Social Action*. Princeton, NJ: Princeton University Press.

Whyte, William F. (1943). *Street Corner Society: The Social Structure of an Italian Slum*. Reprinted Chicago: University of Chicago Press, 1955.

Zannetos, Zenon S. (1966). *The Theory of Oil Tankship Rates*. Cambridge, MA: MIT Press.

Zipf, George K. (1949). *Human Behavior and the Principle of Least Effort: An Introduction to Human Ecology*. Cambridge, MA: Addison-Wesley.

4

Small N's and big conclusions: an examination of the reasoning in comparative studies based on a small number of cases[1]

STANLEY LIEBERSON

This chapter evaluates an approach which is gaining in usage, especially for historical and comparative problems. Namely, we will consider the causal inferences drawn when little more than a handful of nations or organizations – sometimes even fewer – are compared with respect to the forces driving a societal outcome such as a political development or an organizational characteristic.[2] Application of this method to a small number of cases is not new to sociology, being in one form or another a variant of the method of analytical induction, described by Znaniecki (1934:236) and analyzed succinctly by Robinson (1951) and Turner (1953).[3] These conclusions rely on a formalized internal logic derived from Mill's method of agreement and his method of difference [see the discussion of Mill in Nichols (1986:170ff).] The formal rigor of this type of analysis sets it off from other small-sample procedures which also imply causality, as say in *Street Corner Society* (Whyte 1943) or in the development of the model of urban structure and growth of Burgess (1925). It is also different from case studies which seek to point out merely that a given phenomenon *exists* in some setting, as opposed to an analysis of its causes. The comments are, however, to some degree relevant for evaluating the Boolean method proposed by Ragin (1987) for dealing with somewhat larger samples used in comparative and historical research. Moreover, although the analysis is stimulated by recent developments in macrohistorical research, it is pertinent to a wide variety of other studies that use Mill's logic with a small number of cases.

One has no difficulty appreciating the goal of applying formal procedures to make causal inferences in a manner analogous to what is otherwise restricted to studies based on a much larger number of cases. If data were available with the appropriate depth and detail for a large number of cases, obviously the researcher would not be working with these few cases (assuming a minimal time-energy cost). Since the data are not available, or the time-energy cost is too great, one can only approach these efforts with considerable sympathy for their objective. We address three questions: (1) What are the assumptions underlying these studies? (2) Are these assumptions reasonable? (3) What can be done to improve such studies in those instances when they might be appropriate forms of inquiry?

Probabilistic and deterministic perspectives

Let us start by distinguishing between causal propositions that are *deterministic* as contrasted with those that are *probabilistic*. The former posits that a given factor, when present, will lead to a specified outcome. The latter is more modest in its causal claim, positing that a given factor, when present, will increase the likelihood of a specified outcome. When we say, "If X_1 then Y," we are making a deterministic statement. When we say, "the presence of X_1 increases the likelihood or frequency of Y," we are making a probabilistic statement. Obviously, if given the choice, deterministic statements are more appealing. They are cleaner, simpler, and more easily disproved than probabilistic ones. One negative case, such that Y is absent in the presence of X_1, would quickly eliminate a deterministic statement.

Alas, a probabilistic approach is often necessary to evaluate the evidence for a given theoretical perspective, even if we think in deterministic terms. This occurs for a variety of reasons, not the least being measurement errors – a serious problem in the social sciences. The existence of a measurement error means that a given data set may deviate somewhat from a hypothesized pattern without the hypothesis being wrong. In addition to this technical matter, there is an additional problem: complex multivariate causal patterns operate in the social world, such that a given outcome can occur because of the presence of more than one independent variable and, moreover, may not occur at times because the influence of one independent variable is outweighed by other influences working in the opposite direction. Under such circumstances, the influence of X_1 is only approximate (even without measurement errors), unless one can consider all of the other independent variables, through controls or otherwise.

Furthermore, we often do not know or cannot measure all of the factors that we think will influence Y. As a consequence, we are again obliged to give up on a deterministic *measurement* of the influence of X_1 on Y, even if we are prepared to make a deterministic statement about its influence. There are yet other reasons for reverting to a probabilistic rather than a deterministic approach, namely, the role of chance in affecting outcomes. Beyond consideration here is the question of whether *chance* per se exists or is simply a residual label referring to our ignorance about additional influences and/or inadequate measures for the variables under scrutiny. In either case, some form or another of indeterminacy is clearly useful to employ in the physical sciences, let alone in the social sciences [see examples in Lieberson (1985:94–7)]. Any of these factors would lead to probabilistic statements rather than deterministic statements of outcome.

This distinction is more than merely an academic one. Rather, it is embedded in our daily thinking. Suppose we examine the influence of alcohol on automobile accidents. Even if we believe there is such an influence, we still will expect some sober drivers to have chargeable accidents and not all drunk drivers to experience accidents. If we find that some sober drivers did cause accidents and some drunk drivers did not, these deviations would not lead us to reject automatically the proposition that drunkenness causes automobile accidents.[4] Rather, we would look at a set of data and ask if the probability or frequency of accidents were greater for drunk than for sober drivers. Why is this so? Even if taking a deterministic view, we would expect several factors to influence the likelihood of an accident, alcohol being only one of them. Indeed, we would expect an interaction effect for drunkenness, such that one drunk driver might run a red light in a busy intersection and have an accident, whereas another driver might be fortunate to enter the intersection when the light was green. To be sure, we might want to take some of these additional factors into account, and we would then expect the influence of drinking to be more sharply displayed. But it is unlikely that we could isolate alcohol's influence from all of the additional conditions that either prevent drinking from causing an accident or lead a sober driver to have an accident. The net effect is that we will not totally reject our idea about alcoholism and driving if we compare a drunk driver with a sober one and find the latter has an accident and the former does not. Likewise, if we learn of one drunk driver who has an accident and a sober driver who does not, that will hardly be persuasive data that the pattern is indeed in the direction anticipated. The point is clear-cut: *a deterministic theory has deterministic outcomes, but often we can measure it only in probabilistic terms.*

Despite these facts, small-N studies operate in a deterministic manner, avoiding probabilistic thinking either in their theory or in their empirical applications. As one distinguished proponent of the small-N approach puts it, "in contrast to the probabilistic techniques of statistical analysis – techniques that are used when there are very large numbers of cases and continuously quantified variables to analyze – comparative historical analyses proceed through logical juxtapositions of aspects of small numbers of cases. They attempt to identify invariant causal configurations that necessarily (rather than probably) combine to account for outcomes of interest" (Skocpol 1984:378). One good reason for this disposition is the following principle: *except for probabilistic situations which approach 1 or 0 (in other words are almost deterministic), studies based on a small number of cases have difficulty in evaluating probabilistic theories.*

Let us draw an analogy with flying a given airline. Suppose a rude employee is encountered, or luggage is lost, or the plane is delayed. One could, after such an experience, decide to use a different airline. However, one would know that although airlines may differ in their training programs, employee relations, morale, luggage practices, airplane maintenance, and other factors affecting their desirability, a very small number of experiences is insufficient to evaluate airlines with great confidence. If airlines differ, it is in the *frequency* of unpleasant experiences rather than that one airline has only polite employees, never loses luggage, or avoids all mechanical problems. Based on a small number of experiences, one may decide to shun a certain airline, and the decision is not totally wrong, since the probability of such experiences in any given small number of events is indeed influenced by the underlying distribution of practices in different airlines. However, conclusions drawn on the basis of such practices are often wrong. We would know that passengers with small numbers of experiences will draw very different conclusions about the relative desirability of various airlines. This is because a small number of cases is a bad basis for generalizing about the process under study. Thus if we actually knew the underlying probabilities for each airline, it would be possible to calculate how often the wrong decision will occur based on a small number of experiences. The consumer errors are really of no great consequence, since making decisions on the basis of a small number of events enables the flyer to respond in some positive way to what can otherwise be a frustrating experience. Such thinking, however, is not innocuous for the research problems under consideration here; it will frequently lead to erroneous conclusions about the forces operating in society. Moreover, other samples based on a small number of different cases – when contradicting the first sample, and this is almost certain to occur – will create even more complicated sets of distortions as the researcher attempts to use deterministic models to account for all of the results. This, in my judgment, is not a step forward.

Briefly, in most social-research situations it is unlikely that the requirements of a deterministic theory will be met. When these conditions

are not met, then the empirical consequences of deterministic and probabilistic theories are similar in the sense that both will have to accept
deviations: the former because of errors in measurement and controls;
the latter both because of those reasons and because the theory itself
incorporates some degree of indeterminacy (due to inherent problems
in either the measurement or knowledge of all variables or because of
some inherent indeterminacy in the phenomenon).

The implications of this are seen all the time in social research. In
practice, for example, it is very difficult to reject a major theory because
it appears not to operate in some specific setting. One is wary of concluding that Max Weber was wrong because of a single deviation in
some inadequately understood time or place. In the same fashion, we
would view an accident caused by a sober driver as failing to disprove
the notion that drinking causes automobile accidents.

Suppose, for example, there is a single deviation among a small
number of cases or a modest number of deviations among a larger
number of cases. What are the consequences for the deterministic theory under consideration?[5] If the deterministic theory is univariate, that
is, either only one variable or one specific combination of variables (an
interaction) causes a given outcome, the theory can be rejected with a
single deviation if one is confident that there are no measurement errors
(a nontrivial consideration for either statistical or "qualitative" descriptions) and there are no other possible causes of the dependent variable.[6]
As for a multivariate deterministic theory, where more than one variable or more than one combination of variables could account for the
consequence, it can be rejected with a single deviation if there is confidence that there are no measurement errors – as before – *and* also that
all other factors hypothesized to be affecting the outcome are known
and fully taken into account.

The importance of all of this is that the formal procedures used in the
small-N comparative, historical, and organizational analyses under consideration here are all deterministic in their conception. Indeed, small-N
studies cannot operate effectively under probabilistic assumptions, because then they would require much larger N's to have any meaningful
results. This becomes clear when we watch the operation of their reasoning with the methods described by Mill.

Mill's method

As Skocpol (1986) observes, the key issue is the applicability of Mill's
"method of agreement" and "method of difference" to such data. Nichols (1986) agrees, but then criticizes the application of this logic in an

Table 4.1. *Application of the method of difference*

Accident	Drunk driving	Car entering from right-hand direction	Driver speeding	Runs a red light
(Y)	(X_1)	(X_2)	(X_3)	(X_4)
Yes	Yes	Yes	No	Yes
No	Yes	No	No	Yes

earlier study; for example, she shows that it assumes interaction effects but no additive influences. I will build on, and modify, this important critique here.

Let us start with the method of difference, which deals with situations in which the dependent variable (outcome) is not the same for all of the cases. Here the researcher examines all possible independent variables that might influence this outcome, looking for a pattern where all but one of the independent variables do not systematically vary along with the dependent variable. Examples of this might be where X_i is constant in all cases or varies between cases in a manner different from the dependent variable. This method is applied even with two cases, so long as only one of the independent variables differs, while the others are constant across the cases (Orloff and Skocpol 1984). Table 4.1 illustrates this type of analysis. For simplicity, let us assume that all the independent variables as well as the explanandum are dichotomies with "yes" and "no" indicating the presence and absence of the attribute under consideration. To illustrate my points as clearly as possible, I have used an illustration based on automobile accidents. The logic is that followed in Mill's methods and is identical with that employed in these deterministic studies of macrophenomena.

Applying the method of difference to the hypothetical data in Table 4.1, we would conclude that the auto accident was caused by X_2, because in one case a car entered the intersection whereas in the other case no car did. We would also conclude that the accident was *not* caused by drunk driving or the running of a red light, because the variables (respectively X_1 and X_4) were the same for both drivers, yet only one had an accident. Such conclusions are reached only by making a very demanding assumption that is rarely examined. The method's logic assumes no interaction effects are operating (i.e., that the influence of each independent variable on Y is unaffected by the level of some other independent variable). The procedure cannot deal with interaction effects; the procedure cannot distinguish between the influence of inebriation or running a red light and the influence of another constant, such as the benign fact that both drivers were not exceeding the speed limit. Since X_1 and X_4 are constant, under this logic it would follow that neither inebriation nor running a red light had anything to do with the accident occurring. *The procedure does not empirically or logically eliminate interaction effects. Rather, it arbitrarily assumes that they do not operate and that therefore constants cannot influence the dependent variable.*[7] Unless interactions are automatically ruled out a priori, this means that the results in Table 4.1 (and all other small-N applications of the method) *fail* to provide any determination of the influence of variables X_1, X_3, and X_4 on the phenomenon under consideration.[8] Just to make the point very clear, consider another example of the same sort: ten people apply for a job; five are blacks and five are whites. One of the five blacks and all the five whites are hired. Applying the method of difference, one would conclude that race did not affect employment. Rather, it would have to be some variable that separates all of the employed persons from the four who did not get a job. Using a small N with the method of difference, it is not possible to examine interaction effects or multiple causes. Their absence is assumed.

The reader should also note how this method has a certain limited generality unless one assumes, a priori, that only one variable causes the phenomenon under study. For variables that are constant, it is impossible to rule out their influence under different levels simply because there are no measurements. From Table 4.1, for example, we know that an accident occurs although X_3 is constant. Even ignoring the question of interaction effects, it is impossible to conclude that X_3 does not cause accidents unless one assumes there is only one cause of accidents. In this case, and this asymmetry is common in small-N studies, we only know about situations where drivers are *not* speeding. Note again the assumptions that are introduced: if there is any generality to the results, it means that only a single causal variable is operating, otherwise, under the logic used in such studies, the influences of constants are not really taken into account in the method of difference.[9] This has a great bearing on the generality of such small-N comparative studies.

In Table 4.2, we have a new situation in which two drivers both experience accidents. As before, the two drivers are drunk, both cars run red lights, and again in only one instance another car was appropriately entering the intersection, whereas in the other instance there was none. This time, however, the second person was driving at a high speed, whereas the first driver was not. Intuitively, it is not unreasonable that high speed driving could affect the chances of an accident, say causing

Table 4.2. *Application of the method of agreement*

Accident	Drunk driving	Car entering from right-hand direction	Driver speeding	Runs a red light
(Y)	(X_1)	(X_2)	(X_3)	(X_4)
Yes	Yes	Yes	No	Yes
Yes	Yes	No	Yes	Yes

a skid, or the car could have failed to make a turn in the intersection. At any rate, since both drivers have accidents, the logic generated by Mill's method of agreement is applied here, where presumably the causal variable is isolated by being the only constant across the two instances, whereas all of the other attributes vary. However, notice what happens under that logic here. The previous cause, X_2, is now eliminated since it varies between two drivers who both have accidents. Previously, X_1 and X_4 could not have caused an accident, but are now the only two contenders as a possible cause. Since only one driver is going at a high speed now and both drivers have accidents, it follows that the addition of this factor could not have caused an accident, an extraordinary conclusion, too. What has gone wrong? This is an example of how Mill's method cannot work when more than one causal variable is a determinant and there is a small number of cases. Comparison between the two tables shows how volatile the conclusions are about whether variables cause or do not cause accidents. Every fact remains the same regarding the first driver in both cases, but the fact that the second driver was speeding and therefore had an accident completely alters our understanding of what caused the first driver to have an accident. Another shortcoming to such data analyses is that the conclusions are extremely volatile if it turns out that a multideterministic model is appropriate. Moreover, with a small-N study, although it is possible to obtain data which would lead one to reject the assumption of a single-variable deterministic model (assuming no measurement érror), it is impossible for the data to provide reasonable assurance that a single-variable deterministic model is correct, even if the observed data fit such a model.

These comparisons suggest more than the inability of Mill's methods to use a small number of cases to deal with a multivariate set of causes. As Nichols points out, Mill had intended these methods as "certain only where we are sure we have been able to correctly and exhaustively analyze all possible causal factors" (1986:172). Nichols goes on to observe that Mill rejects this method when causality is complex or when more than one cause is operating. Beyond these considerations, important as they clearly are, the foregoing analysis also shows how exceptionally vulnerable the procedure is to the exclusion of relevant variables. In Table 4.2, had we left out X_4, inebriation clearly would have been the causal factor, but it is not clear because X_4 is included. This is always a danger; large-N studies also face the potential danger that omission of variables will radically alter the observed relations, but the susceptibility to spurious findings is much greater here.

Suppose a researcher has a sufficient number of cases such that there are several drivers who have accidents and several who do not. Would the deterministic model based on a small number of cases now be facilitated? In my opinion, it is unlikely. If drinking increases the probability of an accident but does not always lead to one, and if sobriety does not necessarily enable a driver to avoid causing an accident, then it follows that some drunk drivers will not experience an accident, and some accidents will be experienced by sober drivers. Under the circumstances, there will be no agreement for these variables among all drivers experiencing an accident, and there will be no agreement among those not experiencing an accident. This means that neither of Mill's methods will work. A difference in the frequency of accidents linked to drinking will show up, but this of course is ruled out (and more or less has to be) in the deterministic practices involving small-N studies. Multicausal probabilistic statements are simply unmanageable with the procedures under consideration here.[10]

One way of thinking about this small-N methodology is to visualize a very small sample taken from a larger population. Let us say we have a small sample of nations or of political developments drawn randomly from the universe of nations or the universe of political developments.[11] What is the likelihood that the application of Mill's methods to this small sample will reproduce the patterns observed for the larger universe? Rarely, in my estimation, do we encounter big-N studies in which all of the relevant causal variables are determined and there are no measurement errors such that all cases are found so neatly as is assumed here with small-N studies. Yet in order to draw a conclusion, the small-N study assumes that if all cases were equally well known, the patterns observed with the small sample would be duplicated without exception. Is this reasonable? Also ask yourself how often in large-N studies would restrictions to a deterministic univariate theory make sense.

It is also impossible for this type of analysis to guard against the influence of chance associations. Indeed the assumption is that "chance" cannot operate to generate the observed data. Because it is relatively easy to develop a theoretical fit for small-N data, researchers are unable to guard against a small-N version of the ad hoc curve fitting that can be employed in large-N studies [see the discussion of Taylor's theorem in Lieberson (1985: 93)]. Ironically, small-N deterministic analyses actually have the same goal as some types of large-scale empirical research, namely, explaining all of the variance. The former is just another version of this, subject to the same dangers (Lieberson 1985: chap. 5), along with special ones due to their very demanding assumptions necessary when using a small N.

Theoretical concerns

Two implications follow from this review; one is theoretical and the other deals with empirical procedures.

Dealing with the theoretical questions first, obviously the small-N applications of Mill's methods cannot be casually used with all macro-societal data sets. The method requires very strong assumptions: a deterministic set of forces; the existence of only one cause; the absence of interaction effects; confidence that all possible causes are measured; the absence of measurement errors; and the assumption that the same "clean" pattern would occur if data were obtained for all cases in the universe of relevant cases.

At the very least, users must recognize that these assumptions are mandatory in this procedure. The issue then becomes this: Under what conditions is it reasonable to make these assumptions ("reasonable" in the sense that they have a strong likelihood of being correct)? Keep in mind that the empirical data themselves cannot be used to test whether the assumptions are correct or not; for example, the empirical data gathered in the typical small-N study cannot tell us if a univariate deterministic cause is operating or if there are no interaction effects. Theories of large-scale organizations, "qualitative" or not, must direct themselves to these questions before the data analyses begin. Moreover, the theories have to develop ways of thinking about these problems so the researcher can decide if they are reasonable. Admittedly, this is vague advice, and hopefully those dealing with this type of research will come up with solutions. Certainly, the Boolean method proposed by Ragin (1987) is a step in the right direction, although it does require a relatively larger N than the type of small-N studies under consideration here.[12]

The quality of qualitative data

It should be clear how critical it is that small-N studies take extraordinary care in the design and measurement of the variables, whether or not it is a so-called qualitative study. Care is always appropriate, but the impact of error or imprecision is even greater when the number of cases is small. Keep in mind that the deterministic model used in these studies requires error-free measurement. The choice of cases for study is itself critical, requiring great thought about the appropriate procedure for choosing them. Presumably, these are self-evident facts to practitioners of this approach, and the intense scrutiny of a small number of cases should mean exceptional care with the descriptions.

However, exceptionally rigorous practices are necessary to avoid some methodological pitfalls. If a small number of cases are selected using reasonably rigorous criteria, then it makes a great difference whether the outcomes are the same or not in each case. If the same, then the method of agreement is used such that a solution occurs only if one variable is constant in all cases; if different, then the only solution occurs when all but one of the variables are constant across all the cases. All of this is nothing more than a repetition of procedures dating back to Mill. Less obvious, at least as far as I can tell, are the implications this has for the delineation of each independent variable. If an independent variable consists of nominal categories, there should be little difficulty, since presumably trained observers would agree on the classification of each measure. The researcher uses the same checks as would be performed in any large-scale study (e.g., content analysis). But if the independent variable is even ordinal, there is a certain arbitrariness in the way an ordered variable is dichotomized or otherwise divided (polytomized).

To simplify the point, just consider dichotomies. The method of agreement will work only if all the cases for one causal variable fall in the same category *and* if no other variable has such uniformity. This means that the cutoffs are critical. The same holds for the method of difference, but here the results must be such that the results are uniform for all but one variable, with the one critical exception being associated with differences in the dependent variable. Under the circumstances, the delineation of the dichotomies or polytomies is critical and has to be done as rigorously as possible since the boundaries will influence the results enormously. All of this means that rigor is mandatory when locating the variables if they are nominal, and even more so when they are ordinal, for example, careful driver versus careless driver, etc.

With the method of difference, where there is an inverse relationship between the number of cases and the difficulty of finding all but one variable constant across cases, researchers have to guard against using such broad categories as to make it relatively easy for cases to fall under the same rubric. With the method of agreement, where it is vital that all but one variable be different across the cases, the danger is in constructing narrow categories within each variable so that it will be relatively hard for cases to fall under the same rubric. In short, because of the subtle pressure to obtain only one variable that is homogeneous (in the case of agreement in the dependent variable) or only one variable that is heterogeneous (in the case of disagreement in the dependent variable), one must also guard against the bracketing of attributes in the former case, and decomposition in the latter. For this method to work at all, researchers must introduce formal criteria for these decisions which can be followed in advance of a given research project. To my knowledge, they do not exist at this time. (It would be an interesting study in both the sociology of knowledge and research methodology to see if the breadth of categories used in recent studies is related to whether the study involves cases calling for one or the other method.)

Because of the small N's and the reasoning this method requires, it is vital to include all possible causal variables. Yet this will tend to lead to inconclusive results if carried out in a serious way, since the method of agreement will probably turn up with more than one variable that is constant for all the cases and, likewise, the method of difference will have more than one independent variable that is associated with the difference in the dependent variable. Suppose, for example, we find that a drunk driver has no automobile accident, but the sober driver experiences one. In such a case, using the small-N methods practiced in historical sociology, the investigator is in danger of concluding that sobriety causes automobile accidents, or at the very least is the cause in the observed situation. At best, and only if the correct causal factor is included, the study will conclude that either sobriety or some other factor causes automobile accidents. At worst, if the correct causal factor is excluded, sobriety will be the cause. So there is a kind of dilemma here; a "clean" result will tend to occur only with a modest number of independent variables, but this very step is likely to increase the chances of an erroneous conclusion.

Also, the relationship between the independent variables and the dependent variable is distorted if the cases are selected so as to have agreement or disagreement with respect to the dependent variable (rather than simply sampling from all of the cases). It can be shown that sampling in order to obtain a certain distribution with respect to the dependent variable ends up distorting the explanandum's association with the independent variables (unless the ratio of odds is used). Obviously not all cases are equally good, since the quality of the data presumably varies between them, as does the researcher's access to and knowledge about the relevant information. However, this distortion is beyond that problem and makes it even harder to assume that one small sample and another small sample by a second researcher can be combined to generate a more accurate model of the forces under consideration.

Conclusions

A number of assumptions made in these small-N macrocomparative studies are not only very demanding, but to my knowledge they are normally not made explicit or seriously examined. Yet they entail assumptions that are usually indefensible in social research. This leads to a certain curiosity. One possibility is that these assumptions occur because they are the only way of proceeding with such data sets, not because the investigators commonly believe they are correct. In that circumstance, the same assumptions will collapse when studies based on large N's are attempted. Another possibility is that such assumptions are appropriate for certain subject matters such as major institutions, nations, and the like. If that is the case, then a very important step is missing, since these assumptions are rarely justified with empirical data based on a larger number of cases. (That is, as a test, by sampling an extremely small number of cases from large macrosocietal data sets it should be possible to show that the same conclusions would occur with Mill's method as by studying the universe of cases.) At the moment, however, it appears that Mill's procedures cannot be applied to small-N studies. There are strong grounds for questioning the assumptions essential to causal analyses generated by such procedures.

As matters now stand it appears that the methodological needs are generating the theory, rather than vice versa. Put bluntly, application of Mill's methods to small-N situations does not allow for probabilistic theories, interaction effects, measurement errors, or even the presence of more than one cause.[13] For example, in the application shown earlier, the method cannot consider the possibility that more than one factor causes automobile accidents or that there is an interaction effect between two variables.[14] Indeed, if two drivers are drunk, but one does not have an accident, the procedure will conclude that the state of inebriation could not have been a cause of the accident that did occur.

I have selected the automobile-accident example because it should be patently clear that the special deterministic logic does not operate in that instance. Perhaps one may counter that nations and major institutions are neither persons nor roulette wheels; surely their determination is less haphazard, and therefore deterministic thinking is appropriate for these cases. Hence, one might argue, the points made are true for automobile accidents but not for major social institutions or other macrosocietal phenomena. This sounds plausible, but is it true? It turns out that many deep and profound processes are somewhat haphazard too, not so easily relegated to a simple determinism. Elsewhere, I have cited a wide variety of important phenomena which appear to involve chance processes, or processes that are best viewed that way. These include race riots, disease, subatomic physics, molecules of gas, star systems, geology, and biological evolution (Lieberson 1985:94–9, 225–7). One must take a very cautious stance about whether the methods used in these small-N studies are appropriate for institutional and macrosocietal events. At the very least, advocates of such studies must learn how to estimate if the probabilistic level is sufficiently high that a quasi-deterministic model will not do too much damage.

References

Burgess, Ernest W. (1925). "The Growth of the City: An Introduction to a Research Project," pp. 47–62 in Robert E. Park, Ernest W. Burgess, and Roderick D. McKenzie (eds.), *The City.* Chicago: University of Chicago Press.

Isaac, Larry W., and Larry J. Griffin (1989). "Ahistorism in Time-Series Analyses of Historical Process: Critique, Redirection, and Illustrations from U.S. Labor History." *American Sociological Review* 54:873–90.

Lieberson, Stanley (1985). *Making It Count: The Improvement of Social Research and Theory.* Berkeley: University of California Press.

Marini, Margaret Mooney, and Burton Singer (1988). "Causality in the Social Sciences," pp. 347–409, in Clifford C. Clogg (ed.), *Sociological Methodology, 1988, Vol. 18.* Washington, DC: American Sociological Association.

Nichols, Elizabeth (1986). "Skocpol and Revolution: Comparative Analysis vs. Historical Conjuncture." *Comparative Social Research* 9:163–86.

Orloff, Ann S., and Theda Skocpol (1984). "Why Not Equal Protection? Explaining the Politics of Public Social Spending in Britain, 1890–1911, and the United States, 1880s-1920." *American Sociological Review* 49:726–50.

Ragin, Charles C. (1987). *The Comparative Method: Moving Beyond Qualitative and Quantitative Strategies.* Berkeley: University of California Press.

Robinson, W. S. (1951). "The Logical Structure of Analytic Induction." *American Sociological Review* 16:812–18.

Skocpol, Theda (1984). "Emerging Agendas and Recurrent Strategies in Historical Sociology," pp. 356–91 in Theda Skocpol (ed.), *Vision and Method in Historical Sociology.* Cambridge University Press.

    (1986). "Analyzing Causal Configurations in History: A Rejoinder to Nichols." *Comparative Social Research* 9:187–94.

Turner, Ralph H. (1953). "The Quest for Universals in Sociological Research." *American Sociological Review* 18:604–11.

Whyte, William F. (1943). *Street Corner Society: The Social Structure of an Italian Slum.* Reprinted Chicago: University of Chicago Press, 1955.

Znaniecki, Florian (1934). *The Method of Sociology.* New York: Holt, Rinehart & Winston.

Part II
Analyses of research experiences

5
Making the theoretical case[1]

JOHN WALTON

This chapter addresses the question of how cases are construed in the research process – how methodological arguments are fashioned for the purpose of establishing the claim that case studies are related to broader classes of events. My argument is that cases are "made" by invoking theories, whether implicitly or explicitly, for justification or illumination, in advance of the research process or as its result. This interpretation supports a renewed appreciation for the role of case studies in social research and offers a fruitful strategy for developing theory. The argument derives from a research project in which my own understanding of what the case study was a "case of" shifted dramatically in the process of pursuing the study and explaining its results. The research, begun as a study of one thing, later proved to be a study of something quite different. I believe that there is a general lesson here.

Case and universe

The seemingly innocent terms "case" and "case study" are really quite presumptuous. Although they have several connotations revealed in the language of social research, beneath various usages lies a fundamental duality. On one hand, they frankly imply particularity – cases are situationally grounded, limited views of social life. On the other hand, they are something more – not simply glimpses of the world or random instances of social activity. When researchers speak of a "case" rather than a circumstance, instance, or event, they invest the study of a particular social setting with some sense of generality. An "instance" is just that and goes no further. A "case" implies a family; it alleges that the particular is a case of something else. Implicit in the idea of the case is a claim.[2]

Cases claim to represent general categories of the social world, and that claim implies that any identified case comes from a knowable universe from which a sample might be drawn. The case is one point in a sampling frame, and cases are made prepossessing by the universal characteristics which they represent. However modestly researchers advance this claim, it is evident in the way they present their case studies to the audience. To cite only a few well-known examples, sociologists do not represent their work as descriptions of this town, that corporation, or the other public agency, but as cases of *Small Town in Mass Society* (Vidich and Bensman 1958), *The Conduct of the Corporation* (Moore 1967), or *The Dynamics of Bureaucracy* (Blau 1955). Such representations have dual referents. On one side, they obviously enhance the case with the presumption that it stands for certain general features of the social world focused in a particular circumstance. On the other side, and less obviously, they imply known features of the universe from which the case comes – a "mass society," for example, pervaded by impersonality, normlessness, and transient social ties against which small towns persevere in rear-guard actions, or one "bureaucracy" in a maze of formalized, rationalized, and purposive organizations.

Cases come wrapped in theories. They are cases because they embody causal processes operating in microcosm. At bottom, the logic of the case study is to demonstrate a causal argument about how general social forces take shape and produce results in specific settings. That demonstration, in turn, is intended to provide at least one anchor that steadies the ship of generalization until more anchors can be fixed for eventual boarding. To be sure, researchers are careful about this work. We do not want to anchor the wrong ship or have our feeble lines snapped by too heavy a cargo. Better that the case study makes modest claims about what may be on the line. In the logic of research, we endeavor to find fertile cases, measure their fundamental aspects, demonstrate causal connections among those elements, and suggest something about the potential generality of the results. However gingerly, we try to make an argument about both the particular circumstance and the universe. Researchers seldom, if ever, claim that their work deals only with a particular circumstance. And if they sometimes say that they have presented "only a case," the term itself reveals greater ambitions. Cases are always hypotheses.

These observations about the nature of cases seem straightforward. If they do not appear among the conventions of research methodology, that is only because our basic texts neglect to pursue the assumptions made in defense of the case study. The point is demonstrated by two reflections on the evolution of method. First, we should recall that the terminology of cases and case studies appears with particular times and conditions. Weber felt no compunction to subtitle his study of the

Protestant ethic "a case study of John Calvin, his Geneva sect, and the diffusion of their ideas about salvation." The language of cases appears only when sociology begins to reflect on its standing as a social science – to fashion an epistemology of positive science aimed at generalization and the justification of observational evidence for that grander purpose.

Second, we then note in the developing canon of research methodology a conspicuous effort to explain why the newly distinguished category of "cases" may impart valid scientific evidence. Ernest Burgess described W. I. Thomas and Florian Znaniecki's (1918–20) *The Polish Peasant in Europe and America* as "the actual introduction of the case study as a method."[3] In the methodological introduction to that work, Znaniecki argued that scientific social theory is distinguished from common sense by its possession of "a large body of secure and objective knowledge capable of being applied to any situation." Research aimed at developing "a science whose results can be applied" must either "study monographically whole concrete societies" or "work on special social problems, following the problem in a certain limited number of concrete social groups and studying it in every group with regard to the particular form under the influence of the conditions prevailing in this society. . . . In studying the society we go from the whole social context to the problem, and in studying the problem we go from the problem to the whole social context." *The Polish Peasant* was thus conceived as a scientific case study based on objective knowledge which could be shown to apply equally to the social whole and particular manifestations in social groups.

If the foundations of a scientific sociology preoccupied researchers in the United States during the 1920s and 1930s, the canon was forcefully announced in the 1950s in the manual on *The Language of Social Research* edited by Paul Lazarsfeld and Morris Rosenberg (1955). After having explained how social research develops concepts and indices, selects indicators, creates property spaces, and combines appropriately measured variables in multivariate analyses, the editors then note that "this left out a whole other world of research procedures where 'connections' are investigated more directly . . . [where] the crux of the intellectual task lies not in finding regularities, but in applying available knowledge to the understanding of a specific case – be it a person or a collective." In an effort to deal sensibly with the "controversial literature" surrounding this subject, Lazarsfeld and Rosenberg hoped to make headway by going directly to the "problem of causal analysis in a single case." Fortunately, case studies focused on connections and causes yield to systematic methodological treatment because there is a "paradigm behind them" (Lazarsfeld and Rosenberg 1955:387–8).

The paradigm, as it turns out, is the same model of multivariate analysis which Lazarsfeld and Rosenberg advance as the essence of sociological method and the framework for integrating its various operations from conceptual development to statistical analysis. The case-study method is shown to be a less formalized version of the paradigmatic model by identifying the five steps through which it "usually proceeds." In the first step, for example, cases make no sense by themselves until they are linked to something more general. "Certain typological distinctions must be made so that only cases which are fairly compared are treated within the frame of one's study." Next, the causal factors which receive attention within the case should be identified as an "accounting scheme," the evidence gathered, and the "crucial causal assessment" made. Finally, "once the causal factors have been assessed in each single case, all cases in the sample are combined into a statistical result," that is, generalized (Lazarsfeld and Rosenberg 1955:388–9). I submit that the Lazarsfeld and Rosenberg interpretation of the case-study method is, indeed, paradigmatic in social research, even today. The idea is simple. Case studies get at the causal texture of social life, but drift without anchor unless they are incorporated into some typology of general processes, made causally explicit within the case, and ultimately referred back to the universe which the case represents, at least hypothetically.

Yet behind such apparent simplicity lies a more elusive set of theoretical assumptions left unexplored in methodological treatments of the case. The act of making "typological distinctions," of constructing a property space based on key considerations that "frame" the case, involves theoretical choices about the causal forces that distinguish and critically affect the case. Studies of social life in North American communities, for example, focus on places like Muncie, Indiana (Lynd and Lynd 1929), on the assumption that they are typical owing to their location, size, population, industry, civil and religious institutions. Similarly, social relations such as alienation and freedom are studied in several industrial organizations compared on the basis of contrasting production processes (Blauner 1964). In both cases, the typology that identifies a sample of cases also involves causal assumptions, however rudimentary. Population size determines the tenor of community life in some important way; production methods help explain alienation in industry. We justify the choice of cases and distinguish them in certain ways according to some theory of causal relations.

Now the question occurs, Where does the theory about the case come from? The answer implied by Lazarsfeld and Rosenberg, which is to say by methodological convention, is that "typological distinctions" are drawn from a fund of prior general knowledge. That is, cases can be referred to a type, embodied processes identified, and contrasts developed, all because we understand the principles of a well-organized universe. We presume to know what defines a universe of communities or organizations, how one sampled case differs from another, and what is likely to affect their individual behavior. But the presumption is faulty. We do not really know these things at all, we simply make guesses about them – hypotheses. There is nothing wrong with that, provided it is clear that the known universe is an illusion and, with it, that the claim to having a case of something is not supported in any substantial way. Jennifer Platt's essay in this volume (Chapter 1), for example, notes that a study such as Whyte's *Street Corner Society* can be taken as a case of a variety of things.

In actual research practice, of course, cases are chosen for all sorts of reasons, from convenience and familiarity to fascination and strategy. Once chosen, however, the case must be justified – shown to be a case of something important. How is this done? There are at least two ways of making general claims for a given case study. The first is substantive in the sense that the investigator plunges into a "case like other cases," say a hospital or a Third World country, making it clear that the issues presented by the new case are similar to those treated in previous studies of the general case. The new case is justified by showing not only that it pertains to the interpretive issues generated in similar cases, but also that it adds something to substantiate or, preferably, expand earlier understandings. The second form of case justification is analytical in that a strategic argument is developed for the case. A familiar example is Lipset's "research biography" (1964) about the printer's union (which he came to know as a youngster because his father was a member), how it provided a critical "deviant-case analysis" as a democratic labor union that seemed to defy Michels's "iron law of oligarchy." In both approaches, the implicit or explicit claims for the case depend on other cases, not on the known properties of a universe. There is no law of oligarchy. Michels (1915) simply used the phrase rhetorically, and successfully, to summarize his study of European political parties, just as Lipset strategically presented his case as an exception to another case-based generalization.

In fact, as we begin to reflect on the state of general knowledge in social science, it is clear that much of what we know derives from classic case studies. Goffman (1961) tells us what goes on in mental institutions, Sykes (1958) explains the operation of prisons, Whyte (1943) and Liebow (1967) reveal the attractions of street-corner gangs, and Thompson (1971) makes food riots sensible. Examples could be multiplied to show that it is not only the skill and notoriety that these writers bring to their cases that establish them as standard interpretations. Lesser-known works have had the same effect on all of us. Rather, these kinds of case studies become classic because they provide models capable of instructive transferability to other settings. Goffman, of course, suggests an interpretation of the "underlife" for "total institutions" in general, and Thompson's "moral economy" has been used by others as key to other forms of social protest (Scott 1976). It is, therefore, the generalizability of cases that begins to stake out broader typologies and causal processes, not some knowledge of universal sampling properties that frame cases. The universe is inferred from the case.

A logic characterizes this process in which a different kind of universe is posited through generalization of the explanatory principles revealed in the case. Generalization may follow various routes separately or in combination. The phenomenon to be explained may be reconceived as a new family of cases – not mental hospitals but total institutions. Or the explanatory mechanism may be identified in a variety of settings – protest stemming not from absolute or relative deprivation, but from injustice defined by the moral economy. The older universe, itself an expression of theory, is disaggregated and some of its elements combined with newly perceived phenomena in a universe reconstructed as the field of new explanations. It is a logic of robustness. The explanatory principles revealed in case studies are generalized because they can solve new problems, explore new terrain in respecified endeavors analogous to Kuhn's scientific revolutions (1959). In the following section, I examine how these small revolts occur in the research process.

Theory and case formulation

If we take the argument no further, the impression is left that cases are all that we know and that general interpretations in social science are little more than embellished cases. I want to suggest another line that runs between case nominalism and theoretical realism. I shall argue, and then try to demonstrate, that generalizations in social science are developed from case-study methods. Specifically, I contend that we progress from limited to more general interpretations of causal processes through reformulations of the case. Now, it is often true that a provocative case study sets in motion a wave of "normal science" (Kuhn 1959), a rash of studies that replicate and improvise on one case to such an extent that people begin to speak of a "field" with presumptions of general wisdom. This happened, for example, in the decade or so following Floyd Hunter's case study (1953) of Atlanta politics in

Community Power Structure, which spawned hundreds of imitators, commentators, and critics.

No cases are sacred, however. If they are provocative in the first place, inviting models for further application, then they typically lead to conceptual and methodological modifications. Cases are reformulated in at least two ways. One grows directly out of a particular case tradition, while the other begins with a substantive problem and looks for adaptable case models. In practice, the strategies may be combined.

In the first approach, established models gain their appeal from analytical cogency. It is persuasive, for example, to understand that organizations function according to an informal and negotiated order rather than through the formal chain of command, or that communities are run according to the interests of a small group of economic influentials rather than by voter preferences. By highlighting one kind of causal process, the exemplary case study nevertheless neglects others. Kuhn (1959) demonstrates how the essential "facts" of one paradigm may be insignificant in another, and Wieviorka's essay in this volume (Chapter 7) suggests the same figure–ground shift in the analytical categories that inform historical and sociological analyses. New cases become strategic when they challenge or respecify received causal processes. The industrial organization, once interpreted as a setting in which informal work-group norms are generated on behalf of worker control over the production process (Roethlisberger and Dickson 1939), is provocatively reformulated as a place for manufacturing consent among workers in the interests of bosses (Burawoy 1979). Such reformulations may go beyond interpretations of the processes that characterize the case to a redefinition of the case itself. Nigeria, once understood as a national case of advancing political integration and economic development (Coleman 1958), is seen today as a semiperipheral society experiencing class conflict and underdevelopment owing to its place within the proper and holistic world-system case (Lubeck 1986).

In either form, the claim is that the case is about something other than what it was originally conceived to be about. If the new study is convincing, it demonstrates a distinct and robust causal interpretation. Although the Kuhnian metaphor of paradigmatic scientific revolutions is often invoked to describe this kind of reformulation, in social science these shifts emerge in less abrupt or discontinuous ways. New causal interpretations succeed because they supplant previous ones – they explain the old facts and more. The content and boundaries of cases are reconceived precisely in an effort to forge new generalizations that embrace and supersede earlier understandings.

The second avenue of case reformulation adapts available models or fashions new ones to address distinct substantive problems. The old models do not fit, because the new phenomenon is either a different kind of case or one that cuts across conventional boundaries. In an effort to explain agrarian protest movements in developing countries, for example, Paige (1975) abandons peasant society as the appropriate unit and patron–client relations as the decisive causal nexus. National case studies such as Eric Wolf's *Peasant Wars of the Twentieth Century* (1969) fail to get at critical intrasocietal differences in the causes and forms of protest. Variation in the latter, from labor-reform movements to socialist revolutions, is explained by class conflicts as they assume distinctive patterns in "agricultural-export sectors" which become the appropriate units of analysis. Having reformulated the case, Paige goes on to compare statistically 135 export sectors in 70 countries and regional uprisings in three countries (Peru, Angola, Vietnam) which exhibit fine-grained, case-study evidence for the causal interpretation.

By contrast to Paige's problem of redefining and differentiating the case, another researcher may discover that the interpretive key to explaining a phenomenon lies in its generality and timing. Hobsbawm (1981:18) takes that approach to social banditry, "one of the most universal social phenomena known to history, and one of the most amazingly uniform." Although social bandits come in different forms (noble robber, haiduk, avenger), their differences are "relatively superficial [and their] uniformity is not the consequence of cultural diffusion, but the reflection of similar situations within peasant societies, whether in China, Peru, Sicily, the Ukraine, or Indonesia [societies, at the given time] which lie between the evolutionary phase of tribal and kinship organization and modern capitalist and industrial society, but including the phases of disintegrating kinship society and transition to agrarian capitalism." In order to demonstrate the argument, Hobsbawm draws on case-study materials from standard regional histories, biographies of the likes of Dick Turpin and Pancho Villa, and even from poems and ballads collected by ethnographers. Revealed in all these is Hobsbawm's universal case – social banditry conceived as a form of self-defense and retributive justice in peasant societies and caused by depredations in the transition from kinship to capitalist organization. Robin Hood is explained less by the evils of English kings than by the advance of commercial agriculture.

I have used two examples dealing with peasants and protest to show how cases that may be similarly understood in conventional approaches (e.g., processes causally situated in national, rural, or developing societies à la Wolf) are reformulated in radically different ways for new explanatory purposes. Despite the sharply different departures taken by Paige and Hobsbawm, the aims of reformulation are similar. First, the case is reconceived as an empirical instance of something new or previously misapprehended. Second, the new case is precisely made a case by defining it theoretically, by demonstrating its causal connections to a hypothesized general process. Third, the methods and evidence from cases as previously construed are incorporated into the new interpretation – indeed, the old cases may suggest the new idea. Finally, an argument is advanced for the greater scope of the new interpretation.

The question of cases, their designation and reformulation, therefore is a theoretical matter. The processes of coming to grips with a particular empirical instance, of reflecting on what it is a case of, and contrasting it with other case models, are all practical steps toward constructing theoretical interpretations. And it is for that reason, paradoxically, that case studies are likely to produce the best theory. As Stinchcombe (1978:21–2) observes, "if conceptual profundity depends on the deep building of analogies from one case to another, we are likely to find good theory in exactly the opposite place from where we have been taught to expect it. For it is likely to be those scholars who attempt to give a causal interpretation of a particular case who will be led to penetrate the deeper analogies between cases."

Making a case

Although the foregoing argument appears as a general meditation, and I believe that it is valid at that level, it occurred to me only after having wrestled with these questions in a particular research project. Almost ten years ago, I decided that I wanted to do a historical case study of a rebellion that took place in a California rural community during the 1920s. My aims, at least, were clear. I was finishing a comparative study of revolutions in the Third World. That project satisfied my curiosity about the nature of modern revolutions but barely explored other big questions (Walton 1984). I had been studying national revolts that had occurred in such far-flung places as Kenya and Colombia during the 1950s. My own research on Third World development later took me to those places and eventually to a historical study of their revolutions. One of my conclusions about those uprisings was that they stemmed from cultural responses to underdevelopment. Yet my own knowledge of, say, Kikuyu culture was limited and derivative. Next time, I decided, I would study the cultural foundations of political movements in more detail and try to penetrate the motivations for rebellion by using original sources which were more accessible and abundant.

My attention was drawn to an episode known as "California's little civil war," a legendary historical episode of conflict between the Eastern Sierra communities of the Owens Valley and the City of Los Angeles over rights to the valley's water. The events, which took place from 1904 to 1928, were chronicled as an infamous chapter of California history in a wealth of accounts ranging from local histories and journalistic exposés to numerous treatments in popular fiction and film – including, for example, Mary Austin's novel *The Ford* (1917) and Robert Towne's screenplay for Roman Polanski's 1974 film *Chinatown*.

In 1904, Los Angeles initiated plans to build a 240-mile aqueduct running southward from the Owens Valley to the suburban San Fernando Valley that would supply ample water for the city's booming population and commercial development. Through mass meetings and petitions, Owens Valley farmers protested the move, which would supplant a U.S. Bureau of Reclamation project under consideration for local agricultural and hydroelectric development. But they lost the fight in 1906 when Teddy Roosevelt took the city's side by granting a right-of-way for aqueduct construction across federal lands and suspending the reclamation project. Roosevelt was bent on a reorganization of both the national state and the Republican Party. Progressive reform would require allies in the West and the urban middle class in places like Los Angeles in order to wrest power from the Democratic Party machine in eastern cities. Local protest subsided during the construction (1907 to 1913) and early operation of the aqueduct. Indeed, town merchants did not join the initial protest and expected their own fortunes to rise with the city's expansion. But drought in 1919 and city efforts to ensure water rights by purchasing valley farms in the early 1920s prompted a new resistance movement. This time support came from a broad coalition of agrarian and commercial interests who interpreted the city's encroachment as a plan to expropriate and depopulate the entire valley. Throughout the 1920s, the local movement fought for survival against escalating city purchases and economic uncertainty and used a varied protest repertoire: they organized a quasi-public irrigation district under state law to represent all town and farm property owners, appealed to the California legislature, took up arms to defend against city attacks on their canal system, occupied the aqueduct control gates and dumped the city's water during a famous five-day siege, and dynamited the waterworks on ten different occasions between 1924 and 1927. The movement collapsed in 1928, when the local bank failed and citizens turned to cash reparations included in land sales. But the protest was never defeated. Legal and legislative strategies of resistance continued from the 1930s onward, nurtured by a growing legend of the "rape of the Owens Valley," laying the foundation for a modern revival.

As I began to reconstruct these events from untapped primary sources, my initial impulse was to locate the Owens Valley rebellion within the appropriate case-study tradition – to determine what it was a case of. Although several models suggested themselves, none really fit. Pope's classic study (1942) of industrial conflict in a North Carolina textile-mill town, for example, dealt with internal class divisions and absentee ownership, but had little to do with a united community movement directed at the state. The Owens Valley struggle had even less connection to agrarian radicalism, whether in the form of Gamson's "tobacco night riders" (1975) or the Populist movement presented in a number of studies of the Farmers' Alliance (e.g., Goodwyn 1976; McNall 1988; Schwartz 1976). The water war was a product of Progressive Era reforms, and its constituency broadened from farmers in 1905 to town and country participants led by local merchants in the 1920s. Similarly, Lipset's study (1950) of agrarian socialism in Canadian prairie communities focused on a cooperative movement of farmers aimed at prices and markets, rather than a local rebellion against urban incorporation. The available models dealt with cases of agrarian protest, populist mobilization, or community conflict. All of this literature was informative, even relevant in some respects, such as the initial period of protest, but none of it suggested a useful theory.

Considering the available case models, it became clear that I had a case of something quite different, assuming it was a "case" at all or simply a unique historical event. This meant rethinking the causal aspects of the historical case, coming to see that to the extent that the Owens Valley represented something general it must lie in the processes of regional incorporation, the state, and local resistance. Free of old restraints, I was also a bit lost. Persevering in the belief that I had a case, I discovered clear parallels between the Owens Valley and Thompson's study (1975) of the resistance of artisans and smallholders in England's forest communities in the 1720s. The foresters' struggle against the Black Acts, which made capital crimes of hunting and sod-cutting on newly created royal preserves, was generated by a reorganization of the Hanoverian state – specifically by Walpole's efforts to consolidate state support through patronage in the forms of game parks and positions in a new "forest bureaucracy." Local people rebelled against this state usurpation of their common rights with acts of defiance, sabotage, and legal challenges. Nevertheless, Thompson's study had two drawbacks as a model. Although a superb history demonstrating the problems of

English state formation and the role of law in class struggle, it offered no theory of the origin, mobilization, or consequences of protest. The forest uprising, moreover, ended indecisively as local courts supported the recusants and the state went about its intervention in less provocative ways.

Returning to the Owens Valley, the local struggle followed a more distinctive and sequential pattern. In the first place, following the Indian conquest and homestead settlement in the 1860s, the Owens Valley witnessed the development of a frontier culture with its own "moral economy" surrounding questions of state legitimacy which bore some resemblance to the traditions governing Thompson's communities. By 1900, local society embraced the person of Teddy Roosevelt and promises of the Progressive movement as the fulfillment of their pioneer heritage. In the 1920s, it was clear to everyone that the state had betrayed its promised development of the valley. The resistance movement of the early twentieth century drew on legitimating traditions and methods of collective action (petitioning, popular violence, mass mobilization) fashioned historically. Second, the arrested rebellion of the 1920s shifted to a combination of resignation and legal challenges during the Depression and postwar years, but was revived in 1970. A new movement was precipitated when Los Angeles expanded its extractive capability with a second aqueduct at the same time that national and California legislation provided standards for environmental protection. Moving beyond Thompson, the changing state and its new interventions in local society seemed critical to these events (e.g., Skowronek 1982). All these developments became apparent as I decided to widen the time frame of the analysis in search of a model of historical change in the relation of state and community.

By now, I have decided to create a new model of state and local society, drawing on "period studies" such as that of Thompson and the literature on U.S. populism, but moving across several periods of state organization and its changing influence on local society – the differences, for example, between the state at the times of the 1862 Homestead Act, 1902 Reclamation Act, and 1970 National Environmental Protection Act, and the consequences of those differences for local society. The research, now some years on, became a longitudinal case comparison. Local history, rather than any preconceived design, suggested three periods defined by the relationship between state organization and regional development. The expansionary state from 1860 to 1900 witnessed frontier settlement at the behest of the army and public land provision. The progressive state from 1900 to 1930 orchestrated governmental reform and the incorporation of a national society (Wiebe 1967).

And the welfare state from 1930 to the present expanded state intervention and bureaucratic responsibility for managing regional affairs.

Finally, the case came together with the discovery that each period displayed a characteristic pattern of collective action. During the nineteenth century, pioneer society developed the civic means of law enforcement (e.g., vigilance committees) and basic service provision (e.g., cooperative "ditch companies" for irrigation, church schools, and roads built through private subscription), activities which the institutionally weak nineteenth-century state failed to address. Mining corporations and the railroad entered the valley in search of profit, but excluded local producers and merchants from their freight monopolies. A pattern of dependent development generated protest movements along class lines. Farmers formed a populist cooperative union and merchants and teamsters petitioned for access to markets at the mines. Yet the pattern was one of fragmented class action rather than unified initiatives. Classes quarreled, among themselves over who was at fault for dependent development, and across status group lines with Indians over wages and the liquor trade. But they never challenged the legitimacy of the state or the mining companies whose institutional interests governed their lives. The pattern shifted in the Progressive Era, and precisely in a transition from agrarian class action in 1905 to the community rebellion that began in 1919, because the state incorporated a willing frontier society with developmental plans and legitimating promises that were later betrayed. The arrested revolt simmered as the legend of local culture grew, ultimately reasserting itself as a social movement under the banner of environmentalism in the 1970s and 1980s. And this time they won. That is, Los Angeles was forced to make important concessions to local control, development, environmental protection, and joint resource management (Walton 1991).

As the longitudinal case comparison came into focus, so did the theory. These were cases of the changing role of agency in history, apropos of Thompson's moral economy and, even more directly, of Tilly's changing forms of collective action. In his study of French contention, Tilly (1986) discovered a pattern of change over 400 years from local patronized (e.g., food riot, property invasion) to national autonomous (e.g., demonstration, social movement) protest forms. His explanation focuses on the interplay of state formation and capitalist development. Tilly's pattern of historical change in collective-action repertoires provides instructive parallels to the Owens Valley, although the two studies are conceived at the opposite poles of state and local society. Yet the difference proves strategically advantageous by allowing a tighter focus on the interplay of state and local action – how such powerful forces as the state and capitalism affect people on the ground and, indeed, how people organize to resist those influences or turn them to local purposes. The theory of resource mobilization, for example, explains collective action as a product of interests, opportunity, and a capacity to organize (Jenkins 1983). Yet such formulations do not explain how and why Owens Valley citizens rebelled during the 1920s in the face of little opportunity or made their own opportunity in the 1970s by bringing distantly legislated environmental protections to bear on their grievances in an imaginative and protracted legal struggle. Those achievements stemmed from a deeper moral economy fashioned by traditions of popular justice and legitimacy – from organization, to be sure, but through changing forms of organization expressing the values and capabilities of a local culture.

In this study, as Stinchcombe observes, theory is developed through a causal interpretation of the particular case and analogies between cases. Changing forms of collective action in the Owens Valley are explained by the intersection of evolving state policies (expansion, incorporation, environmental welfare) and local mobilization responding to grievances in ways suggested by the moral economy. In different aspects, the process is analogous to Thompson's treatment of local resistance to state incorporation and Tilly's longitudinal analysis of changing protest forms. Indeed, the interpretation here is informed by a synthesis of cases which become cases through application of the causal analogy. Analogies identify similar causal processes across cases, meaning that cases are those bundles of reality to which analogies apply. Causal processes discovered in cases and generalized through analogies constitute our theories. Thinking about cases, in short, is a singularly theoretical business.

This formulation of the Owens Valley case around issues of state, culture, and collective action is but one of a variety of conceivable theoretical choices. The region or portions of its history could be "cased" (in the sense of the noun-verb described in Charles Ragin's essay, Chapter 10) as something altogether different in another interpretive project – as a case, for example, of frontier settlement, environmental conflict, or incorporation of the urban hinterland. The choice of one strategy or another is not decided on the basis of what is a "better case," but on the explanatory advantages produced by formulating a case in one way or another. This implies, of course, that certain elements of a given empirical situation can be construed as different kinds of cases.

Conclusion

I come back to the theme of my initial remarks. If my experience at coming to understand a case resembles that of other researchers, then the introductory sections of this essay may describe a general strategy. The Owens Valley study began with the ambition of probing in more depth the causes of rebellion analyzed in previous cross-national case studies. In the early going, my assumption that the Owens Valley presented a case of something familiar in U.S. history or in the sociological literature on local uprisings was frustrated. The episode belonged to no known universe from which typological distinctions could be drawn and causal explanations hypothesized. On the contrary, suggestions about what it might represent came from other case studies and causal analogies. Because they were inexact, those analogies forced a reformulation of the Owens Valley case. Indeed, I realized that it was usefully reconceived as three cases of collective action linked in a longitudinal process. This methodological shift opened the way to theoretical progress. Changing forms of collective action, addressed in insightful national and social-movement case studies, required emendation. Mobilization, interest, and opportunity in standard interpretations become intervening analytical categories in an explanation that focuses on the cultural and ideological foundations of action. A theory of state and culture may enhance the explanation of collective action insofar as it is examined where people live – on the ground in local societies. If the analysis accomplishes anything, it does so by pursuing the deceptively simple question "A case of what?"

Any case, of course, may offer a variety of answers to the question "A case of what?" Rather than arguing that there is a single or ideal answer, I am saying that any answer presumes a theory based on causal analogies. What constitutes the best answer at a given time will be decided by those communities of social scientists who confirm today's theoretical fashion and will surely change as new questions are put to old cases. Indeed, the great value of so many of our classical case studies is that they continue to provide the material of new interpretations – to provide a case of many things depending on the vigor of new theories.

References

Austin, Mary (1917). *The Ford*. Boston: Houghton Mifflin.
Blau, Peter M. (1955). *The Dynamics of Bureaucracy*. Chicago: University of Chicago Press.
Blauner, Robert (1964). *Alienation and Freedom*. Chicago: University of Chicago Press.

Burawoy, Michael (1979). *Manufacturing Consent: Changes in the Labor Process Under Monopoly Capitalism.* Chicago: University of Chicago Press.

Coleman, James S. (1958). *Nigeria: Background to Nationalism.* Berkeley: University of California Press.

Gamson, William (1975). *The Strategy of Social Protest.* Homewood, IL: Dorsey Press.

Goffman, Erving (1961). *Asylums: Essays on the Social Situation of Mental Patients and Other Inmates.* Garden City, NY: Anchor Books.

Goodwyn, Lawrence (1976). *Democratic Promise: The Populist Movement in America.* Oxford: Oxford University Press.

Hobsbawm, Eric (1981). *Bandits,* rev. ed. New York: Pantheon.

Hunter, Floyd (1953). *Community Power Structure: A Study of Decision Makers.* Chapel Hill: University of North Carolina Press.

Jenkins, J. Craig (1983). "Resource Mobilization Theory and the Study of Social Movements," *Annual Review of Sociology* 9:527–53.

Kuhn, Thomas P. (1959). *The Structure of Scientific Revolutions.* Chicago: University of Chicago Press.

Lazarsfeld, Paul F., and Morris Rosenberg (1955). *The Language of Social Research.* New York: Free Press.

Liebow, Elliot (1967). *Tally's Corner: A Study of Negro Streetcorner Men.* Boston: Little, Brown.

Lipset, Seymour Martin (1950). *Agrarian Socialism.* Berkeley: University of California Press.

(1964). "The Biography of a Research Project: Union Democracy," pp. 111–39 in Phillip E. Hammond (ed.), *Sociologists at Work.* New York: Basic Books.

Lubeck, Paul M. (1986). *Islam and Urban Labor in Northern Nigeria: The Making of a Muslim Working Class.* Cambridge University Press.

Lynd, Robert S., and Helen M. Lynd (1929). *Middletown.* New York: Harcourt, Brace & World.

McNall, Scott G. (1988). *The Road to Rebellion: Class Formation and Kansas Populism, 1865–1900.* Chicago: University of Chicago Press.

Michels, Robert (1915). *Political Parties: A Sociological Study of the Oligarchical Tendencies of Modern Democracy.* Reprinted New York: Dover, 1959.

Moore, Wilbert E. (1967). *The Conduct of the Corporation.* New York: Random House.

Paige, Jeffrey M. (1975). *Agrarian Revolution: Social Movements and Export Agriculture in the Underdeveloped World.* New York: Free Press.

Platt, Jennifer (1988). "What Can Cases Do?" *Studies in Qualitative Methodology* 5:1–23.

Pope, Liston (1942). *Millhands and Preachers: A Study of Gastonia.* New Haven, CT: Yale University Press.

Roethlisberger, Fritz J., and W. J. Dickson (1939). *Management and the Worker.* Cambridge, MA: Harvard University Press.

Schwartz, Michael (1976). *Radical Protest and Social Structure: The Southern Farmers' Alliance and Cotton Tenancy, 1880–1890.* New York: Academic Press.

Scott, James C. (1976). *The Moral Economy of the Peasant: Rebellion and Subsistence in Southeast Asia.* New Haven, CT: Yale University Press.

Skowronek, Stephen (1982). *Building a New American State: The Expansion of National Administrative Capacities, 1877–1920*. Cambridge University Press.

Stinchcombe, Arthur L. (1978). *Theoretical Methods in Social History*. New York: Academic Press.

Sykes, Gresham M. (1958). *The Society of Captives: A Study of a Maximum Security Prison*. Princeton, NJ: Princeton University Press.

Thomas, William I., and Florian Znaniecki (1918–20). *The Polish Peasant in Europe and America*, 5 vols.; 2nd ed., 2 vols., New York: Knopf, 1927.

Thompson, Edward P. (1971). "The Moral Economy of the English Crowd in the Eighteenth Century," *Past and Present* 50:76–136.

(1975). *Whigs and Hunters: The Origin of the Black Act*. New York: Pantheon.

Tilly, Charles (1986). *The Contentious French*. Cambridge, MA: Harvard University Press.

Vidich, Arthur J., and Joseph Bensman (1958). *Small Town in Mass Society: Class, Power, and Religion in a Rural Community*. Princeton, NJ: Princeton University Press.

Walton, John (1984). *Reluctant Rebels: Comparative Studies of Revolution and Underdevelopment*. New York: Columbia University Press.

(1991). *Western Times and Water Wars: State, Culture, and Rebellion in California*. Berkeley: University of California Press.

Whyte, William Foote (1943). *Street Corner Society: The Social Structure of an Italian Slum*. Reprinted Chicago: University of Chicago Press, 1955.

Wiebe, Robert H. (1967). *The Search for Order, 1877–1920*. New York: Hill & Wang.

Wolf, Eric R. (1969). *Peasant Wars of the Twentieth Century*. New York: Harper & Row.

6
Small N's and community case studies

DOUGLAS HARPER

As John Walton (Chapter 5) suggests, cases in sociology have the dual character of situational groundedness and theoretical generality. The case, as an example, implies a larger category. My contribution to this discussion suggests how an inductive method, focused on individuals or small groups, may get at what Walton has called the "causal texture" of the social life of communities. That implies that the deductive, natural-science model, with specific hypothesis testing and statistical analysis, may not allow us to see the most sociologically meaningful boundaries of cases or the complexities of their social processes. I will also discuss methodological issues which arise from using a small N to build a theory of community. I will use as points of reference my study of railroad tramps (Harper 1982), the work of a rural mechanic (Harper 1987), and an ongoing study of a dairy-farm community.

The question of how we conceptualize and study cases has given sociology a dual character since it began. Auguste Comte, writing in the early nineteenth century, asserted that the new field of sociology was a natural extension of natural science. Social facts, he argued, were indistinguishable from physical facts; the same methods could be used to measure them, and sociological study "would ultimately generate the same kinds of law-like propositions and explanatory coverage believed to be present in the natural sciences" (Truzzi 1974:1). From the beginning of sociology, this view has been balanced by the belief that understanding human action requires a more complex set of tools than those employed in natural science, and that the goals of social science should move beyond the search for "recurrent sequences" of social life to include an understanding of the point of view of the subjects of study. Wilhelm Dilthey began this dialogue in response to Comte, and Weber later developed the idea of *verstehen* – the importance of understanding the full dimensions of social life in social and historical research.

139

Weber, in fact, remained committed to the scientific method, but understood that "as soon as we attempt to reflect about the way in which life confronts us in immediate concrete situations, it presents an infinite multiplicity of successively and coexistently emerging and disappearing events, both within and outside ourselves" (Shils and Finch 1949:72). Thus we should avoid a method which radically simplifies in the search for laws. Weber wrote that "in the social sciences we are concerned with psychological and intellectual phenomena the empathetic understanding of which is naturally a problem of a specifically different type from those which the schemes of the exact natural sciences in general can [solve] or seek to solve" (Shils and Finch 1949:74). We should not abandon science, Weber cautions, but should transcend scientific reasoning and methodology, which reduce human life to simple causal sequences.

From these earliest debates, sociology has maintained an ambivalent stance toward the narrowly defined scientific method, composed of distinctive levels of abstraction (theory, hypothesis, case) and explicit procedures for hypothesis testing. The logic and methods of scientific sociology were applied primarily to the study of the social characteristics and processes of large-scale, industrial society. For the most part it was left to anthropologists, working among smaller groups in traditional, nonindustrial societies, to develop the case-study methods appropriate for the kin group, informal network, or small community.[1] Ethnography (as the case study of the small group came to be known) typically begins with description of settings, objects, and the behavior and classifications of individual and groups, and ends with an analysis of the structural relationships among the elements of the group. VanMaanen (1988:7) calls these "realist tales [which] provide a rather direct, matter-of-fact portrait of a studied culture, unclouded by much concern for how the fieldworker produced such a portrait."[2]

A more complex level of cultural description involves learning and communicating the point of view of those we study, first identified as an appropriate sociological focus by Weber, as mentioned earlier. Weber identified the problem as one of understanding the "historical other," and he did not develop research methods for the study of living, contemporaneous culture. Ethnographers who have sought to understand the point of view of their subjects have had to fashion (and continue to fashion) means by which this goal can be approximated. Thus, while methods used in conventionally empirical case studies have become fairly standardized (primarily in the form of the social survey), ethnographic methods continue along experimental lines. And, while the confidence of scientific method underlies "modernist" and "scientific" sociology, a tentative and incomplete claim for knowledge lies at the basis of "postmodern" ethnography (Clifford and Marcus 1986). While the postmodern critique has blurred the boundaries between ethnography and other forms of discourse such as autobiography and literature, the critique does not suggest that we abandon ethnography altogether. Its usefulness is in reminding us of the frailties of our claims for knowledge and the need for an ever-evolving experiment in ethnographic description and analysis. VanMaanen (1988:120) concludes his analysis of ethnographic practice with the suggestion that "we need more, not fewer, ways to tell of culture. The value of ethnography from this standpoint is found not in its analysis and interpretation of culture, but in its decision to examine culture in the first place; to conceptualize it, reflect on it, narrate it, and, ultimately, to evaluate it."

To summarize this section, ethnographic case studies represent the evolution of a mandate identified by Weber for an "interpretive sociology." The ethnographic case study has become the post-modern "tale of culture," in which description is taken as problematic, and in which theory, rather than an edifice from which hypotheses may be mechanically derived, assumes a more tentative, inductive character. The goal of description remains, however, to arrive at theoretical understanding. The "point of view" of the individual informant is the basis for understanding the shared points of view of the group (in this case, the community) to which the subject belongs.

Achieving this understanding includes hypothesis testing but is not limited to the strictly empirical renderings of social life. We may think of it, rather, as a reasoned analysis of such questions as "Do the data (nonquantifiable as well as quantifiable) tend to or appear to support the hypothesis?" Blumer suggested that concepts which are the elements in such hypotheses be thought of as sensitizing instruments – guides for looking that do not overwhelm the situational particularity of the circumstances, settings, or groups under study. Using the inductive approach grounds concepts in ensuing rounds of observation and analysis (Blumer 1969:148–50). In other words, the theoretical understanding which emerges from ethnographic case studies is gradual, tentative, and grounded in ensuing rounds of data gathering (Glaser and Strauss 1967). I have used this reasoning process in the case studies of several communities.

Cultural definitions of place in the community case study

The community case study, unlike case studies of such phenomena as "mass society" or "bureaucracy," is grounded in concrete, identifiable settings. Yet the boundaries and sociological characteristics of settings are often taken for granted, or defined in an ad hoc manner, meaningful to the researchers but perhaps not to the subjects under study. For example, sociologists often use bureaucratically derived boundaries, such as those defined by census tracts, to define a community. Or they may use commonsense assumptions about organizations to mark boundaries of units such as bureaucracies. Lining up the sociological definition with bureaucratic definitions makes data accessible and comparable. Yet such definitions may overlook boundaries or characteristics which emerge from an inductive approach grounded in the points of view of community members. In the following I consider the process of defining community and the nature of community in my studies of railroad tramps, a rural artisan, and dairy farmers.

Space and tramp community

To understand the social life of the homeless man I found it necessary to enlarge upon what had been taken for granted as the "community" of the homeless. The commonsense idea, at the time I completed the study (well before the current crisis of homelessness), was that the homeless man lived in dilapidated areas of cities usually called skid rows. Sociologists who studied the homeless man limited their study to institutions found in skid row: the mission, flophouse, single-room-occupancy hotel, jail, or social service agency. While some sociologists produced a rich and multidimensioned understanding of the world of the homeless by immersing themselves in these settings, particularly Wiseman (1970), most studied the homeless at a distance, using surveys and other standard procedures to test hypotheses derived from quite explicit theories about such topics as alienation and family structure. The surveys increased our knowledge about the social etiology of homelessness, but did not lead to an understanding of the community of the homeless as defined by those on the streets.

James Spradley (1970) was one of the first to see the cultural importance of "place," as defined by the homeless man. Employing "ethnoscience," a method which reveals the natural language categories of a culture, Spradley discovered that tramps (the term the homeless men Spradley studied used to describe themselves) see themselves and each other largely in terms of how they inhabit several quite different settings. "Homeguards" are tramps who remain, during their tramping career, in the same locality. "Bindle-stiffs" move about on freight trains and carry all of their possessions in gunnysacks tied to sticks. "Rubber tramps" move about in old cars. Spradley discovered, in fact, that the tramp defined himself in at least thirteen different ways, based primarily on their typical settings and modes of transportation.[3] Prior to that time, skid-row men had been characterized as "anomic," "normless," and "socially disorganized." Spradley's research demonstrated that the group possessed culture in the sense of shared categories, signaled by words, and intricate plans for action, indicating purposefulness. This line of reasoning, grounded in the point of view of the subjects, led me to study a wider set of the cultural settings that had, for one reason or another, been left out of the extensive research on the homeless man.

As I began field research on the homeless I realized that the "community" of the homeless[4] was not a boundaried, settled population, but a group on the move geographically and through cycles of working, drinking, and migrating. Community, in this case, more accurately described bundles of cultural expectations than populations in a location. For example, as the homeless man moved through a cycle of drinking, migrating, and working, he faced a series of different norms, values, and expectations. Each setting called upon a different facet of the whole community of the tramp, and each implied a different set of behaviors. The freight train was not simply a means to get to a different place, but a setting in which one either succeeded or failed to act out cultural norms. These included such mundane issues as proper ways to ride, including what freight cars to select or what gear to carry. More importantly, the norms indicated codes from which to fashion one's own behavior, alone and with others. Thus the tramp defined himself through such actions as not drinking on a train, even if his life included periodic long drunks on skid rows. A tramp with whom I traveled during my fieldwork commented on an incident in a freight car in which this cultural "sorting out" took place:

[referring to events in a boxcar we had been riding] "Now you saw how quick some of those guys took that wine. . . . That one didn't have no clothes – no nuthin'. He's just goin' from town to town bummin'. Probably got his clothes from the Salvation Army, or else he's workin' somewhere around here, out on a drunk and started runnin'. . . . But you tell me – what was different about all those guys that were bummin' on the train? . . . Those bums had low-quarter shoes with stockings falling over their ankles. Holes in the shoes, holes in the pants. Your tramps, even if they were dirty, had working man's clothes – and they wore boots and a hat. Did you see that guy across the car? *That's* your tramp. He don't talk much – he don't speak until he's spoken to. Did you see how he was carrying his bedroll? Tied like mine. Clean shaved." [Harper 1982: 84, 89]

The strategies for catching a train, dodging rail police, and finding one's way from one end of the country to another, and the norms that guided behavior among tramps on freight trains and in railroad jungles, are bodies of cultural knowledge which define who is a member of the community, and who is not.

The cultural definition leads to an understanding of the structural role of the tramp community. This includes an understanding of the tramp as agricultural laborer in economies which depend on intermittent, intense labor. The tramp rode to the apple harvests in the isolated river valleys of western Washington on local freights that were connected to main lines in Spokane and Wenatchee; they harvested the apples and spent their wages (or had them stolen by jackrollers or police) in the local towns, and they rode out of the harvests – generally penniless, after finishing the harvest – on the same trains that had brought them to the area two months earlier. Many of the tramps experienced a regular cycle of events through which they participated in quite different "communities" on the freight, in the hobo jungle, and during the harvest. Only the failures of the tramp world – those defined by the tramp as "mission stiffs" – lived permanently on skid row. Those had been the only homeless men who had been studied by sociologists, and thus the limited view of the community of the homeless had severely narrowed what had been known about tramp life.[5]

Community as social networks

I emphasized the role of social networks in the community built by Willie, a rural mechanic, in his shop (Harper 1987). The specific boundaries and characteristics of the setting – a mechanical shop on a quarter acre of land cut out of agricultural fields, filled with a homemade Quonset-hut shop, several rusting cars, a wrecked school bus full of engine blocks, and miscellaneous pieces of farm machinery and metal – are easily documented. The community created by the shop, however, is better understood as a network of farmers and low-income rural people who depend on the mechanic to keep old agricultural implements, automobiles, and house-systems in repair. The network consists of reciprocal relationships which extend from the shop through the surrounding area. This can be conceptualized as a moral community within which quite distinct norms operate. To become a customer is to enter into the normative community, rather than to engage in a contractual, one-dimensional relationship, as is the case in typical service relationships. Entering the community means accepting such things as the mechanic's definition of time. This means, for example, that the length of time a repair will take will not be defined ahead of time; nor will Willie's work be hurried for a worried customer. When a crisis happens, however – the breakdown of a farm machine needed immediately for seasonal work, or the breakdown of an automobile owned by an individual who has no other means of transportation – Willie will work nearly around the clock to "get the farmer back to work," or to "get a person back on the road." As the center of the community, Willie determines what forces will motivate him to work. To be in that community means accepting his definitions, waiting in line with the realization that a sort of moral queuing up has taken place as Willie confronts the problems of many more people than he can immediately help.

The reciprocal relationships of the shop also allow Willie to replenish the material he uses for repairs and restorations. Relationships extend for years, and even decades, and a gradual evening-up process is accepted as normal. As an illustration, Willie and I were examining a photograph of an upturned truck box in the middle of his yard. Our conversation reflects this process:

Willie: A guy brought a truck in and wanted it cut down into a trailer. I made the trailer – that's the trailer I was using in the woods. Someday he'll come and pick it up. I cut the cab off, narrowed the frame up, and put a hitch on it. Then he gave me the front part of it for the work I did on the trailer. I'm going to make another trailer out of it. From the frame where it was cut off to make his trailer you've got your whole front end that carried the motor. You can make a trailer out of that too. Put a draw hitch on it – see, this is off the frame already. The other part sits up there in the parking lot.
Doug: It looks like he was getting a better deal than you were.
Willie: Not really. He's one of these fellas – he's done a lot for me. If I need something done and he knows I want it done and I'm not in too good a shape to do it – *he* does it. He wouldn't let me go onto my roof to put the shingles on – he did it. So it's one of those deals – well, I've known him, oh, thirty years. . . . You work with your friends and your neighbors and you work out a lot better. . . . [Harper 1987:158]

Willie's community extends to several square miles and through the personal histories of many of the people who live there. Stories told in the shop become a tradition of folklore through which community norms are enforced.

Just as with the rail tramp, an understanding of the cultural definition of community illuminates larger issues. In the case of Willie's shop, these forces are economic and social. Farmers who have depended on Willie's particular skill and values are in steady decline due to factors far removed from the immediate community. Newcomers to the area, who are used to and are able to afford specific, contractual arrangements when buying services such as automotive repair, have little need for or interest in a blacksmith's skill or membership in an informal community as part of fixing their cars or machines. Social change at a different level leads to new zoning laws that slowly redefine a repair shop with a lot of spare parts around as a small junkyard, a blight on the landscape. The space of the shop shrinks; the shop proprietor becomes isolated, and his subtle power in a group of interdependent people fades. The work of an individual, in this sense, is much more than skilled actions. It is social action enmeshed in a fragile web of community, itself a function of social forces operating at a macrolevel, an impersonal level.

To understand the community which radiates out of an individual's working world one must see it from the point of view of the individual, emergent in the normal talk and actions of the shop. It is not discernible through censuses or commonplace assumptions. Its fundamental feature is change – ongoing redefinition of social networks through the actions of people who play out one of several options available to them in any given social interaction. In Durkheim's terms, it is social integration measured in the number and intensity of social contacts, and its moral integration is understood as the extent of the shared beliefs which direct and guide the social interaction.

Community and hypotheses in case studies

Definitions of community may be quite different in more conventional case studies. I am currently surveying one of several New York State dairy communities in order to see the impact of differing human-capital resources and environments on agricultural productiveness and farm viability. I have agreed with my colleagues in the study to define "community" as an area containing fifty farms. Each community, to be comparable, needs to contain the same number of farms. Community thus becomes an equivalent unit in different regions, differing in easily measured ways. However, this largely expedient manner of defining community masks important differences between study populations. At the simplest level, the dairy farms may constitute a small percentage of the rural residences in one community and nearly all rural residences in another. The dairy community may cover a hundred square miles in one community and fifty in another. These, and other more complex dimensions, strongly influence what is meant, in a cultural sense, by "community."

We face a dilemma. Defining community one-dimensionally allows us to measure comparable elements, test specific hypotheses, and thus extend or criticize social theories. But doing so confuses a definition reached for expedient reasons with a concept, built from the ground up, which takes into account the points of view of community participants. Such a study might reveal community as networks of cooperating farms

(Stadtfeld 1972), linked together by shared labor or common use of support institutions. Kin networks may have great importance in these dairy communities (Salamon 1982), or they may be organized around ethnicity (Salamon 1985) and religion, perhaps sharing a folklore based on common heritage as the basis for individual farm identities (Glassie 1982). Thus, if we were to do an ethnographic case study of a community of dairy farmers, we would begin by having these people define the networks through which they participate in social life. A study of a single community would inform studies of subsequent communities, but those studies would not be strictly comparable.

Perhaps the best resolution to this issue is to maintain a close focus on the purpose of specific research. The inductive approach may create a portrait which most closely resembles the social reality of the setting, but may limit the comparative usefulness of the case study. Social surveys of communities which are defined from a kind of research expediency foster hypothesis testing and comparative analysis. Depending on the questions asked, this approach may yield useful data. But such an approach does not exhaust the potential definitions of community, nor does it treat the concept of community in terms grounded in the subjects' definitions or experiences.

Method and small *N*'s in the community case study

Conventional case studies generally focus on the institutional or group level: communities, religious groups, voluntary organizations, occupations, and the like. Because of the complexity of these phenomena, hypotheses and theories need to be clearly defined, and data gathering tends to favor explicit methods such as census analysis or social surveys. The focus is on the behavior of the aggregate; the individual is reduced to a sequence of responses to a questionnaire or to a set of formal attributes on a census (see Abbott, Chapter 2, for a critique).

The ethnographic case study may begin and end with the individual and his or her small group. Most sociologists' lists of important case studies based on the individual include Nels Anderson's *The Hobo* (1923), Clifford Shaw's *The Jack-Roller* (1930), Whyte's *Street Corner Society* (1943), and Carl Klockers's *The Professional Fence* (1975). I would add John Berger and Jean Mohr's *A Fortunate Man* (1967) and Bruce Jackson's *Thief's Primer* (1972) as particularly interesting examples. In the following comments I will raise questions about how we gain access to cultural knowledge and justify our trust in its truthfulness. These are, in different terms, the issues of reliability and validity.

Finding informants

Intensive focus on an individual or small group presupposes field methods rather than surveys, analyses of census data, and other forms of data gathering which lead to quantitative analysis. In the quantitative study, the representativeness of the sample is determined statistically. In the ethnographic case study the representativeness of the "sample" (which can be a single individual) is determined informally. One must gain deep knowledge of a setting to judge whether or not the individual who has become one's informant can be taken, in any of several ways, to represent the group. This is usually an indefinite and often an arduous process. The initial informants one happens on in a new setting are often deviants in their own group, happy to find an audience with a newcomer. When I began studying rail tramps, for example, I soon learned to avoid the tramp who was quick to be friendly. These men, I learned, were outsiders in a group which protected its privacy and established limited and regulated relationships. It took several months and several thousands of miles of travel to find and recognize an informant who carried on the traditions of tramp life and was willing to express them to me. The process of "buddying up" (a tramp category for establishing a relationship of the road), however, happened informally and in the process of fieldwork, rather than as a result of a formal evaluation. We both got on the wrong train in Minneapolis, heading for the apple harvest two thousand miles distant. He was coming down from a two-week drunk; I had enough food to tide us over the days of our meandering trek across Montana. Slowly, and very grudgingly, the tramp accepted my company, which he took great pains to define for me in tramp terms:

[Carl] "Yeah, there's a lot of tricks on this road, but only a few important ones. You have to learn to stay away from the rest. Set up camp after dark. I never let anybody know where I'm goin' – I wait until the campfire's out and then I disappear. I don't want nobody to follow me!" Then he looked me straight in the eye. "Some people on this road are helpless. When you start helpin' it's just like having a son – they don't know where it stops! You got to support them – take care of them – you got to provide the hand and I won't do that. If a fella is on this road and he can't learn – then to hell with him!" [Harper 1982:35]

In this case, finding an informant required establishing a culturally typical relationship. Such relationships may require that we leave behind our own values relating to social interaction and patterns of association, that we define something such as "buddying-up" as do those we choose as subjects. This can cause a great deal of emotional and psychological distress, especially when the new expectations strongly violate the cultural baggage we bring to the field. In the case of the tramp study I was not successful at maintaining this separation. The tramp, who knew me as an outsider, rebuffed my attempts to establish something more like "friendship" with constant reminders of how people treat each other on the road. While the subject is often passed over in ethnographic writeups, it is extremely important in that the things we learn are deeply influenced by the nature of the social bonds we maintain with those we study.

When I studied the community of Willie's shop, for example, my ideas grew gradually and naturally out of a typical "client–provider" relationship. I learned about the subject of the study, Willie, as I hired him to fix the old cars, house, and machines we needed to live in the area and set up a rural business. As I learned about my informant, I also learned how to live in a culture with decidedly different norms than I had experienced. Coming from the hustle of urban anonymity, I had to learn to act in a traditional community, where one's actions are watched closely and remembered for years (and may, in fact, become part of community folklore). I learned slowly to queue up in this community, to take my turn and quell my impatience. The process of "finding an informant" became, in part, a process of examining and redirecting my own life in a culture I now studied.

Finding an informant, however, need not follow such arcane, informal, and, one can say, inefficient procedures. For several years, I hesitatingly began and paused on a field study in the sociology of agriculture. I tried to find a "way in" to the culture by volunteering several weeks of labor one spring to a farmer. There was not, however, an easy role to assume on the farm as a volunteer laborer. All farm tasks were assigned to family members or hired hands; anything I did in the normal routine of farm work was resented by the individual who usually did the job. My work was limited to out-of-the-routine tasks like unloading fertilizer sacks or building a chimney, which the farmer was glad to get done but which did not teach me much about farming. Occasionally I did minor tractor work, but the specialized jobs of cropping and milking were off limits. After about five weeks I had not learned enough about the issues which had drawn me to the field to justify continuing, and I summarily withdrew.

After several experiments with open-ended interviewing of farmers that did not lead to in-depth cultural understanding, or lead me to a pool of informants from which I would finally "do ethnography," I completed a rather conventional survey of the farmers of a dairy community. In order to add ethnographic depth to the survey, however, I have spent several hours with each farm family, and while interviewing

in the dead of a cold winter there have usually been tasks – retrieving
hay, shoveling manure – that I have been able to do to help out a little
and gain a fuller understanding through informal talk and observation
than I would have by simply asking the questions on the form. The
survey has been the vehicle through which I have learned the characteristics of a population, which I am now studying in order to choose, in a
"rational" and "formal" manner, subjects for more in-depth study. I
mention this example because it is a reversal of the usual means by
which case studies are done. Typically a brief period of fieldwork precedes a survey, which is the fundamental data gathering activity. The
idea of using the survey as the means by which to identify informants
for a more in-depth, ethnographic case study is unusual. It does, however, offer a way in which the systematic treatment of a population
through a survey may be married to a qualitative, in-depth examination.[6]

These are, then, some of the issues which influence finding subjects
for ethnographic case studies. We begin with little or no knowledge of a
setting; either through immersion or through a procedure such as formal data gathering we learn what is culturally "typical." With luck we
find an individual or a small group willing to act as a subject, an
informant. Only then begins the process of learning.

Relationships and learning

We live in a world in which increasing amounts of our time and our
relationships are formally organized. Most of us are inundated by surveys – phone surveys, mail surveys, and an occasional in-person survey, seeking information on an incredible array of topics. Many of us
resent being interrupted, taken from the small periods of time left over
in our increasingly complex lives. Enter the fieldworker. What reason
does a subject have for cooperating with a stranger seeking "knowledge
for knowledge's sake"? There are usually no compelling reasons for
cooperating. As I reflect on transforming a friendship into a researcher/
informant relationship, which characterized my study of Willie's work,
I wince at the complexity, subtlety, and sometimes painfulness of the
process. And as I confront farmers, who are the busiest people I have
ever met, it is never clear to either of us why they should pause to talk.

The answer has to do with the irrational rewards of human relationships. If we are successful in the relationships we establish with those
we study, people will cooperate. In each study the circumstances change.
When I studied tramps I learned to leave most of my own cultural
baggage about relationships out of the picture and to interact with my
informants on their terms. I did not like the limitedness of the relation-

ships and my ability to redefine "friendship" in the narrowed sense of tramp bonds, but I learned to recognize these qualities as appropriate for the setting and consistent with what was expected of me. When I used my neighbor as a subject, part of the understanding which created our "research relationship" was that I would portray Willie in the terms that we had agreed upon. This meant, for Willie, that the topic of the study was a category of work rather than his private life. I felt the book we wrote largely accomplished that purpose. The moment of truth came, however, when the publisher's marketing director announced his intention to call the book *Willie: Portrait of* (something like "the last American Independent," although I don't recall the exact title). I knew such a title would offend Willie and violate our informal "terms of agreement." The marketing director persisted; if I wanted the book marketed more widely, I needed another title. I had learned enough from my years around the shop to know that one's actions can have a long-standing impact on people's reputations and identities. Willie was not a member of a faraway tribe; my characterization of his life would have a genuine and powerful effect on how he was seen by his peers and himself. We retained the original title, *Working Knowledge*, which has indeed helped make the experience satisfying for Willie.

That we learn through human relationships forces us into a kind of emotional/rational schizophrenia. Relationships of the type I speak of here are of the heart; sociology is supposed to be of the mind. In the field, we develop empathy or antipathy for our subjects; yet we observe and record with the cold dispassion of a physicist. It becomes necessary to live in both worlds, motivated and affected by the genuinely subjective feelings (meaning that they have meaning for the observer only) that grow up in all intimate human contact, yet able to draw back sufficiently to treat one's subject in sociological terms. It is never possible to maintain that dualism completely. In one of the most compelling accounts of this dilemma, Jean Briggs (1970) tells of how her dislike for one of her Eskimo subjects caused her, eventually, to act in a way which temporarily destroyed her relationship with the group. She made her study an examination of Eskimo emotions in order to come to grips with their way of dealing with each other, but also in order to understand her emotions as an outsider and fieldworker, and as a human being.

Finally, it is only partially honest to use the term "relationship" to characterize the research process in ethnographic case studies. Relationships are typically run on a logic which comes from human give-and-take. When research ends, however, we break our connections with the group in an arbitrary and one-sided manner. These endings can be painful for both sociologist and subject. They show the fiction that underlies the connection between the studied and the studier. The subject has welcomed you into his or her life; you've learned there and come to care yourself; and then, when the research is over, typically you break it off and go about your business.

Reporting the small-N community study

I've suggested that relationships are the basis for the research, and they influence whom you find to learn from and how you present your information. In this sense, relationships are necessary but not sufficient for the ethnographic case study. They lay the basis for learning, but they are not learning. How then, if we go about our research with an inductive, theoretically tentative approach, do we learn in the case study?

Each case study demands a different mixture of observation, participation, and interviewing. There are tools that facilitate these operations: cameras have been used to record observations; tape recorders or video cameras have made interviewing a more controllable method. How these three elements come together, as I suggested earlier, varies greatly.

For example, to study railroad tramps I began with large doses of participation and observation. I had to learn how to live in the places they normally lived in, public spaces like skid rows, or illegal places like freight trains that you could use if you gained the right cultural knowledge. I gained that knowledge by hit-and-miss but rapid learning during longer and longer visits to the setting. During initial experiences in the field I recorded observations in a small notebook and in black-and-white photographs. Because I was participating by the rules of the group – I slept out with tramps, risked arrest, mixed with the jackrollers as well as tramps, and had to learn to avoid or evade the local hoods who frequently beat up rail tramps – I photographed very little. The photography, as one might guess, attracted attention. I did not broadcast that I was usually a graduate student rather than a tramp, but I did tell the truth if anyone asked. Since I was sharing the externalities of the life, it did not seem to matter much to anybody.

I spent several months over three years participating and observing the life of the railroad tramp. While I gradually became adept at managing life on the road at the practical level, my data were limited to written observations and photographs. No interviews with tramps had revealed more than the nuts-and-bolts information about riding freights and avoiding police, and I had not encountered, in my travels, an informant who would take on the headier issues of the culture. I despaired of getting further and considered abandoning the project.

Looking back at it now I can see that the long gestation was necessary for this particular study. When I finally did "buddy-up" with a tramp, I knew the role sufficiently to hold up my end of the relationship. The "interviewing" that emerged from our month-long trip across the country to the apple harvest was natural conversation about shared experience. Our relationship, for whatever combination of reasons, got deeper than many on the road, and the tramp told me a great deal about his life that he probably had not revealed to other men with whom he had traveled. I recorded conversations mostly by remembering and writing. I did not write in the company of others; there were plenty of hours waiting for trains when I wandered off to be by myself and to get down as much as I could remember. I also carried a small tape recorder and used it to record a few hours of talk; mostly at night during the end of our trip, when we camped in the orchards we were eventually to harvest.

The talk that was our interviewing had a natural beginning and ending. It grew out of our shared experience of finding our way several thousand miles on freights, waiting in hobo jungles with other tramps for the harvest to begin, and eventually landing a job. Once the work began, our time together was limited to a few evening hours in an orchard cabin we shared as workers. The purpose which had brought us together was accomplished, and what had been (to me, at least) intimate conversation quickly dried up. I worked long enough in the orchards to make enough money to get back to Boston, where I was in graduate school, and considered that stage of the fieldwork finished. While this sounds rather cut-and-dried, the reality is that the letdown at the end of our experience was very difficult personally. For me, our month-long trip had been a ritual of male bonding (and I instinctively expected our relationship to continue). For the tramp it was but another moment in a repeating cycle of events and temporary companions.

I describe the process of the fieldwork in some detail to show how interviewing, in some research projects, is an organic part of shared experience, impossible to pluck, upon command, from life. In other words, when the relationship upon which fieldwork depends disappears, so does the basis of talk from which we learn.

Most sociological fieldwork is different from what I have described. Most participation and observation are arranged formally and take place in institutions. Interviewing is generally a systematic examination of topics which the sociologist wishes to explore. The interaction between the interviewer and subject is usually for one session (or interview) only. The assumption is that one-time interviewing will produce information in sufficient depth to accomplish the research goal.

In the ethnographic case study the researcher will look in more depth with a smaller number of subjects; perhaps, in extreme cases, even one. But how is one to achieve this "greater depth"? Most subjects are willing to be interviewed a single time, but many researchers (myself included) have found that subsequent interviews often seem to circle back to initial subjects or to run into dead ends. On a similar vein, interviews which record simple reactions to events or straightforward descriptions pose little problem; interviews which probe more subtle meanings and values are correspondingly more difficult to achieve. One method that ethnographers have used to solve these problems has been to employ visual images (generally art objects from the culture, or photographs of the culture) as a kind of "Rorschach test," or projective device to which subjects respond in extended and ongoing interviews. John Collier (1967) described how this process of "photo-elicitation" (leaving the art side out of it, for the time being) was used in several anthropological studies done during the forties and fifties. Despite Collier's careful and enthusiastic documentation of the successes of this method, photo-elicitation has been little used in ethnographic case studies.

I turned to photo-elicitation to explore the subjective definitions of work in my study of Willie's shop. I sensed that by understanding Willie's work in detail, I could learn about how he had gained his knowledge from his father's store of traditional knowledge, how his work had evolved as the technology he dealt with changed over time, and how his relationships with his neighbors were orchestrated and mediated through barter and other means of exchange. I expected that I could learn about Willie's relationships with his family by first understanding how the family unit was organized around accomplishing the work of the shop. Our initial conversations, however, seemed to get stalled at the same quite simple level. I also began to understand that the first photographs I took of the shop reflected my culturally uneducated perspective, and thus lacked much ethnographic meaning.

It seemed reasonable to apply Collier's ideas both to inform my photography and to probe Willie's point of view. Over a three-year period we worked in this way: of the many hundreds of photographs I took at the shop I assembled groups of images which generally documented the flow of work on individual jobs. We discussed these photographs in tape-recorded interviews which built on each other over a several-month period. The photo-elicitation interview worked in this instance because the subject began as a material, visible process. (I can imagine sociological topics where it would not yield much.) The interviews had a different character and feeling from other in-depth interviews. Rather than focusing on an individual as subject (which usually makes people uncomfortable), the interview is organized around a physical artifact (the photograph). The subject becomes the teacher, explaining in greater and greater detail (as encouraged by the researcher) the several layers of meaning in the image. A simple repair of a tractor, for example, leads to a discussion of barter, the evolution of technology and farming practices, the nature of Willie's relationship with his son, his engineering knowledge and hand skill applied to transforming discarded machine parts into a usable machine, and finally his sense of his own identity and his role in the community.

As I suggested earlier, photo-elicitation offers a solution to getting beneath the surface in some in-depth interviewing. In the past few years, several sociologists have successfully applied the method.[7] I have found the technique useful in student projects on everything from a study of the student's parents' divorce (in this case using the family album to gain several family members' definitions of the social dynamics of the family) to a study of the social meanings of professors' offices. The technique has several steps, and it calls on a wider repertoire of skills than many sociologists possess. It does offer, however, rich potential in research problems where the core of the study can be made visible.

Reporting the results of more conventionally empirical case studies is seldom a problem. Researchers learn to eliminate editorial or subjective elements from their writing by writing in the third person or the passive voice and by using qualifiers. In the narrowest sense, the point of the research report is to describe "objective social facts," which are elements of the world that an independent audience would define in the same way. Researchers subtract themselves, as much as possible, from the report.

This issue once again raises the question of how "scientific" our methods are or can be. If we believe that human behavior can be dealt with in essentially the same manner as objects in the physical world, then we can describe research results in the same language we use to analyze experiments in natural science. Because we use the language of science, our findings seem to carry the authority of science. A small trick is being played here: we agree to accept sociology as science (in the narrow sense of hypothesis testing I have referred to throughout this essay) because it uses the tools of science and sounds like science when it is written.[8]

I have suggested that the ethnographic case study draws on both affective and rational sentiments enmeshed in many-dimensioned human relationships. If this is correct, we must find a way to describe not only what happened "out there," but also what happened "in here."

Working through these issues has been one of the most challenging problems I have faced in my research. An unavoidable dilemma underlies the issue: if you write like a sociologist, other sociologists will recognize what you do as sociology. If you seek experimental forms of writing and presenting information (such as by using photographs or film), your work will be rejected or treated as a curiosity – certainly not real sociology. And yet enough social scientists continue to question the implications behind scientific presentation that experimental forms of presentation continue, and even gain a grudging respect. Part of the experiment with presentation, as I suggested earlier, derives from the postmodern critique of ethnographic authority, and part of the experiment consists of a long but nearly underground tradition of what John VanMaanen has called "confessional" and "impressionist" tales (VanMaanen 1988:73–84). In my own work, I have felt, for example, that writing in the first person is an honest and accurate way of reporting what I have done and seen in ethnographic research. Writing in the first person naturally leads to narrative in which you write not only what you observed, but also what you felt. I chose to present my ethnography of rail tramps in this way: a single field trip represented a typical moment in repeating cycles, for the tramp, of drinking, migrating, and working. I sought to present the cycle of events from my own point of view as well as the point of view of those I met. My fears, anxieties, and emotional highs were as much a part of what I learned as were the rituals and rules of tramp life. Still, I did not have the confidence to transform my field notes into narrative until I was encouraged by Everett Hughes, my thesis advisor, to "tell the whole story." The resulting documents, both thesis and book, retain the narrative emphasis, which is separated from more conventional sociological presentation by chapter breaks. It is one way of doing it, but certainly not a final answer.

As I have thought about the problem of telling in subsequent projects, it has seemed appropriate to preserve several voices in the final text. This, too, is consistent with ongoing discussion within ethnographic theory about "polyvocality," text as dialogue, and other admonitions to abandon the traditional notion of scientific authority in ethnographic presentation. I have thought about these issues in terms of solving concrete problems in presenting ethnographic knowledge. When I wrote about Willie, several voices emerged. The voices were Willie's in formal interview, Willie's as storyteller (represented as vignettes about shop life), and my voice as social theorist, observer, and interviewer. I thought of writing the book more as assembling these several voices (each with a distinctive perspective) rather than creating a linear and one-dimensional analysis. To preserve the voices we presented the text in several formats: some italicized, some justified right and left, others left with unjustified right margins. It is a simple solution. The physical presentation of data becomes part of the message of the text.

Final statement

The question of "What is a case?" is a complex inquiry into how we conceptualize the social world, how we gather data, how we establish relationships with our subjects, and how we report our findings. In the preceding comments I have allowed myself the pleasure (but hopefully not self-indulgence) of reflecting from my own research experience how I have resolved several of these issues. Some social scientists see the process of defining problems and research techniques as unproblematic. More and more, however, social scientists address the deep complexity of these issues. The "small-*N*" community case study may provide a particularly apt setting in which to develop and refine our ideas about our work.

References

Anderson, Nels (1923). *The Hobo: The Sociology of the Homeless Man*. Chicago: University of Chicago Press.
Becker, Howard (1980). "Culture: A Sociological View." *Yale Review* 71:513–27.
    (1986). *Writing for Social Scientists: How to Start and Finish Your Thesis, Book or Article*. Chicago: University of Chicago Press.
Berger, John, and Jean Mohr (1967). *A Fortunate Man*. New York: Pantheon Books.
Blumer, Herbert (1969). *Symbolic Interactionism: Perspective and Method*. Englewood Cliffs, NJ: Prentice-Hall.
Briggs, Jean (1970). *Never in Anger*. Cambridge, MA: Harvard University Press.
Bunster, Ximena (1977). "Talking Pictures: Field Method and Visual Mode." *Signs* 3:278–93.
Clifford, James (1983). "On Anthropological Authority." *Representations* 1:118–46.
Clifford, James, and G. E. Marcus (eds.) (1986). *Writing Culture: The Poetics and Politics of Ethnography*. Berkeley: University of California Press.
Collier, John (1967). *Visual Anthropology: Photography as a Research Method*. New York: Holt, Rinehart & Winston.
Glaser, Barney, and Anselm Strauss (1967). *The Discovery of Grounded Theory: Strategies for Qualitative Research*. Chicago: Aldine.
Glassie, Henry (1982). *Passing the Time in Ballymenone: Culture and History of an Ulster Community*. Philadelphia: University of Pennsylvania Press.
Harper, Douglas (1982). *Good Company*. Chicago: University of Chicago Press.
    (1987). *Working Knowledge: Skill and Community in a Small Shop*. Chicago: University of Chicago Press.

Jackson, Bruce (1972). *A Thief's Primer.* New York: Random House.

Klockers, Carl (1975). *The Professional Fence.* New York: The Free Press.

Salamon, Sonya (1982). "Sibling Solidarity as an Operating Strategy in Illinois Agriculture." *Rural Sociology* 47(2):349–68.

(1985). "Ethnic Communities and the Structure of Agriculture." *Rural Sociology* 50(3):323–40.

Shaw, Clifford (1930). *The Jack-Roller.* Chicago: University of Chicago Press.

Shils, Edward, and Henry Finch (eds.) (1949). *Max Weber: The Methodology of the Social Sciences.* Glencoe IL: Free Press.

Spradley, James (1970). *You Owe Yourself a Drunk: An Ethnography of Urban Nomads.* Boston: Little, Brown.

Stadtfeld, Curtis (1972). *From the Land and Back.* New York: Scribner's.

Suchar, Charles S., and Richard A. Markin (1990). "Forms of Photo-elicitation: Narrative Reflections of Micro-social Realities." Paper presented at the annual meetings of the International Visual Sociology Association, Whittier College.

Truzzi, Marcello (ed.) (1974). *Verstehen: Subjective Understanding in the Social Sciences.* Reading, MA: Addison-Wesley.

VanMaanen, John (1988). *Tales of the Field: On Writing Ethnography.* Chicago: University of Chicago Press.

Whyte, William Foote (1943). *Street Corner Society: The Social Structure of an Italian Slum.* Reprinted Chicago: University of Chicago Press, 1955.

Wiseman, Jackie (1970). *Stations of the Lost.* Boston: Little, Brown.

7
Case studies: history or sociology?[1]

MICHEL WIEVIORKA

Anyone familiar with the practice of medicine in hospitals has, in France at least, heard talk about "good" patients. When you ask what is meant, the reply may be unexpected for a sociologist. The "good patient" is not necessarily the one who fits into the health-care system's roles and norms as described by Parsonian sociology. Nor is he necessarily the one who takes good care of himself, wants to "get better" and trusts in modern science. No, the "good patient" may also be a "case." But what does this mean? A "case" is an illness that a doctor, though seldom encountering it, can either recognize, because it has been listed in medical literature, or describe in all its originality so as to be considered to have "discovered" it (or a variant) and have it named after himself.

This spontaneous medical usage has the advantage of combining distinct elements. A case is defined by its occurrence, which, in the example cited, is exceptional. But the doctor takes a case to be significant only if it refers to a phenomenon (an illness) that has been or can be described in the professional literature and that other medical practitioners have encountered or will encounter. A "case" designates, on the one hand, a specific patient and, on the other, an illness independent of this patient. Usage thus refers this word to its practical, historical unity (the patient) but also to its theoretical, scientific basis (the illness as described and listed, or as can now be listed for the first time). Hence, a case is both unique in that it affects the patient, an individual, and reproducible, though seldom so, in that it has to do with an illness. Both characteristics are necessary to talk about a case. A case that is unique in the history of medicine does not as such appear in medical repertories; and a patient with an ordinary syndrome is not so singular as to represent a significant case. Notice that this double characteristic holds only for medical professionals. For the sick person, his illness, whether exceptional or ordinary, is unique since it bears on his own existence. It concerns himself, a single person, at a precise time and affects, even if

159

temporarily so, his personal history, experience, relations, and work. A "case" is a case for an observer, not for the affected person, unless he has internalized medical pronouncements about his condition.

These preliminary remarks provide a starting point for an inquiry into the notion of a case study in the social sciences. For a "case" to exist, we must be able to identify a characteristic unit, whose unity is given (at least initially) in concrete historical experiences. This unit must be observed, but it has no meaning in itself. It is significant only if an observer (like the forementioned doctor) can refer it to an analytical category or theory. It does not suffice to observe a social phenomenon, historical event, or set of behaviors in order to declare them to be "cases." If you want to talk about a "case," you also need the means of interpreting it or placing it in a context. Though necessarily referring to a stock of factual knowledge, a case study cannot be merely empirical. Regardless of the practical approach for studying it, a case is an opportunity for relating facts and concepts, reality and hypotheses. But do not make the mistake of thinking that it is, in itself, a concept. A case draws its unity not from the theoretical tools used to analyze it, but from the way it takes shape, namely as a social or historical fact combining all sorts of elements into a set comprising social roles, an institution, a social movement, or a logic of community action. But it is not, in itself, these roles, this institution, or this social movement.

By talking about a case, we propose bringing theory and practice together in a special way. This sets us apart from two approaches. First of all, as pointed out, it sets us apart from purely empirical ones, or rather from those reduced to pure empiricism. For example, participant observation is sometimes (though rarely) content with collecting data and then presenting them as such without theorizing. Secondly, talking about a case sets us apart from a purely speculative approach that, looking away from facts, concentrates on ideas alone. In this sense, it leads us afar from philosophy and resolutely places us inside sociology and history. This is where the problems really start.

Historical versus sociological aspects of cases

An event, or situation, does not, alone, constitute a case, at least not as long as it is defined by its singularity. Since the same event, or situation, can be observed neither before nor afterward, we are forced to admit that it is, in fact, a historical phenomenon. To understand such a phenomenon, we have to see it as a combination of elements (which a historian calls causes or factors) that, taken separately, may not be exceptional. These elements are multiple and diverse; and their combination is always new and irreproducible. Even when history stutters, it does not repeat itself exactly, as Marx (1969:15) said when referring to Hegel:

Hegel somewhere stated that all major historical events and persons are, we might say, repeated. He forgot to add: the first time is a tragedy; the second, a farce.

Methodologically speaking, the idea of history as a synthesis of distinct elements may mean that reality can be seen more clearly from several viewpoints than from any single perspective. In this sense, Simmel, at the beginning of this century, championed methodological "relativism," which some scholars prefer calling "relationism." It is worthwhile to emphasize that, whatever the method adopted, history cannot be the science of cases, and everything that is historic is not a case. As suggested by the remarks about the "good patient," there must be something else, which enables us to see a larger phenomenon or interpret it with the help of a broader category, something transcending the experience itself.

As an initial approximation, we can say that scholars adopt one of two approaches to a case study.

First, a case may serve to signal the presence, in a historical experience, of a simple element or particular characteristic that the social scientist wants to bring to light and that constitutes an analytical category, just as chemists try to isolate a pure element out of a compound. From this same approach, a case may also (this already implies a larger perspective) be selected for what it represents in an abstract or theoretical construction. For example, a concrete case may be the starting point for building a Weberian ideal type. Both these choices, and their many variants, are essentially sociological. The intent is either to interpret the case with a sociological tool (the analytical category hypothesized as present) or to use the case at hand to develop a tool for handling other cases as well. Of course, these two sociological intents are not contradictory. They may govern, together, a scholar's endeavor to simultaneously test a sociological hypothesis (or even quantify it) and improve the means of testing.

Secondly, a scholar's viewpoint may no longer be aligned with a sociological perspective. He may examine a case not in order to discover an elementary analytical category (e.g., a logic of action or a process), nor to see what theoretical structure (e.g., an organizational form or ideal type) it can be used to build or consolidate, but to learn what it teaches concretely about a reality defined from the outset as a complex synthesis. This does not mean that the case is a link in a succession of events, or situations, to be explained only by their chronology, their place in the chain of history, but rather that it is selected for study because it can be used to make a diagnosis in history or to exemplify a historical hypothesis. In this respect, someone might talk about the Romanian, Czechoslovakian or Polish cases in order to illustrate general historical hypotheses (e.g., that the events in late 1989 signaled the decline of Communism or the end of Soviet imperialism). Such research may be sophisticated, like the classical study of the "affluent worker" by Goldthorpe et al. (1968–9). To disprove the thesis that the working class, having reached middle-class status, was dissolving into a society without class conflict, these authors chose a special situation: not one favorable to their position, but one as apparently unfavorable as possible. They wagered that, if the thesis could be proved false in such an extreme case, then it would not hold for intermediate ones. Hence, Luton, a prosperous industrial center with companies known for high wages and social stability, was selected as the test case. Although the working class seemed much more integrated there than elsewhere, long fieldwork enabled these scholars to discover an autonomous working-class culture and thus prove the persistence of a class identity.

When referring to a case, scholars seem to be divided between sociological and historical approaches. Of course, the study of a single case may combine both, and some scholars do not distinguish clearly between them. Nonetheless, there is no reason to confound these two approaches, even though they may complement each other.

Historical and sociological aspects of terrorism

From 1976 to 1981, I participated in a team, directed by Alain Touraine, that addressed a twofold objective, historical and sociological, for studying social conflicts.[2] Our research illustrates the possibility of combining these two approaches without confusing them.

In pursuit of a sociological objective, we hypothesized that it would be possible to discover, buried under actors' crisis behaviors as well as institutional and organizational preoccupations, the marks of a social movement – of an action with a lofty plan involving general cultural choices wherein actors recognize their own and their opponents' social identities. The notion of conflict was empirical – referring to such concrete experiences as students on strike or antinuclear activists organizing a demonstration. The concept of a social movement was theoretical – referring to a purely analytical category to be isolated within the complex reality of conflicts.

Our approach implied another hypothesis, namely, that in the late 1970s France ceased being an industrial society, wherein social movements referred to the working class, and turned into a postindustrial society, whose central protestors would be new social movements defined in terms of culture, communication, or science, not just in relation to the world of work and industrial production. As it shed light on the presence (though slight) of these new movements in the conflicts under study, this research also sought to validate this hypothesis about societal change. This was our historical objective.

If a case is to be studied under the tension of combining these two approaches, a major obstacle crops up that does not exist as long as a case is defined in only historical or else sociological terms. As our research showed, sociological and historical approaches can be brought together to study a single case or set of cases. But can this combination be more than mere juxtaposition? How far can these two approaches, which complete and shape each other, be combined?

Historically defined, a case involves all sorts of elements, each of which, taken separately, may be related to a discipline, theory, or analytical level within a theory, but they cannot all be unified by a conceptual analysis alone. Coherency comes exclusively from historical totalization – from the convergence, in the experience under study, of perhaps unrelated factors. Sociologically defined, a case has no significance unless referred to a precise, coherent theory or method. Sociology helps us understand history dimly at best. It can focus but a narrow beam of light on events, a beam all the narrower because of the discipline's relatively distinct, even fragmented, paradigms, methods, and approaches. This may explain why sociologists are so poor at making predictions – why, for instance, no American sociologist had foreseen the widespread civil-rights movement[3] or why, more recently, no great social or political scientist foresaw the Soviet bloc's rapid breakup. Historical synthesis and sociological deconstruction are not alike, even though each may be applied to a single unit of study. A case study will, therefore, continuously oscillate between these two disciplines without necessarily being fully drawn to one or the other. The exemplary, paradigmatic, or representative nature of a case is one thing; its unity as a historical synthesis, something else.

Nonetheless, I believe research will advance not by confusing but by combining these approaches. By circumscribing a field of investigation in time and space, a case study may even be the best way to justify making a combination. Commenting on sociological classics such as *Street Corner Society* and *The People's Choice*, Platt has pointed out that these can be read as oscillating between historical and sociological poles of analysis (see Chapter 1). Walton too has implicitly distinguished between these two poles (see Chapter 5). A case thus provides the opportunity for pursuing the effort to bring together, without mixing them up, historical and sociological approaches.

My own research on terrorism (Wieviorka 1988) illustrates this idea, but first a few preliminary remarks about my method of sociological intervention. During the initial phase of this research in 1981, I asked a group of seven former terrorists (Italian leftist refugees in Paris) to participate in a process, lasting several months, during which they would successively meet various other actors in their experiences. Group members talked freely and deeply with about fifteen guests, each invited to a session that lasted three hours on the average. Were they fighting capitalism? I arranged a meeting with the head of a big company. Were they leading a fight in the name of the proletariat? I arranged a meeting with a union member. Did the press manipulate information and deviate their actions? I arranged a meeting with the director of an Italian daily. And so forth. Following this, the group met without any guests, and I presented my own hypotheses about its members' experiences as terrorists. Lively, often tense, discussions followed, which helped me improve my hypotheses, which the group then used to interpret its own historical experience and analyze the armed struggle in Italy during the 1970s. To refine my analysis, I undertook a second sociological intervention with another group of former terrorists, who, also Italian, represented another major tendency, to use the jargon of the times; they were less working class or Marxist-Leninist and more "spontaneous" or "autonomous." In like manner, I studied the Basque separatist revolutionary organization by meeting with both former and then-still-active members of ETA. Whereas the major reference marks in the Italian phenomenon had been the social movement and revolution, Basque references were to a national consciousness as well as Marxism-Leninism, to the working-class movement as well as new social movements.

From 1981 to 1988, I thus developed the means for sociologically analyzing terrorism and tried to apply them to important or significant cases. I had to examine existing concepts and arguments and use them either directly or indirectly so as to construct new ones. In particular, I had to sort them out, eliminate the inappropriate, and establish a hierarchy of the apparently useful. For example, functionalist theories of political violence as a response to a crisis (of the state, the political system, etc.) or as a frustrated actor's reactions seemed weak and sometimes did not even fit. The instrumental perspective of the so-called sociology of resource mobilization, though insightful when dealing with violent actors' strategies, seemed incapable of shedding light on the delirious nature of extreme, pure terrorism. The idea that a "culture of violence" is a factor in the adoption of radical behaviors or the formation of a terrorist personality was stimulating but did not seem applicable to all situations. And so forth.

Finally, I came upon the idea that full-blown forms of terrorism come out of a complicated process I called *inversion*. I developed this concept, which did not exist in the sociological literature, because I was facing a twofold problem. For one thing, I realized that, although many terrorist groups speak in the name of a social movement or real community, there is no direct connection between the recourse to violence and the reference group's (people's, class's or nation's) concrete life and expectations. Terrorism could be explained in relation to such a reference group, but it also seemed to be in contradiction with it (for instance, when workers felt that their interests were hindered by the actions of a terrorist group speaking in their name). For another thing, I also realized that, although terrorism is linked to an ideology or religion, it is, at least in extreme cases, not a direct expression of an ideology or religion. In other words, it takes categories from Marxism-Leninism or Islam, for instance, but distorts, even inverts, them. Lenin would have condemned the violence committed in his name, just as many Moslems do not recognize their religion in the actions committed by certain radical Islamic groups. With this concept of inversion, I designated a twofold phenomenon that consisted of both speaking "artificially" in the name of a reference group and distorting an original source of inspiration in ideology or religion. This concept emerged in the course of research when I realized this twofold phenomenon was at work in different cases of terrorism and that the unity of all these cases lay in this very process.

The analytical concept of inversion, applied to various cases, enabled me to make a sociological diagnosis. I could thus indicate and interpret major phases in certain terrorist groups' trajectories and show how far these groups were from the theoretical limit of a pure, blind terrorism disconnected from the reference groups for whose sake they claimed to be acting. This did not meet with everyone's approval, especially not when I concluded that the ETA in Spain was not purely terroristic from a sociological viewpoint. Many Spaniards found this conclusion hard to accept.

Can the analysis of cases help us understand terrorism from a historical viewpoint? In my opinion, we can thus focus attention on usually underestimated or overlooked aspects and, thereby, gain original insights. For example, to understand the 1978 kidnapping and assassination of Aldo Moro by the Italian Red Brigades, we might not think of measuring the distance separating working-class struggles and the Italian far Left at that time. Nonetheless, a key to understanding this episode lies therein.

A major point needs to be made. The way I arranged various arguments in a hierarchy led me to assign sociological value to factors of little account historically. By placing the process of inversion at the center of my thinking, by maximizing it, I minimized factors that might be determinants in history, such as leaders' personalities, that capability of the police and judicial system to manage violence, or the primary networks of solidarity through which activists are recruited. In other words, the sociological approach undoubtedly exposed a process that produces terrorism; but it could explain neither why nor how this phenomenon occurs in one place but not another, and it was of practically no use for making predictions. In my study of Basque and Italian terrorism, I tried to combine sociological and historical approaches. When I look back at this research, I cannot help seeing that the one approach exposed a central process, whereas the other worked out a synthesis for understanding the cases at hand. This might explain the trouble I encountered when writing up these case studies. Was I to start with a historical chapter so as to introduce readers to the whole situation? Or rather, should I not conclude with such a chapter in order to show how sociological research contributes to history? I am not sure I fully resolved this inevitable tension between two approaches that it is both necessary and impossible to combine in case studies.

A purely sociological analysis does not explain history, and a purely historical one risks overlooking the most significant and meaningful processes, or factors, because these do not come into play by themselves and may even have a minor role in the succession of events or in the most decisive episodes. For instance, the sociological analysis of the Basque armed struggle will emphasize the Basque national consciousness and opposition to Franco's dictatorship; but, when explaining an event such as the 1974 assassination of Admiral Carrero Blanco, other, circumstantial factors must be taken into account (for example, that the commandos had wanted to kidnap the victim but decided to kill him only when they realized it would be technically impossible to kidnap him).

Delimiting cases

The more we admit that a case calls for a twofold effort of understanding, analytical and synthetic, sociological and historical, the less obvious its practical unity appears. As pointed out, a case forms a whole circumscribed in time and space. But what criteria justify cutting this "whole" unit out of reality? Two examples will show that we must avoid naive empiricism and be capable of theoretically justifying the categories used to thus cut out something we deem a case.

How to cut a case out of space? To answer this question, let us turn, once again, to my study of contemporary far-Left terrorism. There are several arguments, underlain by hypotheses, for or against selecting Italy during the 1970s and 1980s as a unit for study. Let us look at a few of them.

One argument, more historical than sociological, chooses this territorial unit because of the extent of terrorism there, and then seeks to relate this violence to the country's specific characteristics (for instance, a Western land with a strong tradition of social banditry, a weak state, a powerful Communist Party and a dominant Catholic church). It thus becomes necessary to explain the whole terrorist phenomenon in Italy – without forgetting far-Right terrorism, which, much more deadly during the period in question, cannot be separated from its counterpart on the Left.

A second, very different argument hypothesizes that, in the Western world, far-Left terrorism mainly concerns societies having experienced a totalitarian government before the imposition of democracy following a military defeat. Since such violence was specific to Japan, West Germany, and Italy; the last is, at most, representative of this larger set. (This hypothesis has lost considerable force since the 1980s, when far-Left terrorist groups sprang up in France, Belgium, Greece, and Portugal.)

A third argument takes the Italian case to be part of a larger process whereby groups, politicized by Marxist-Leninist ideology, speak in the name of an institutionalized working class that rejects or ignores the violence mythically committed in its stead.

Several arguments could be added to this list, but that would be pointless. What is important is that, depending on the type of argument used, the case under consideration will be approached from a specific angle (such as the country's general history, political culture, or the working class movement and its political parties). It is also important to recognize that the case at hand (Italy) could either represent a certain type of problem or form a unique, incomparable historical unit. But what is most important is to admit that the territorial unit under consideration is not necessarily very relevant. If the aim is to study far-Left terrorism in countries having experienced totalitarianism, defeat, and then democracy, this past determines the lands to be studied, and a full demonstration calls for examining, if not all, at least more than one of them. Thus, as will be shown hereafter, a case study often entails comparison. If the aim is to examine scientifically a process whereby a political elite loses contact with the working class, which serves as its reference mark, then anything complicating this examination must be avoided, and it is not wise to choose Italy, where other factors obviously came into play. It would be better to take a simpler or purer case, such as the Belgian Communist Combat Cells or the major terrorist group (Red Brigades) in Italy rather than all such groups.

Similar considerations arise if reality is cut up as a function not of space but of time. This can be shown through the workers' movement, in particular behaviors during its formative phase. With regard to this phase (throughout the eighteenth and early nineteenth centuries in Great Britain and later in France), it would be bold indeed to talk about a labor or social movement based upon collective action directed against those who control work or production, and involving the progress and control of a society defined as industrial. In one place, workers were breaking their machines. In another, currents of thought were arising that, despite their confusion, were pushing for a socialistic utopia. Elsewhere, groups that foreshadowed political parties were taking shape, and activists were trying to set up cooperatives and friendly societies. Meanwhile, society still seemed rural and mercantilist rather than industrial. Later, much later, trade unions were formed, and political parties too. Furthermore, a working-class consciousness emerged that recognized the identities both of the actor, defined by his labor and efforts in production, and of his adversary, who organizes work. For this consciousness, the issues in this social conflict were defined as being the control of industry or, more broadly, the goal of socialism. During the long chaotic phase winding up to this moment however, these various elements stayed separate. They did not project the image of a social movement, not even of a splintered one. Instead of respecting their machines, some workers were destroying them. Instead of talking about a social adversary and recognizing they were struggling for the control of production, other workers were shutting themselves up inside their own culture and defining themselves not as social actors but as communities or metasocial forces representing good against evil, angels fighting the devil. In other words, what could be observed during this formative phase looked more like an "antimovement" than a movement. By antimovement, I refer to any phenomenon wherein actors define themselves as a community or an essence rather than as a dominated group, and see themselves as fighting an enemy rather than striving with an adversary. Only by placing these events in a very long term perspective, as proposed in Thompson's classic study (1963), do we see that they were the forerunners and first manifestation of a social movement, but in an inverted, splintered, or weakened form.

What time span is appropriate? If various of the forementioned elements are analyzed in their context from a short- or even middle-term perspective, the only conclusion is that they demonstrate ways of acting or thinking that were still very far from or even contrary to the emergence of industrial society or a working-class movement. If we adopt a long-term perspective, however, our analysis changes, and these cases take on another significance. This may puzzle anyone who, like me, claims to be a sociologist but is so focused on his own society that he cannot stand back to see the historical picture. The long-term perspective does have the advantage of forcing us, during a case study, to assess the stability over time of our analyses and inquire into the appropriateness of a different time scale. It should be mentioned (although this leads too far from my present purpose) that we must be aware of the risks of anachronism – of studying a case in the light of events that, occurring afterward, were unknown to social actors, events that they probably could not even have imagined. For example, does it help us understand the case of Marrano Jews facing the Spanish Inquisition if we have in mind modern anti-Semitism and Nazi barbarity? Probably not.

Case study and comparative analysis

For a long time, an evolutionary model prevailed in the social sciences. Accordingly, societies were progressing on a single path of progress in the direction of history. Opposed to this model was the less prevalent idea, which I shall call historicism, that any collective historical experience was absolutely original. Accordingly, comparisons between societies and cultures were forbidden. A major variant of this opposition cropped up in anthropology between universalism and cultural relativism. Both of these models granted a very special status to case studies. Whereas a case is isolated so as to be seen, from a historicist viewpoint, in its radical originality, it is considered, from an evolutionary or universalist viewpoint, to be part of a general process with a meaning determined from outside – by an economic, natural or divine law. It can at most illustrate this law's validity and be classified with other cases governed by the same law. Of course, scholars' evolutionist convictions might be shaken when a case invalidates the law. For example, the notion of an Asiatic mode of production caused major problems for Marxism as a philosophy of history.

Whichever viewpoint is adopted, making comparisons is useless or, at best, secondary. From the evolutionist viewpoint, the problem of studying several cases is to show that all are explained or determined by the same cause, are part of a single chain of events. Increasing the number of case studies does not, therefore, add much to the stock of knowledge about the general law of evolution, which transcends any case. At most, additional studies serve to validate this law quantitatively. From the historicist viewpoint, the very principle of comparison is unacceptable since it requires drawing up classifications, hierarchies, and correlations about what cannot, from the start and by definition, be reduced in such a way.

Since the early twentieth century, social thought, without definitively abandoning these two viewpoints, has strayed ever further from them as it has developed the idea of a system, inquired into the rupture/continuity opposition, raised new questions about the relationship between innate and acquired behaviors or between the universal and particular (Atlan 1979; Morin 1973; Moscovici 1972), and reassessed the notion of modernity by analyzing its crisis and examining whether it can be extended to postmodernity. Case studies have now acquired a different status. No longer located in an evolutionary perspective that transcends it, nor defined by its incomparability, a case becomes the opportunity to discover knowledge about how it is both specific to and representative of a larger phenomenon. Its originality does not keep us from making comparisons, and its representativeness does not refer to a metasocial law, but to analytical categories. Hence – and in partial response to Lieberson's complaints (in Chapter 4) about "small-N determinism" – the complement of case study is comparative analysis.

A comparison may have at least two main functions. It may help deconstruct what common sense takes to be unique or unified. On the contrary, it may construct the unity of what seems to be broken up into practical categories. It is never so useful as when it combines these two functions and thus justifies both the deconstruction of a preconception and the construction of a scientific category.

I would like to illustrate this by, once again, referring to my work on terrorism. The word "terrorism" means something to everyone. Spontaneous definitions abound. During meetings of experts and academic colloquia, the commonplace is that the terrorist for one person is the freedom fighter for another, and it seems impossible to lay down a precise, operational definition.

In this situation, the scholar faces two possibilities. Turning toward those who use the notion of terrorism to refer to a menace, he may examine not the menace itself but the way the image of it is produced. Accordingly, terrorism is a social construct, and comparing distinct national experiences makes it possible to observe the processes, or actors' games, that widely diffuse the perception of the phenomenon (for example, political efforts to draw up antiterrorist policy). This is how I analyzed the American and French cases (Wieviorka 1990, 1991).

But, if the aim is to deconstruct the preconception of terrorism, there is a more effective possibility. It consists of using sociological hypotheses to study the behaviors and actors generally qualified as terrorist, without, initially, being concerned about whether this labeling process is justified or not. Given the diversity of these cases, we are soon forced to make out at least two types of experiences: those wherein violence is a method adopted by an actor capable, if the situation changes, of using other, political or diplomatic, means, and those wherein terrorism seems to be a logic of action from which the actor can escape only through death, exile, or imprisonment. In the latter type, we can discern pure terrorism, a logic of action apparently fully disconnected from the population the actor claims to incarnate. Its absolute, unlimited, and radical nature can be described by various characteristics. At this point, comparing several cases enables us to isolate inversion, the process whereby an actor is taken up in terrorism as a logic of action, from all other factors, which vary from case to case. It also helps us define this process, which, at the start of research, was but a rough and poorly formulated hypothesis. Henceforth, each case can be analyzed in its generality by referring to terrorism not as a commonsense notion but as a process of inversion that is more or less advanced depending on the case. Moreover, it can, at the same time, be described in its historical originality, where inversion is mixed up with all sorts of other variables that constitute so many conditions favoring terrorism.

Such an approach, which seems somewhat in line with Abbott's recommendations in Chapter 2, can be applied to many other social problems (for instance, racism, insanity, or AIDS). The scholar can use a single case to deconstruct preconceptions and reconstruct scientific categories, as D. Jodelet (1989) has done in her remarkable study of insanity in the village of Aunay-le-Chateau. A number of carefully chosen cases can serve to broaden the scope of reconstructed categories. Consequently, the categories of spontaneous, or commonsensical, sociology can be undermined, and experiences can be grouped in unforeseen ways.

References

Atlan, Henri (1979). *Entre le cristal et la fumée.* Paris: Editions du Seuil.

Goldthorpe, John, David Lockwood, Franck Beckhofer, and Jennifer Platt (1968–9). *The Affluent Worker.* 3 vols. Cambridge University Press.

Hughes, Everett (1963). "Race Relations and the Sociological Imagination." *American Sociological Review* 28:879–90.

Jodelet, Denise (1989). *Folie et représentations sociales.* Paris: Presses Universitaires de France.

Marx, Karl (1969). *Le 18 brumaire de Louis Bonaparte*. Paris: Editions Sociales.

Morin, Edgar (1973). *Le paradigme perdu: la nature humaine*. Paris: Editions du Seuil.

Moscovici, Serge (1972). *La société contre nature*. Paris: UGE Collection 10:18.

Thompson, Edward P. (1963). *The Making of the English Working Class*. London: Victor Gollancz.

Touraine, Alain, Zsuzsa Hegedus, François Dubet, and Michel Wieviorka (1983). *Antinuclear Protest: The Opposition to Nuclear Energy in France*. Cambridge University Press.

Touraine, Alain, Michel Wieviorka, and François Dubet (1987). *The Workers' Movement*. Cambridge University Press.

Wieviorka, Michel (1988). *Sociétés et terrorisme*. Paris: Fayard.

(1990). "Defining and Implemeting Foreign Policy: The U.S. Experience in Anti-Terrorism," pp. 171–201 in Y. Alexander and H. Foreman (eds.), *The 1988–1989 Annual on Terrorism*. Netherlands: Kluver Academic Publishers.

(1991). "France Faced with Terrorism." *Terrorism* 14:157–90.

8

Theory elaboration: the heuristics of case analysis[1]

DIANE VAUGHAN

A colleague once confessed that since getting his degree he seemed "progressively to know more and more about less and less." He referred to his transition from a graduate student required to demonstrate competence in several diverse areas to a professional sociologist who selectively focused his reading and research around a particular interest. Perhaps many sociologists experience this same narrowing of focus. Our early interest, whether our own impassioned choice or fortuitous circumstance, tends to get reinforced as we seek a professional identity. Although our teaching may push us to diversify, and we often create courses for exactly that purpose, most of our teaching innovations harmonize with our research focus. Moreover, once we've given a paper at a professional meeting or published on a topic, other opportunities tend to come to us in the same area. Ties to colleagues with similar interests further reinforce our career path. These professional networks, plus the extensive knowledge accumulated from reading and research experience, bind us to our chosen specialty. To change specialization involves intellectual, professional, and social costs that few are willing to pay. Although over the course of a career many people's interests do change, those shifts tend to be gradual transitions that slowly and subtly rearrange our intellectual, professional, and social commitments (trace, for example, the intellectual course of the major writings of Howard S. Becker and Rosabeth Moss Kanter) rather than sudden, dramatic (and costly) jumps from, say, theories of the state to the dynamics of interpersonal relationships.

Our tendency to stick with a particular problem or field of inquiry and know it both intensively and extensively undeniably expands our ability to develop theory. Yet, ironically, specialization often results in fixed preconceptions about the organizational form appropriate for case analysis, and these preconceptions, in turn, can result in unacknowledged disadvantages for theorizing. We tend to tie our research questions to some organizational form that has a particular function: educational institutions, nation-states, business organizations, families, elite networks, social revolutions, communities, courtrooms. But the lack of variation in our choice can inhibit the discovery and development of theories, models, and concepts that are broadly applicable. This is not to deny the potential of quasi-experimental comparative analysis of comparable organizational forms varying along some dimension for generating formal theory (e.g., Przeworski and Teune 1970). Rather, I am suggesting that when we limit our sociological questions to particular organizational forms, we tend to build on existing theory or generate new theory in fragmented rather than integrative ways.

In the sociology of organizations, for example, theory is biased by the predominance of research done in hierarchical organizations, generally business firms. How would organization theory change if it were grounded in research that delved into nonprofits, worker-managed firms, small organizations, and nonhierarchical organizations to a similar extent? In the sociology of the family, those who study violence typically do not explore violence within and between other organizational forms – delinquent gangs, schools, communities, terrorist groups, prisons, nation-states. They strive for a theory of family violence, rather than working toward a general theory of violence. While their selectivity suits their interest and conforms to disciplinary standards for generating formal theory, omitting other types of violence from consideration precludes finding both support for and challenges to their own theories. Moreover, they obviate their own use of theories, models, or concepts particular to violence in these alternative organizational forms that might have explanatory potential in the special case of the family.

Breaking away from our preconceptions about appropriate cases can stimulate theoretical innovation. If there is a possibility for developing general theories of particular phenomena, it lies not only in acknowledging social organization as a context for behavior, but in empirical examination and comparison of the dependent variable of interest in a variety of organizational forms. In this essay, I describe how to elaborate sociological theory by using case studies of organizational forms of differing size, complexity, and function and improving/altering theory by alternating between units of analysis. The goal is to work toward general theory that spans levels of analysis by refining theoretical constructs and clarifying their relevance for different organizational forms. After illustrating the method's potential with examples from some well-known sociological studies, I demonstrate the strategy in greater detail by showing how I elaborated Merton's "social structure and anomie theory (SSAT) into a theory of organizational misconduct (Merton 1968).

Then I show how I am elaborating this theory further through case analyses of misconduct in three organizational forms: the National Aeronautics and Space Administration (NASA) and the Space Shuttle *Challenger* accident, police misconduct, and family violence. Finally, I will discuss one of the methodological issues that can confound theory elaborated by this method: the problem of forcing fit.

Method

Theory elaboration is a method for developing general theories of particular phenomena through qualitative case analysis. By theory, I mean theoretical tools in general (theory, models, and concepts) rather than a more restricted formal meaning (a set of interrelated propositions that are testable and explain some phenomenon). By elaboration, I mean the process of refining a theory, model, or concept in order to specify more carefully the circumstances in which it does or does not offer potential for explanation. By cases, I mean organizational forms that are analyzed regarding some similar event, activity, or circumstance: for example, social control in family, nation-state, or professional association. The cases can be ethnographies, analyses based on interviews and documents, or historical comparative studies.

We begin by using a theory, model, or concept in a very loose fashion to guide the research. Cases are chosen because (1) they are potential examples of research topic *X*, (2) they vary in size and complexity (e.g., groups, simple formal organizations, complex organizations, subunits within them, or networks), and (3) they vary in function (e.g., accounting department, church, environmentalist group, research institution, symphony orchestra). We analyze the cases sequentially. We treat each case independently of others, respecting its uniqueness so that the idiosyncratic details can maximize our theoretical insight. As the analysis proceeds, the guiding theoretical notions are assessed in the light of the findings. As in analytic induction (Cressey 1953; Lindesmith 1947; Robinson 1951), the data can contradict or reveal previously unseen inadequacies in the theoretical notions guiding the research, providing a basis for reassessment or rejection; the data can confirm the theory; the data also can force us to create new hypotheses, adding detail to the theory, model, or concept, more fully specifying it.

Because more than one theoretical notion may be guiding an analysis, confirmation, fuller specification, and contradiction all may result from one case study. Under these circumstances, each construct can be elaborated to specify more carefully the circumstances in which it does or does not offer potential for explanation. In subsequent case analyses, we use the more fully elaborated theoretical notion (or notions) as a guide. In keeping with Kaplan's warning (1964) about "premature closure" and his stress on the importance of "openness of meaning," we continue to treat them as hypotheses to be further elaborated in future research. While greater specificity is one hoped-for goal (in terms of both clarification of theoretical notions and the limits of their applicability), *greater ambiguity* is another. Each case analysis will consist of intricate, interconnected detail, much of it perhaps unexpected. It is the "loose ends," the stuff we neither expect nor can explain, that pushes us toward theoretical breakthroughs. If the guiding theoretical notion truly is used heuristically, case analyses should raise additional questions relevant to understanding the concept, model, and/or theory being considered.

Walton (Chapter 5) makes the point that the first goal in case analysis is to find out exactly what we have a case of. He notes that we tend to select our cases based upon "typological distinctions" grounded in prior assumptions about what defines a case or a universe of particular cases:

> But the presumption is faulty. We do not really know these things at all, we simply make guesses about them – hypotheses. There is nothing wrong with that, provided it is clear that the known universe is an illusion and, with it, that the claim to having a case of something is not supported in any substantial way.

Having chosen a case on the basis of certain typological distinctions, we may find we were mistaken. Our data may show that the organizational form we thought was an example of X is not an example of X at all, but something very different. In the event we are surprised in this manner, we may decide to develop a parallel theory of the new dependent variable. In the interest of theory generation, whether that theory is the one that initiated the inquiry or some new theoretical notion that we develop from the data, the integrity of the individual case analysis takes primacy. Future research may prove the case to be a member of a class of similar objects, or it may be that the class has only one member. Whichever is true, identification of the defining patterns of each case is a necessary first step. Once defined for that case, the pattern can be treated as a model. Its relevant features may be found in other cases selected by the same selection criteria that selected that case.

Varying both organizational form and function is crucial to this method. Stinchcombe points out that "lots of facts" are "good hard stones for honing ideas" (1978:5). The transformative powers of this approach lie not only in having lots of facts, but in the radically different kinds of facts that varying cases can produce, which result in three major benefits for theory elaboration. First, because shifting units of analysis can produce qualitatively different information, case comparison can generate startling contrasts that allow and, in fact, demand us to discover, to reinterpret, and ultimately to transform our theoretical constructs. Second, selecting cases to vary the organizational form sometimes permits varying the level of analysis. Because of the different sorts of data available from microlevel and macrolevel analysis, choosing cases that vary both the unit of analysis and the level of analysis, when possible, can lead to the elaboration of theory that more fully merges microunderstanding and macrounderstanding. Third, this method can be particularly advantageous for elaborating theories, models, and concepts focusing on large, complex systems that are difficult to study. Shifting to a different organizational form may create access to data previously unavailable; or it may create a possibility for measurement previously precluded by the size, complexity, or norms of privacy of the organizational form chosen as the research setting.

Suppose we are interested in the concept of culture, originally developed through studies of societies but more recently applied to business organizations as "organization culture" (e.g., Frost et al. 1985). We can alter or enhance what has been learned about culture in these complex organizations by comparing it with analyses of culture in families (e.g., Stacey 1990) or in simple formal organizations (e.g., Fine 1987). Then, having elaborated the concept in some organizational form where microanalysis is possible, we may refine it further by working again at the macrolevel, using the adjusted culture concept to guide analysis of a community or a nation-state. What we know about culture (or "organization culture") can be reevaluated in light of the data produced by this latter macrolevel iteration.

But our application of this method is not restricted to analysis *between* organizational forms; we can apply it within, as well. For example, some concepts, theories, or models developed to explain relations between an organization and its environment can be examined intraorganizationally, and vice versa. Here is where creative conceptualization comes into play in choosing cases as alternative research settings. Consider the work of Miles and associates (1982), who explored two competing theories concerning organizational survival: strategic choice and population ecology. They examined five tobacco companies' responses to the surgeon general's announcement that cigarette smoking is hazardous to health. Instead of studying five complex organizations facing the same environmental constraint, as they did, the efficacy of these same two theories can be explored intraorganizationally. Suppose, in the interest of theory elaboration, we choose five internal subunits of a complex organization that face some similar constraint originating from the environment. Now, however, we define the environment as the organization to which the subunits belong. We explore strategic choice and population ecology in a context that will permit interviews and analysis of internal documents. In this setting, we get microlevel data that, when weighed against the original work of Miles and associates, allows us more fully to integrate individual behavior and structural factors in an explanation.

Critical to elaborating theory by this method is the development of an anthropology of organizations. An essential component is systematic comparison of one case with the next. Part of the rationale of theory elaboration is that organizational forms are sufficiently analogous for use as alternative settings for some dependent variable. However, in our search for empirical regularities across settings, we need to know, as best we can, why we achieve different or similar results in our inquiries. Consequently, we must make clear the characteristics of our cases with explicit attempts to (1) distinguish similarities and differences in the organizational forms that are the locus of our inquiry, (2) consider how they affect the findings, and (3) specify the theoretical consequences for comparisons between cases. These conclusions need to be published with the case analyses. When we do not take this final step, we discourage others from building on what we've done, reducing the method's potential for cumulative theory development. Rational-choice theorists, for example, study rational choice in a variety of organizational forms. However, the consequences of these different substantive contexts seldom are assessed. Any claim that instances of X are "the same" or "different" or that findings from one case are confirmed in a different setting is itself an empirical question. While we may never be able to answer it completely, we gain understanding by careful articulation of the characteristics of the organizational form that is the research locus and the theoretical consequences for case analysis. Further, organizations (or organizational forms) do not exist in a vacuum. At the same time that they provide a context for individual behavior, they have a context – an organizational environment – that must be taken into account. If we locate the organizational form chosen as our case within its environment, we expand our understanding of similarities and differences between cases.

Taking into account the environment in case comparison requires that this somewhat nebulous concept be grounded in some manageable empirical reality. Always, the researcher carves up social reality in order to study it, but it is the research problem that dictates how the carving is done. Therefore, we selectively can identify and isolate the social structural contingencies that seem relevant for the event, activity, or circumstance with which we are concerned. We can examine such contingencies at two levels: interactional and contextual (e.g., Vaughan 1983). We examine the immediate social structure, delineated for research purposes by interaction between the organizational form (or actors within it) and other organizations acting as competitors, consumers, controllers, or suppliers. Then we identify influential factors in the broader social structural context: the history, politics, economics, and/or culture of the community, region, nation, or global system in which the case occurs. By so doing, we situate our case. Not only does this strategy highlight what might prove to be idiosyncratic explanatory factors, but it also forces us to take into account contingent social relations.

Rationale

Theory elaboration based upon alternating units of analysis is possible because of the hierarchical nature of organizational forms. Emergent groups tend to develop around previous interaction patterns, which provide the basis for further structural differentiation and organizational development. The varieties of group life, treated as ideal types, can be conceptualized hierarchically on a continuum according to increasing structural complexity: patterned interactions, groups, simple formal organizations, and complex organizations. When so conceptualized, each form exhibits the characteristics of the simpler form that precedes it and adds to them. The simplest forms of social organization are patterned interactions: crossing the street, waiting in line, applause at a concert. Groups (i.e., crescive organizations) are distinguished from simple patterns of interaction by common values and norms (which lead to interaction on a regular basis) as well as consciousness of kind. But, in addition, the patterns of interaction are altered by the introduction of structural complexity. Because groups are task-oriented, they are composed of a number of persons whose interactions are based on a set of interrelated roles and statuses. As a consequence, we note the development of simple division of labor and hierarchy. The family stands as the traditional example of the crescive organization, but all groups exhibit these same characteristics.

The simple formal organization, next on this continuum, exhibits patterned interactions, consciousness of kind, common values and norms, and, in addition, set goals and formalized rules for achieving these goals. Like a crescive organization, a formal organization has a relatively simple structure and a simple division of labor, but is distinguished by formal goals and rules. Finally, the complex organization bears all the defining characteristics of crescive and formal organizations, but also additional levels of hierarchy, more specialized division of labor, increased tendencies toward centralization, greater degree of formalization, geographic dispersion, and so forth. A network may develop from linkages between the several organizational forms on this imaginary continuum. Consequently, we may have a network consisting solely of crescive, complex, or simple formal organizations, or some combination. We may have intraorganizational networks, composed of the subunits of a complex organization or informal group alignments. Some networks may be formalized, some not. Because networks assume myriad forms and develop from a variety of the basic forms of social organization, they do not have a place of their own on this continuum. Nonetheless, they are relevant for this method: e.g., a network theory can be elaborated by studying an international alliance and/or by treating internal subunits of a corporation as a network.

These forms have elements in common that have implications for theory elaboration. They share aspects of structure. In addition, they have in common processes that are natural concomitants of organizational life: conflict, social integration, deviance, cooperation, power, socialization, social control, decision making, social change. Certainly, the varieties of organizational forms are not strictly comparable. We know, for example, that as structural complexity increases, the possibilities for internal dynamics also increase (Simmel 1950). Differences exist between them, yet they are sufficiently analogous to offer us alternative settings in which to explore a particular phenomenon and compare the findings. As sociologists tend to pose either structural or normative theories to explain behavior (Hechter 1983:4–6), whenever we do empirical work, we selectively study some aspect or aspects of social organization as they relate to our research problem. Thus our research always can be thought of as organizational, although the form of social organization, the aspects of it selected for investigation, and the researcher's acknowledgment of the importance of the organizational context vary. It is the researcher who chooses the case – the locus for exploring the research question – and then makes the theoretical case for it (see Walton, Chapter 5 in this volume). Since a case is whatever we decide it is (on this the authors in this volume seem to agree), we can vary the organizational settings we select to explore our research questions and systematically assess and compare the findings. Wieviorka, discussing comparative analysis of idiosyncratic cases, states in Chapter 7 of this volume that "a case becomes the opportunity to discover knowledge about how it is both specific to and representative of a larger phenomenon. Its originality does not keep us from making comparisons, and its representativeness does not refer to a metasocial law, but to analytical categories."

Historical precedents

Much of this method no doubt will sound both familiar and self-contradictory. On the one hand, the examination of data with theory elaboration as the goal is seen by some as a major (if not *the* major) building block of a positivistic science (e.g., Kendall and Lazarsfeld 1950). On the other hand, the ideas of Blumer (1969) and Glaser and Strauss (1967) are evident. Theory elaboration incorporates aspects of both these traditions. Positivism's recent fall from grace notwithstanding, I think theory development and testing are central to sociology. Theory elaboration is aimed at (1) developing theory that spans units and levels of analysis and (2) explaining particular sets of findings. Testing is involved, but it is not testing of formal theory as conducted in the deductive positivistic tradition. Theory elaboration depends on testing by comparison: data from each case are used to assess ("test") some theoretical apparatus. At the same time that theory elaboration leads to more fully specified constructs, it allows us to proceed with explaining similarities and differences among collectivities and the processes that create, maintain, and change patterned behavior – which I believe is our fundamental task, whether our theories get formally tested or not.

Theory elaboration is grounded in the work of Blumer and Glaser and Strauss, but deviates from their approaches in some important ways. Blumer believed that "every object of our consideration – be it person, group, institution – has a distinctive and unique character and is imbedded within a context of a similarly distinctive character. [We] have to accept, develop, and use the distinctive expression in order to detect and study the common" (1969:148, 149). He argued that using concepts as a reference point with which to assay the empirical world would lead to the improvement and refinement of those concepts, for they would be corrected "in light of stubborn empirical findings" (1969: 150). This method of theory elaboration incorporates these Blumerian beliefs, but diverges in its extension to relationships *between* concepts, as they are framed within theories and/or models.

Like that of Glaser and Strauss, this approach relies extensively (but not exclusively) upon qualitative data and constant comparison for theoretical discoveries. Like that of Glaser and Strauss, it involves alternation of induction and deduction. And it relies upon cases chosen to maximize differences in the contexts of similar phenomena, so that what is common appears more clearly and its relevance to different contexts, its generalizabilities, can become clear. But it directly contradicts Glaser and Strauss's position that verification and discovery cannot go on simultaneously. This method of elaboration is based on the assumption that the "discovery" of another example of X *is* "verification." Moreover, within the same case analysis we may verify one theoretical notion, contradict another, and discover some new theory, concept, or model. Although comparison of groups is the foundation of both approaches, in theory elaboration we diverge by comparing (1) the findings from case analyses with theories, models, or concepts in order to subject the latter as well as the former to challenge and change, (2) diverse groups (which Glaser and Strauss suggest only when striving for formal theory), and, whenever possible, (3) findings between levels of analysis. While theory generation is a common goal of both approaches, this method diverges again (and perhaps most importantly) from Glaser and Strauss by aiming to

1. develop concepts, models, or theories whose limits and applicability to various organizational forms become increasingly specified,
2. develop a bridge between our study of behavior in and of small groups, on the one hand, and complex systems, on the other.

The macro/micro connection
This latter goal of forging a link between our understanding of small groups and complex systems may prove to be an advantage of this method that is significant beyond the elaboration of any particular theory, model, or concept that we seek. Individual choice and structure are inextricably related. Hence, our ability to offer a full causal explanation of any phenomenon rests upon exploring the macro/micro connection: What structural factors govern or influence patterns of individual choice, how are those choices constructed, and what are the structural consequences? Although many have recognized the importance of the macro/micro connection (e.g., Coleman 1986; Collins 1981; Fine 1988; Giddens 1979, 1984), theory remains bifurcated. We generate either macrolevel or microlevel explanations, ignoring the critical nexus. Moreover, empirical work follows the same pattern. Instead of research that systematically attempts to link macrolevel factors and choices in a specific social phenomenon, we tend to dichotomize. Both macro and micro get their fair share of attention, but in separate projects, by separate analysts. Those who do join them in empirical work most often do so by theoretical inference: data at one level of analysis are coupled with theoretical speculation about the other. Because the macro/micro connection seldom has been traced empirically, knowledge has remained fragmented.

The macro/micro connection is not an insurmountable problem, and, in fact, may not be a problem at all. It simply may be an artifact of data availability. Sometimes we do not have access to information about individual actions and the structural determinants of those actions in the same research project, so we are unable to arrive at integrated explanations. We may be denied formal access to people or records, restricting our inquiry to one level of analysis. Or perhaps necessary people, documents, and records no longer exist or cannot be found. But sometimes what appears to be formally available is unavailable in practice. Even when we do have access to both microlevel and macrolevel data, often we are prevented from working at both levels simultaneously because doing so is a difficult, unwieldy task. The social historian tracing the evolution of social-welfare legislation cannot manage both data demonstrating the influence of a changing political economy and the diaries, biographies, and legislative records that might demonstrate how these influences played themselves out in the lives of decision-makers. The field-worker investigating the interactional basis of culture in a community or a small group cannot simultaneously account for the structural influences originating in the external environment that shape the evolution of that culture and still craft a clear, incisive microanalysis.

But data that would allow us to make macro/micro theoretical connections may be unavailable for less obvious reasons. We develop paradigm preferences that restrict our ability to integrate structure and process in our research. In the same way that our preconceptions of cases appropriate as units of analysis can become fixed, so can our ideas about what constitutes useful information and how to go about getting it. We develop very personal research styles that become comfortable, and while we may get better at finding the information we seek and interpreting what we find, we may be blind to other sorts of information because our ability to see it is undeveloped. We readily "see" either micro or macro, but not both. When this is the case, the problem still legitimately can be framed as one of data availability: we tend to define and conceptualize our problems at one or the other level of analysis, making certain data available and not others. Such patterned ways of seeing surely are the product of graduate education (e.g., social psychology and political economy are separated in the curriculum), dichotomous departmental emphasis, specialized journals, and intradisciplinary reward structures. While these professional schisms may enhance our ability to answer questions at either the macrolevel or microlevel, they can create learned disabilities that constrain us from making macro/micro connections.

If the macro/micro problem is an artifact of data availability, then perhaps this method of theory elaboration is one way of closing the gap. The elaboration of existing theories, models, and concepts is grounded in qualitative data. The data come from analysis of cases chosen for suspected similarities, but their differences are equally important. When we vary cases for size, complexity, and function, data formally unavailable to us in a case study of one organizational form may become available in another. When we sequentially alternate units of analysis so that the level of analysis varies as well, we automatically put ourselves in touch with data and theories at both levels. Moreover, by doing so we are forced to take into account factors that we otherwise might not, given our learned disabilities. We must contend with data that lie outside our individual paradigm preferences in order to explain the event, circumstance, or activity central to the particular case. The result can be a dramatic contrast with other cases, forcing us to amend the guiding theoretical notions in sequential case analyses.

Further methodological considerations

One limitation of this approach is that it is more oriented toward identifying the presence/absence of factors in different cases than evaluating the relative importance of those factors. But their relative importance can be explored in subsequent research constructed for that purpose. This limitation also can be counted as an advantage, however, for organizational settings can be selected precisely because the researcher is interested in a particular factor believed to be present. Carol Heimer, for example, is elaborating a theory of taking responsibility by studying several settings, chosen because they are examples of significant theoretical variations (personal communication 1990). She first examined taking responsibility in the Norwegian state oil company during a crucial transition (Heimer 1987). Because she wanted to look more closely at gender differences in taking responsibility, she next investigated families with babies in neonatal intensive-care units, also a crucial transition (Heimer 1988).

Another potential problem is that a case-oriented methodology may give inappropriate weight to cases where an expected factor is not found (F. Cullen, personal communication 1989). The risk is to assign these cases a special or idiosyncratic theoretical status when, in fact, they may simply be cases where the probability of the factor's occurrence did not hold. The absence of a factor in a particular case cannot lead us to conclude that overall the factor does not play a significant role in other cases of that category. But its absence still clarifies our thinking by forcing us to acknowledge that the role is that of a sufficient rather than a necessary cause. Another concern about this approach may be the time it requires. One person trying to do a sequential analysis of varying organizational forms may have difficulty completing the work. Most certainly, the time required for fieldwork, a comparative historical study, or documentary analysis of a particular organizational form may vary with the size and complexity of the organizational form serving as the unit of analysis, the scope of the problem, available data, etc. Nonetheless, for many the time required may be prohibitive, or at the least, the prospect of spending years analyzing each case may be daunting, especially for the untenured or those who prefer variety rather than what may be a single career-long enterprise.

One alternative is a team of researchers, each person studying the same theoretical notion in a different organizational setting. Or the single researcher may choose a single case, using, for example, a theory of family violence to guide analysis of violence in one other organizational form. Another possibility is for the single researcher to use a mix of original work and the published work of others. For example, Stinchcombe (1970) developed a model composed of seven conditions that determine the degree of dependency of inferiors in different types of organizations. He conceptualized the seven conditions from several research projects he did in the 1950s and 1960s. In the 1970 article, he used these organizations to demonstrate variability in the conditions, filling in with a few additional examples (personal communication, 1990). He then ranked them by degree of dependency of inferiors (some cases ranked: concentration camps in Nazi Germany; craft production; oligarchic unions; modern armies in garrison).

Another researcher could now analyze Stinchcombe (1970), exploring the several ranked organizations, first specifying more precisely the variation in size, complexity, and function of the several organizational forms he chose and how the seven conditions vary within and between organizations. The second phase would be original research exploring the degree of dependency of inferiors in other organizational forms that would allow Stinchcombe's model to be considered at the microlevel. But theory can also be elaborated from secondary analysis done in its own right. No doubt many case analyses, using the same theories, models, or concepts, exist that have never been systematically compared. The work of Blau (1964) is exemplary: he began at the microlevel, defining social exchange in intimate dyads, then applied the principles he developed to groups, complex organizations, and some inter-organizational forms. Many others have used these ideas in both microanalysis and macroanalysis in a variety of organizational settings, e.g., Scanzoni (1972) and Pfeffer and Salancik (1978), respectively. These findings have never been juxtaposed and scrutinized for similarities and differences that would promote elaboration of Blau's original ideas.

Elaborating a concept: loose coupling

The concept "loose coupling" has a long history in the literature on complex organizations (Corwin 1981). A "loosely coupled system" is a complex organization characterized by a high degree of autonomy among its interdependent parts and isolation between the strata (Corwin 1981:262). Weick (1976) used the concept to explain educational organizations, remarking that because of measurement difficulties, the concept of loose coupling lacks precision, yet still can be used heuristically. Here is an example of this method's advantages for elaborating theoretical constructs focusing on large, complex systems that are difficult to study. The concept loose coupling could be refined by using it to analyze the relationships of cohabiting couples. Despite vast differences in size and complexity, cohabiting couples and complex organizations have sufficient characteristics in common [see also McCall 1978)] that variation in the degree of integration of the parts can be explored in both settings. When we shift from complex organizations to cohabiting couples, we see the advantage that varying the level of analysis produces. We not only have abundant information, but qualitatively different information to contrast with macrolevel studies like Weick's exploration of educational institutions.

By analyzing families, the degree of integration of the "separate parts" of an organization can be studied in greater detail. Multiple methods can be brought to bear on the problem: interviews, observation, lab studies, content analysis of autobiographical accounts. At the microlevel, it is possible to explore not only the extent to which partners in a relationship are interdependent, but also how that interdependence varies by task, and over time. Quantitative analysis also can be incorporated. Through measurement, greater specificity can be attributed to the terms "loosely coupled" and "tightly coupled," clarifying the meaning of a loosely coupled or a tightly coupled organizational unit, the range of variation between extremes, and the factors associated with variation. The more fully elaborated concept could then be reapplied in macroanalysis, examining the relationship between the subunits of another type of complex organization: e.g., an alliance of nation-states in an international governing body. Measurement at the macrolevel may become possible. Block modeling, the definitional tool developed by White, Boorman, and Breiger (1976), is one possible method for establishing variation in the relation between units at the macrolevel. A network of organizations would be loosely coupled if the units had few connections, for example. We can begin to identify the range of connective possibilities in a given organizational form and across collectivities. Even if macrolevel application remains heuristic, more sophisticated insights are possible as a consequence of previous refinement at the microlevel through research on cohabiting couples. The next step would be to take whatever new insights are gained by the macrolevel application of loose coupling and reconsider the degree of integration in small groups.

Elaborating a theory of organizational misconduct

In developing a theory of organizational misconduct, I used this method of theory elaboration for the first time. Automatic and implicit at first, it was not until the manuscript was nearly complete that I could see that I was shifting units of analysis mentally as I theorized, and how that had influenced my development of ideas. I wanted to take what I seemed to be doing implicitly and make it explicit. Also, I wondered if we all intuitively do the same thing when we theorize, and whether something might be gained by being more systematic about it. Since then, I have been using the method in a more conscientious, rigorous way so that I can understand how to use it better and at the same time refine the theory. I have continued to explore misconduct with three case studies of organizational forms that vary in size, complexity, and function: NASA and the Space Shuttle *Challenger*, police misconduct, and family violence. My purpose now is to go beyond the preceding suggestive examples of this method, showing my early use of it and how I am continuing to develop both the method and the theory in my current work. The examples that follow are necessarily brief and schematic. The promise of this method is better understood through examining the original texts. Interested readers may follow my first application (Vaughan 1983:54–104). Those passages show the possibility for confirmation, fuller specification, and contradiction that can result from shifting units of analysis. Also you will find the promised "greater ambiguity": many new research questions as well as questions about other concepts and theories that subsequently required reinterpretation. For examples of applications of the theory to the NASA case study, see Vaughan (1989, 1990).

Developing the theory

In 1983, I completed a case study of Medicaid–provider fraud in which one organization victimized another. Relying on the findings of the case study and integrating them with existing theory and research on complex organizations and on deviance and social control, I developed a structural explanation of the unlawful behavior of organizations. The major elements of that nascent explanatory scheme were

1. the *competitive environment*, which generates pressures upon organizations to violate the law in order to attain goals (1983:54–66),
2. *organizational characteristics* (structure, processes, and transactions), which provide opportunities to violate (1983:67–87), and
3. the *regulatory environment*, which is affected by the relationship between regulators and those they regulate, frequently minimizing the capacity to control and deter violations, consequently contributing to their occurrence (1983:88–104).

I argued that each of these three is related to violative behavior, but, more significantly, they are interrelated: misconduct results from the three in combination. Because the competitive environment, organizational characteristics, and the regulatory environment are all necessary to a causal explanation, and because they work together to affect decision making in organizations, they constitute an integrated theory for understanding unlawful organizational behavior. Many other theories, models, and concepts appear throughout the text, but these three concepts are the major building blocks.

This theory of organizational misconduct began with my heuristic application of Merton's "social structure and anomie theory" (SSAT) (1968) to business organizations. American society was the organizational setting in which Merton studied individual deviance. While working on the Medicaid–provider fraud case study, my data and the literature I was reading kept bringing to mind Merton's notion of "blocked access to legitimate means." Although his conceptualization sought to explain the violations of individuals, a lot of it resonated with what I knew about the violations of business organizations. In fact, because of Merton's emphasis on culturally approved goals for economic success, SSAT seemed a better explanation of the behavior of organizations than the behavior of individuals. I studied his theory, along with its many applications and assessments, reinterpreting everything I read by mentally substituting organizations as the units of analysis. Applying the theory to business organizations exposed weaknesses in Merton's conceptualization and at the same time suggested how SSAT might be altered to increase its explanatory potential. The key to this was reconceptualizing both "means" and "ends" as scarce resources for which organizations may compete. This reconceptualization not only did away with the troublesome theoretical and empirical problems associated with "means" and "ends," but allowed the theory to be extended to a variety of organizations, not just business organizations (Vaughan 1983:55–64). Another significant theoretical result was contradiction of the social-class implications in Merton's original exegesis (Vaughan 1983:54–66, 70–3, 84–7).

Once I had worked out the elaboration of SSAT by considering organizations as the units of analysis, the obvious next step was to reconsider the applicability of Cloward and Ohlin's *Delinquency and Opportunity* (1960), a theory proposing the availability of illegitimate opportunity structures as a corrective to SSAT. Like SSAT, Cloward and Ohlin's theory focused on the structural determinants of individual deviance in American society. I reassessed it with organizations in mind. Cloward and Ohlin suggested that Merton's idea of restricted access to legitimate means didn't go far enough; his theory must take into account the availability of illegitimate means, in the form of organized crime. Their work started me thinking about business as well as other organizations as opportunity structures for misconduct; obviously, these were legitimate, not illegitimate, opportunity structures. This realization resulted in my integration of "organizational characteristics" into my schema. Considering their theory with organizations in mind generated many new insights: for example, Cloward and Ohlin's ideas on standards for individual success became the basis for articulating how organizational standards for success engender continuous structural strain for all organizations, regardless of size, wealth, age, experience, or previous record (Vaughan 1983:59). Most important, illuminating organizations as legitimate opportunity structures for misconduct contradicted the social-class implications of Cloward and Ohlin's original work, confirming my reconceptualization of SSAT. I grounded my social-class argument in the hierarchical nature of organizational forms (Vaughan 1983:85–7, and 54–66, 70–3).

The problem remaining to be resolved was patterns of individual choice: Why do some who are subjected to competitive pressures and surrounded by opportunities act unlawfully on behalf of an organization while others do not? Since rewards and punishments influence choices people make on behalf of their organizations, the ability of other organizations to impose costs affects the probability that opportunities for misconduct will be used. Thus, the regulatory environment became the final conceptual building block of the theory (Vaughan 1983:88–104).

Theoretical gaps

At the time of publication, I believed that my explanatory scheme was limited in two major ways. First, while I was aiming for a theoretical explanation of the violative behavior of organizations in general, most of the existing theory and research focused upon only the violations of corporate profit-seekers. Although I relied heavily upon the more broadly based theory and research on organizational behavior, sociological analysis of violations by organizations other than corporations was scant. Second, while I believed that the link between individual choice and the structural determinants of those choices was paramount to understanding misconduct (1983:68–73, 84–7), we knew very little about how structural factors translated into the internal dynamics of organizations and affected decision making. The explanation of decision making most frequently supported in the literature on "white-collar crime" is the "amoral-calculator" model: the violating business firm is portrayed as an amoral, profit-seeking organization whose actions are motivated by managers rationally calculating costs and opportunities. Research, however, has focused on structural factors associated with violative behavior, not the decision to violate itself (e.g., Clinard and Yeager 1980). We have not been able to trace the connection between structural factors and individual decisions to violate, so the amoral-calculator model is untested. Although some scholars aimed at the connection between macrolevel and microlevel analysis, these attempts mainly were theoretical, empirical work being limited by lack of access to information about individual decision making and the structural determinants of those decisions (Vaughan in press).

The results of applying theories from one organizational setting to another in case analysis led me to believe that both the ambiguous micro/macro connection and the business-firm bias in my explanatory scheme could be corrected by (1) analysis of the violative behavior of organizations other than corporations and (2) employing the case-study method in situations where qualitative analysis was most likely to produce new information. I had been teaching an undergraduate course in criminology, in which I taught a unit on corporate crime as organizational misconduct. The course also included lectures on police misconduct and family violence, and over several semesters I noticed analogous causal factors between these three forms of misconduct. I experimented in the classroom, creating a unit about organizational misconduct using the 1983 theory as a tool for analyzing all three. The success of this as a teaching strategy and what I was learning from it convinced me that research was the next step. Police misconduct and family violence looked like exciting cases to include, but I wanted a complex organization of another type to replace the often-studied corporate profit-seeker.

NASA and the Space Shuttle *Challenger*

In the early testimony during the 1986 Presidential Commission's investigation of the *Challenger* tragedy, many of the factors having known association with violative behavior were uncovered. My preliminary analysis, based upon published accounts and the first volume of the commission's report (1986), suggested that internal rules and industry rules were violated in the events leading up to the accident. The NASA case provided an opportunity to move beyond previous understanding because of the unusual data available. First, the case involved the combined activities of a government agency and several private-enterprise organizations (e.g., Morton Thiokol, Inc., the manufacturer of the flawed Solid Rocket Booster), a combination providing desirable variation in size, complexity, and function. Second, the investigations of the Presidential Commission and the House Committee on Science and Technology – and the reactions to the event by the media, employees of both NASA and Thiokol, scientific experts, space historians, and others – produced information in abundance. Much of this information was directly relevant for an organizational analysis: tables of organization, rules and procedures, the history and goals of NASA, and its relations with other organizations (competitors, suppliers, customers, regulators). More to the point, much of the information pertained to NASA's decision making, not only for the *Challenger* launch, but for previous launches. Here was an opportunity to explore the macro/micro connection in a single case study. Perhaps the case would shed light on the amoral-calculator hypothesis.

I began analyzing the various sources, filing information on 4 × 6 cards. To organize the data, I reduced the theory to skeletal form, reconstituting it as an analytic framework composed of the three building blocks and significant sensitizing concepts within each:

Environment: competition, scarce resources, norms
Organization characteristics: structure, process, transactions
Regulatory environment: autonomy, interdependence

I used these very broad categories, rather than a more detailed organizing schema, in order to maximize discovery. The point of a heuristic device is to sensitize, to open the researcher to possibility. Beginning with a few major concepts that are provocative and seem typologically distinctive allows us a first rough sorting and sifting of data that illuminates the variation and ambiguities within categories. This rough sorting is then followed by fine tuning at regular intervals in order to elaborate these categories as we go along [for a detailed example, see Vaughan (1986:197–202)]. The concepts that are not included in the skeletal form of the explanatory scheme remain the subject of inquiry, but not all the concepts that compose the theory can be assessed by every case study, for each empirical investigation will yield insights that inform some but not all. Thus, depending upon the data available from the case being explored, one of the three building blocks rather than the entire explanatory scheme may be the focus, or even a single concept or model within one of them.

One conceptual change resulting from the NASA case analysis is that I now find "organizational misconduct" a more useful analytical tool than "unlawful organizational behavior" (the term used in my 1983 research). The violation of internal rules and industry rules in this case study occurred within a constellation of organizational factors, justifying expansion of the conceptual definition to include internal rule violations rather than restricting study to illegalities. The more encompassing concept of organizational misconduct adheres to the principle of beginning broadly to maximize discovery. It promotes contrast and refinement of differences and similarities between behavioral types. The definition of organizational misconduct I am using is

violation of laws, administrative regulations, or internal or external rules by an act of omission or commission by an individual or group of individuals in their organizational roles acting on behalf of the organization or some subunit of it.[2]

This definition is merely a selection rule to guide my choice of cases for analysis, so is open to alteration or rejection as the findings dictate, in keeping with the goal of elaborating theory through discovery. Although violative behavior is the fundamental criterion for selecting cases, deciding whether a case is a case of "misconduct," "deviance," "crime," "illegality," "unethical behavior" – or simply "conduct" – awaits full analysis (see Walton, Chapter 5).

In fact, perhaps the single most definitive finding of the NASA case analysis is my revised understanding about what the case is a case *of*. Although I selected the case as a possible case of misconduct as defined earlier, the data contradicted the starting theory. The circumstances surrounding the rule violations at NASA were not explained by the amoral-calculator model that fills the literature on violative behavior by organizations. Consequently, I treated the rule violations as negative cases *within* my case that had to be explained (Lindesmith 1947). I concluded that the rule violations were a consequence of the social construction of risk, not amoral calculation (D. Vaughan, unpublished data). The data compelled me to redefine my case. Thus, the case shifted from an example of misconduct (at least, as traditionally represented in the literature) to an example of the social construction of risk. The discovery does not negate the NASA case as an example of misconduct, but instead suggests that the mechanism by which rules are violated in organizations is far more complex and socially determined than a rational-choice model posits.

Here, in brief, are some of the directions in which my original explanatory scheme has been elaborated by analysis of the NASA/*Challenger* case.

The competitive environment. No findings contradict the various theoretical notions included in the original conceptualization. Indeed, the finding that the Space Shuttle program was born into an environment of scarce resources, with the burden of carrying out the U.S. government's goals of primacy in the international competition for scientific and military supremacy in space, is strong confirmation for the general relevance of two of the major concepts, competition and scarce resources. My attempt to examine environmental norms pertaining to misconduct in and by organizations produced only greater ambiguity: How can we trace the connection between norms external to an organization and the behavior of individual actors? Do organizations create internal normative environments that are distinctive, or do they incorporate elements of external normative standards? If the latter, how do we distinguish one from the other? What about intraorganizational and extraorganizational variations in normative standards and how their effectiveness is mediated by individual willingness to abide by them?

Organizational characteristics – structure, processes, and transactions. By virtue of the extraordinary historical documentation of internal NASA affairs, this case produced rarely available microlevel data. Many of the new insights from the study are about what happened intraorganizationally. One example is the elaboration of Spence's model (1974) of market signaling. Spence described how organizations make decisions in a world of incomplete information. He argued that because of the number and complexity of transactions in which organizations engage, and the amount of information necessary to complete each one, they are unable to know each individual case thoroughly. Observation costs are high. As a consequence, organizations tend to use a shortcut assessment method when considering a transaction where product uncertainty exists, relying on signals and indexes rather than bearing the costs of a thorough inquiry. Spence used transactions in the job market as an example: an employer, confronted with a pool of potential employees and unable to gather complete information on each one, relies on indexes and signals, like the prestige of a person's school and/or letters of recommendation. Although Spence's model explained how organizations interpret information originating from individuals, in the 1983 Medicaid–provider fraud case I applied his principles to exchanges between organizations. Because of the new information from that case, I was able to see how high observation costs create the possibility of manipulating signals, and thus fraud between organizations (Vaughan 1983:78–81).

In later research on intimate relationships (Vaughan 1986), the key question was how one person in a relationship could leave the other person socially and psychologically without that other person being aware of it until too late in the uncoupling process. In that research, I had microlevel data. I discovered that individuals in cohabiting intimate relationships evolved a method of communicating information that had the characteristics that Spence originally pointed out and that I had elaborated at a structural level in my previous book. Uncertainty and high observation costs led to a reliance upon signals rather than intensive monitoring of each and every exchange. Again, fraud was a possible consequence. Because analyzing intimate relationships produced a different kind of data, I learned more about the sending and receiving of information: the *characteristics* of signals sent by unhappy initiators in a troubled relationship and how they were *interpreted* (or misinterpreted, as was generally the case) by still-contented partners in a dyad (Vaughan 1986:62–78).

This discovery was truly a surprise. I did not enter into my research on uncoupling with any ideas about the comparability or noncomparability of communication in these two situations, nor did I have the idea at the time that the two research projects would have anything in common at all, other than the fact that both focused on organizations. Only after I had analyzed the data and written a chapter draft did I see the parallels among Spence's ideas, my research on Medicaid–provider fraud, and information exchange in coupled relationships. Indeed, this discovery was what prompted me to begin thinking more systematically about theory elaboration by alternating between units and levels of analysis.

Having applied Spence's model at the macrolevel to interorganizational relations and then at the microlevel to intraorganizational relations, I again was surprised to find the elaborated model applicable in the NASA study. Almost every available source documented that communication problems at NASA contributed to the *Challenger* tragedy. I did not set out to intentionally apply Spence's elaborated model, but *Uncoupling* (1986) had sensitized me to the importance of the characteristics of signals. So I was curious about information about the flawed Solid Rocket Booster Joints, how it was distributed, presented, and interpreted at NASA. The data allowed me to (1) refine my previous notions about the sending and receiving of information in complex organizations, (2) use the elaborated version of Spence's model to explain intraorganizational and interorganizational communication at NASA, and (3) offer a plausible explanation of why *Challenger* was launched despite signals of danger. The theoretical significance is that the NASA case provides microlevel data that contradict the amoral-calculator model. This finding does not disprove that model, but does challenge it, suggesting the need for more studies with microlevel data about misconduct in organizations.

The regulatory environment. While the foregoing allowed me to begin filling a theoretical gap of which I was keenly aware, the data on safety regulation at NASA drew my attention to a subject that hadn't even occurred to me. Theory and research on regulation are based almost exclusively on government agencies regulating business firms. The NASA case was an instance of a government agency regulating itself and its own product. Moreover, safety at NASA was regulated by one external and two internal regulatory bodies. Consequently, it was a rare opportunity to study self-regulation reinforced by external control. The concepts of autonomy and interdependence, previously used to explain regulatory relations between legally empowered agents of so-cial control and business firms, guided the analysis. The case study confirms the effects of autonomy and interdependence in the regulation of a government agency. In addition, it shows that these two concepts are useful for analyzing intraorganizational as well as interorganiza-tional relations [for the analysis, see Vaughan (1990)].

The problem of forcing fit

The paradox of theory is that at the same time it tells us where to look, it can keep us from seeing. Glaser and Strauss argue against initiating qualitative analysis with any preconceived theory that dictates relevan-cies in concepts and hypotheses prior to the research (1967:33). They warn that proceeding in this manner creates a tendency for a researcher to "force-fit" the data to the theory. But this method of elaboration relies upon comparing data with some sensitizing theory, concept, or model. It rests on the assumption that a researcher never begins with a clean slate. Even when we believe ourselves to be unfettered theoretically, we always begin a research project with an arsenal of preconceived theoret-ical notions accumulated from our own research, our reading of the work of others, personal experience, literature, and conversations that shape our perceptions and ideas in spite of ourselves. Having once read labeling theory, for example, or DiMaggio and Powell (1983) on institutional isomorphism, we cannot block or isolate these ideas from interpretive use, for they remain part of our worldview, activated unexpectedly in response to situations where, rightly or wrongly, we "see" their applicability. Furthermore, once in touch with our data, we tend early to develop a "theoretical fix": an explanatory scheme that guides the remainder of the work.

Because theories, models, or concepts are points of departure in this method of elaboration, does it create a propensity to see a "fit" – or create a "fit" – when none exists? Does approaching a case with a possible explanatory scheme in mind, as suggested here, block discovery of the fresh and new? The argument could be made that this method poses no such danger. Here we use theories, models, and concepts as sensitizing devices, rather than translating them into formalized propositions that are tested; consequently, working within this mode is no different from, say, beginning a study of a prison-release program with an array of conceptual tools (e.g., labeling theory, deterrence theory) as a part of our background reading. On the other hand, isn't there a greater tendency for bias when the predetermined task is to look for, examine, and possibly apply a particular theoretical notion, or assemblage of theoretical notions?

Bias is inherent in both the foregoing situations. Undeniably, theoretical notions affect our interpretation of information, and the information we select to interpret. My affinity for an organizational paradigm, for example, means a particular reading of the data, not the only reading possible. But I am concerned here with *unacknowledged* biasing effects, which raise the possibility of some distortion being introduced into the work so great as to make it useless or invalid (Becker 1967). The requirement of this method – that, to the best of our ability, we make our theoretical notions explicit from the beginning – creates the possibility of control. We take an intuitive practice – using theories about the world to organize and understand it – and make the practice overt so we can better direct our analysis of social situations. By acknowledging our theoretical tools (i.e., our "biases") as best we can at the outset, we can better guard against the tendency for our worldview to affect our interpretation of information in unacknowledged ways.

In addition, two safeguards against the unwitting force-fitting of data to theory are built into this method. The cases selected produce unique data that draw the researcher away from the theory, model, or concepts that are guiding the analysis. First, different organizational forms produce variation in the data that exerts a control. Examining organizational forms diverse in size, complexity, and function as opposed to choosing similar organizational forms (studying only families) will lead to information that will not immediately confirm our views. Second, each case has some circumstance, activity, or event that must be explained. Abbott (Chapter 2) notes the complexity and narrative order of cases, suggesting they "engage in a perpetual dialogue with their environment, a dialogue of action and constraint that we call plot." Each case analysis must have internal integrity, explaining as fully as possible its plot. A full explanation can be achieved only by exploring the relationships among all the parts of the whole (Ragin 1987). Because of this interconnectedness, the researcher cannot isolate a portion of the findings that appear to be an example of a guiding theory or concept without also taking into account the whole. This necessity acts as a check upon unintentional distortion to fit preconceived notions.

The resolution of contradictions (selective dropping of information that doesn't fit, versus rejecting the theory, versus conceptual innovation) cannot be left to chance, however. The researcher needs to initiate strategies that guard against unacknowledged biases. Of course, reliance on the tools and techniques of the discipline to ensure that the research meets the standards of good scientific work is necessary. But, in addition, the researcher actively can incorporate strategies into the investigation that specifically monitor the subtle influence of biases by forcing consideration of contradictory points of view.

Systematic generalization

Systematic generalization heightens a researcher's sensitivity to biases in an ongoing work.[3] It consists of three procedures that make the researcher confront alternative explanations directly and regularly: collegial exchange, using insiders and outsiders, and comparisons with existing documented cases. For systematic generalization to keep the researcher effectively in touch with bias, these procedures should be integrated into the research process at scheduled intervals (hence, "systematic"). The primary purpose is not ultimately to generalize, but to free the researcher's mind from total preoccupation with the intricacies and influences of the case at hand and to force attention to considerations of broader scope (hence, "generalization").

Collegial exchange. As the data are gathered and analyzed, regularly airing the case analysis with colleagues (preferably in a small seminar environment) as the work progresses subjects the researcher's ongoing mental processes to analysis by others who are neither wedded to the researcher's theoretical viewpoint nor seduced by the particular case that becomes so central to the researcher's life. The subtle acquisition of bias can be exposed in discussion with colleagues who suggest alternative interpretations. For the sociologist working alone, the regular integration of collegial exchange throughout the entire research process is a key mechanism for sensitizing the researcher to unknown bias in interpretation. This may also be an important strategy for a team of field researchers. Though regular exchange among them can provide a check on biasing influences, the group can develop a "theoretical fix" so that they evolve an analysis that reflects the theoretical premises of the group as a whole. The predisposition to fit the data to the theory may be fulfilled unless they seek regular exchange with noninvolved sociologists or people from other disciplines.

These conversations also can be important correctives for our understanding of the theories, models, and concepts guiding our work. As Platt and White argue (Chapters 1 and 3), we unintentionally can distort these theoretical notions. From our reading and research experience, we tend (as in all other matters) to remember selectively. We condense our readings of the work of others, remembering main points, forgetting others, perhaps misinterpreting or missing something useful in the process. We can self-correct by rereading periodically. But our colleagues, perhaps remembering other aspects of a given work or even other relevant works that we've ignored, will remind us of what we've forgotten or never noticed in the first place.

Using insiders and outsiders. Insiders are participants in the event under study who are interviewed as primary data sources. Chosen because of their involvement in the case under study, their review of the work in progress can correct both factual and interpretive errors. In the NASA study, I circulated early drafts of papers or chapters for comment to insiders who were primary data sources, which led to both correction and new information. Some of what they said (and equally important, what they didn't say) gave me perspective on the biasing effects of *their* worldview. In order to evaluate insider data, the researcher not only must be informed about the context, but must know the source of the data as thoroughly as possible, must wonder why people agreed to cooperate, must consider how information was selected to be given to the researcher. Consequently, insider information should be balanced by incorporating the perspectives of outsiders.

Outsiders are individuals informed about the subject matter who, because of position within the group, in another group, ideology, occupation, or even in varied proximity to the event or setting, may have different perspectives than the primary data sources. In examining NASA's regulatory environment, for example, insiders were people who worked in the three safety regulatory units I studied. Outsiders were people who regulated NASA but were not in the three units, journalists who wrote about safety at NASA, "whistle-blowers," and NASA employees who were subject to regulation. Data from outsiders (interviews, internal documents, published accounts) help us know the organizational setting or event from the perspective of others in the environment. Outsiders, of course, have their own biases; consequently, submitting preliminary drafts to them not only can reveal biases in the analysis by forcing us to consider alternative points of view, but also can enlighten us about the biases of these outsiders.

Case comparisons. Comparing the ongoing case analysis to existing documented cases forces us to maintain a keen sense of the idiosyncratic qualities of the work in progress, preventing us from selective attention to data that conform to our theoretical hunches (Glaser and Strauss 1967). We can quickly acquire comparison cases through historical documents, journalistic accounts, or other written materials by nonsociologists. For example, Phyllis Rose's engaging biographies in *Parallel Lives: Five Victorian Marriages* (1983) were wonderfully useful for comparison with my interview data for *Uncoupling.* Another source is systematic analysis of other sociological research using the same concept, theory, or model. Earlier I discussed the role of secondary analysis in theory elaboration, but analyzing the work of others deserves mention again as a bias-reduction strategy: it forces us to confront facts that do not readily fit our preconceptions. Useful for comparison with research on corporate crime, for example, is a collection of seventeen cases of government illegality (Grabosky 1989). When relying on written materials as comparison cases, however, we must bear in mind that, like ourselves, other people selectively organize information into memory and into documentary form (Smith 1974).

Because data gathering and analysis are simultaneous and we tend to develop hypotheses during all stages of our work, systematic generalization is most effective when regularly integrated into the research process. Of course these suggestions will need to be tempered to fit the problem being studied as well as the number of researchers participating, but frequent direct confrontation with contradictory evidence can monitor bias developing in the research. Careful inspection and record keeping are essential. We tend to forget those bits of information that do not conform to our own worldview. With careful inspection and record keeping, we can keep in touch with the idiosyncratic characteristics of the research, reducing the possibility that sensitizing theories, concepts, or models will lead to dropping of information that does not fit. In this way, we can maximize the heuristics of case analysis.

References

Becker, Howard S. (1967). "Whose Side Are We On?" *Social Problems* 14:239–47.
Blau, Peter M. (1964). *Exchange and Power in Social Life.* New York: Wiley.
Blumer, Herbert (1969). *Symbolic Interactionism: Perspective and Method.* Englewood Cliffs, NJ: Prentice-Hall.
Clinard, Marshall B., and Peter C. Yeager (1980). *Corporate Crime.* New York: Free Press.
Cloward, Richard A., and Lloyd E. Ohlin (1960). *Delinquency and Opportunity.* New York: Free Press.
Coleman, James S. (1986). "Social Theory, Social Research, and a Theory of Action." *American Journal of Sociology* 91: 1309–35.
Collins, Randall (1981). "On the Microfoundations of Macrosociology." *American Journal of Sociology* 86:984–1014.
Corwin, Ronald G. (1981). "Patterns of Organizational Control and Teacher Militancy: Theoretical Continuities in the Idea of 'Loose Coupling,'" pp. 261–91 in Alan C. Kerckhoff (ed.), *Research in Sociology of Education and Socialization.* Greenwich, CT: JAI Press.
Cressey, Donald R. (1953). *Other People's Money.* New York: Free Press.
DiMaggio, Paul J., and Walter W. Powell (1983). "The Iron Cage Revisited: Institutional Isomorphism and Collective Rationality in Organizational Fields." *American Sociological Review* 48:147–60.
Fine, Gary Alan (1987). *With the Boys: Little League Baseball and Preadolescent Culture.* Chicago: University of Chicago Press.
    (1988). "On the Macrofoundations of Microsociology: Constraint and the Exterior Reality of Structure." Paper presented at the annual meetings of the American Sociological Association, Atlanta.
Frost, Peter J., L. F. Moore, Meryl R. Louis, C. C. Lundberg, and Joanne Martin (eds.) (1985). *Organization Culture.* Beverly Hills, CA: Sage.
Giddens, Anthony (1979). *Central Problems in Social Theory: Action, Structure, and Contradiction in Social Analysis.* London: Macmillan.
    (1984). *The Constitution of Society: Outline of the Theory of Structuration.* Berkeley: University of California Press.
Glaser, Barney G., and Anselm L. Strauss (1967). *The Discovery of Grounded Theory: Strategies of Qualitative Research.* New York: Aldine.
Gouldner, Alvin W. (1968). "Reciprocity and Autonomy in Functional Theory," pp. 251–70 in Llewellyn Gross (ed.), *Symposium on Sociological Theory.* New York: Harper & Row.
Grabosky, Peter N. (1989). *Wayward Governance: Illegality and Its Control in the Public Sector.* Australian Institute of Criminology.
Hechter, Michael (ed.) (1983). *The Microfoundations of Macrosociology.* Philadelphia: Temple University Press.
Heimer, Carol A. (1987). "Producing Responsible Behavior in Order to Produce Oil." Report # 76. Bergen, Norway: Institute of Industrial Economics.
    (1988). "Institutions, Rights, and Responsibilities in the Neonatal Intensive Care Unit." Paper presented at the Conference on the Emergence, Maintenance, and Effects of Social Institutions, Werner-Reimers Stiftung, Bad Homburg, West Germany.

Kaplan, Abraham (1964). *The Conduct of Inquiry*. San Francisco: Chandler.

Kendall, Patricia L., and Paul F. Lazarsfeld (1950). "Problems of Survey Analysis," pp. 133–96 in Robert K. Merton and Paul F. Lazarsfeld (eds.), *Continuities in Social Research: Studies in the Scope and Method of "The American Soldier."* New York: Free Press.

Lindesmith, Alfred R. (1947). *Opiate Addiction*. Bloomington, IN: Principia Press.

McCall, George J. (1978). "The Social Organization of Relationships," pp. 3–34 in George J. McCall, Michal M. McCall, Norman K. Denzin, Gerald D. Suttles, and Suzanne B. Kurth (eds.), *Social Relationships*. Chicago: Aldine.

Merton, Robert K. (1968). *Social Theory and Social Structure*. Glencoe, IL: Free Press.

Miles, Robert H. (in collaboration with Kim S. Cameron) (1982). *Coffin Nails and Corporate Strategies*. Englewood Cliffs, NJ: Prentice-Hall.

Pfeffer, Jeffrey, and Gerald R. Salancik (1978). *The External Control of Organizations*. New York: Harper & Row.

Presidential Commission on the Space Shuttle *Challenger* Accident (1986). *Report of the Presidential Commission on the Space Shuttle Accident*, 5 vols. Washington, DC: U.S. Government Printing Office.

Przeworski, Adam, and Henry Teune (1970). *The Logic of Comparative Social Inquiry*. New York: Wiley.

Ragin, Charles C. (1987). *The Comparative Method: Moving Beyond Qualitative and Quantitative Strategies*. Berkeley: University of California Press.

Robinson, W. S. (1951). "The Logical Structure of Analytic Induction." *American Sociological Review* 16:812–18.

Rose, Phyllis (1983). *Parallel Lives: Five Victorian Marriages*. New York: Knopf.

Scanzoni, John (1972). *Sexual Bargaining: Power Politics in the American Marriage*. Englewood Cliffs, NJ: Prentice-Hall.

Schrager, Laura Shill, and James F. Short, Jr. (1978). "Toward a Sociology of Organizational Crime." *Social Problems* 25:405–19.

Simmel, Georg (1950). "Dyads and Triads," pp. 122–69 in Kurt Wolff (trans.), *The Sociology of Georg Simmel*. Glencoe, IL: Free Press.

Smith, Dorothy (1974). "The Social Construction of Documentary Reality." *Sociological Inquiry* 44:257–67.

Spence, Michael A. (1974). *Market Signaling*. Cambridge, MA: Harvard University Press.

Stacey, Judith (1990). *Brave New Families*. New York: Basic Books.

Stinchcombe, Arthur L. (1970). "Organized Dependency Relations and Social Stratification," pp. 95–9 in Edward O. Laumann, Paul M. Seigel, and Robert W. Hodge (eds.), *The Logic of Social Hierarchies*. Chicago: Markham.

   (1978). *Theoretical Methods in Social History*. New York: Academic Press.

U.S. House of Representatives, Committee on Science and Technology (1986). *Investigation of the Challenger Accident, Report, Hearings*, 2 vols. Washington, DC: U.S. Government Printing Office.

Vaughan, Diane (1983). *Controlling Unlawful Organizational Behavior: Social Structure and Corporate Misconduct*. Chicago: University of Chicago Press.

   (1986). *Uncoupling: Turning Points in Intimate Relationships*. Oxford: Oxford University Press.

(1989). "Regulating Risk: Implications of the *Challenger* Accident." *Law and Policy* 11:330–49.

(1990). "Autonomy, Interdependence, and Social Control: NASA and the Space Shuttle *Challenger*." *Administrative Science Quarterly* 35:225–57.

(in press). "The Macro/Micro Connection in 'White-Collar Crime' Theory," in Kip Schlegel and David Weisburd (eds.), *Essays on White-Collar Crime*. Boston: Northeastern University Press.

Weick, Karl (1976). "Educational Organizations as Loosely Coupled Systems." *Administrative Science Quarterly* 21:1–19.

White, Harrison C., Scott A. Boorman, and Ronald L. Breiger (1976). "Social Structure from Multiple Networks." *American Journal of Sociology* 81: 730–80, 1384–446.

Part III
Reflections on "What is a Case?"

9
Cases, causes, conjunctures, stories, and imagery

HOWARD S. BECKER

Cases

The problems associated with doing and understanding case studies involve, apparently necessarily, the question of explanation or description, which might be translated as the problem of what we can say about what we've found out in our research. Can we say that something we discovered causes or produces or influences or comes before or in some other way affects what happens to some other thing? We produce a lot of "results" and then have to arrange them so as to "say something." What kinds of "somethings" can we say? Where do they come from? What criteria do we use to judge them?

Causes

One way we approach this problem is to say that something "causes" something else. The notion of cause is very tangled philosophically, at least (to my meager knowledge) since Hume, and it is especially hard to separate from the simple fact of sequence, of one thing following another. Billiard ball *A* hits billiard ball *B*. Billiard ball *B* moves. Did *A*'s hitting it "cause" it to move?

Leave these philosophical tangles aside. Sociologists have typically solved the problem of cause by embodying it in procedures which we agree will serve as the way we know that *A* caused *B*, philosophically sound or not. These procedures have the status of paradigmatic methods. They are parts of packages of ideas and procedures which some community of scientists has agreed to accept as plenty good enough for the purpose of establishing cause. For all the reasons Thomas Kuhn (1962) pointed out, these paradigmatic ideas are double-edged. Without them we can't get anything done. But they never really do what they say they do. They leave terrible anomalies in their wake. They have terrible flaws in their supporting logic. They are thus always vulnerable to attack, to being shown to be less and do less than they pretend.

Sociologists have agreed on paradigms for establishing causality many times, usually describing their procedures in the language of variables. The analyst identifies a "dependent variable," some phenomenon which varies along some dimension, and then attempts to identify the "independent variables" whose own variation "causes" the variation in the dependent variable. The definition of cause is covariation. If the measure of dependent variable A changes in some regular way when the measure of the independent variables changes, cause has been demonstrated or, at least, researchers who accept this paradigm agree that evidence of causation has been produced.

Naturally, such procedures have many difficulties. Students learning correlation techniques traditionally also learn that correlation is not causation. A long list of standard troubles can derail the easy identification of covariation and causality. Nevertheless, sociologists routinely use this form of explanation, in a variety of forms, particularly in such paradigmatic applications as figuring out, say, what factors affect social mobility: to what degree do parental social position, education, occupation, and similar variables covary with (and thus cause) someone's class mobility?

One standard procedure (or, better, family of procedures) has been a kind of quasi-experimental factoring out of the relative influence of the several causes we can imagine might explain or account for (a variety of terms have been used to describe this connection) the outcome we are interested in. Lieberson (1985) has criticized this family of statistical procedures profoundly, arguing that the notion of estimating the influence of a variable by holding other factors constant is untenable, because of the nonrandom distribution of the variables so introduced, the "selection" problem. He has, in his essay in this volume, nevertheless tried to keep that logic going by cleaning up the occasions of its use.

The procedures used in studies based on this logic depend on comparing cells in a table (the cells containing cases which embody different combinations of the variables being studied), and the comparisons will not withstand standard criticisms unless they rest on large numbers of cases. The results of such studies consist of probabilistic statements about the relations between the variables, of the kind Abbott discusses in his chapter, statements whose subjects are not people or organizations doing things but rather variables having an effect or producing some measurable degree of variation in the dependent variable. The conclusions of such a study – that the cases studied have a particular probability of showing this or that result – are intended to apply to a universe of similar cases.

The logic of this approach, even in the cleaned-up version advocated by Lieberson, requires us to imagine that all the causes involved in the production of an effect operate more or less simultaneously and continuously, as in the well-known laws governing the relations among pressure, temperature, and volume of gases. Even when we know better and know that *A* must precede *B*, the analytic procedures require us to treat them as though that were not true.

These procedures also require us to imagine that the variables proposed as causes operate independently. Each makes its own contribution to the variation in the dependent variable. To be sure, the analyst may have to contend with interaction effects, the effects on the dependent variable of the effects the independent variables have on each other. But these too are treated as though they are all operating simultaneously and continuously.

Lieberson's analysis of automobile accidents in his chapter in this volume exemplifies the point. Any automobile accident is a complex multistep event: the drivers (there are two in the accident he analyzes, although he is only interested in the one alleged to have been drinking) either drink or don't drink; they start their cars; they proceed to the intersection where they will meet; the traffic light at the intersection shows red in one direction, green in the other; one driver proceeds to enter the intersection legally, the other enters it illegally, each of these acts composed of a sequence of more detailed acts, such as looking for other cars and speeding up or slowing down on seeing another one in the intersection (one or more of these acts perhaps related to the drinking that may have occurred earlier); and so on. At each point, the drivers involved may proceed to the next step in the sequence leading to the accident, or they may take some other action that averts the accident. Lieberson's analytic tables, however, treat these events, which in fact are temporally dependent on one another, as though they occurred simultaneously and continuously.

To say that this family of techniques treats causes as operating in these ways does not imply that analysts using them are so stupid as not to recognize that variables have a temporal order, that they occur in recognizable and variable sequences, but rather that the techniques offer no simple way of dealing with this knowledge. The analysis proceeds "as if" all the foregoing were the case. The logic of the techniques does not provide any special way of dealing with these problems. Such visual devices as path diagrams, which lay variables out in a diagram connected by arrows, purport to deal with temporal sequence, but time is only a visually represented metaphor in them. Later I deal with this failure further.

Conjunctures

Another approach recognizes that causal variables are typically not really independent, making their independent contributions to some vector which produces the overall outcome in a dependent variable. This approach, analyzed by Ragin (1987), suggests instead that causes are effective when they operate in concert. Variable X_1 has an effect, but only if variables X_2 and X_3 and X_4 are also present. In their absence, X_1 might as well have stayed home.

This approach is often seen as necessary in studies which accumulate a great deal of information about a small number of cases, as is typical of detailed cross-national historical studies (in the instance Lieberson considers, studies of revolution or the development of state welfare policies in a few countries). Here, the analyst tries to deal with all the complexity of real historical cases, rather than the relations between variables in a universe of hypothetical cases. The conclusion is intended to make historical cases intelligible as instances of the way the posited variables operate in concert.

We do not have many rigorous numerical methods for the assessment of this kind of conjunctural influence of variables. Ragin's Boolean algorithm, which describes the likelihood of a particular outcome given the co-occurrence of specific values of the relevant independent variables, is one such device. He and his colleagues (Ragin, Mayer, and Drass 1984) have, in a paradigmatic example, shown how probabilities of promotion in a federal bureaucracy vary for people with different combinations of values for such variables as race, gender, education, and seniority. This differs from an approach which produces numbers said to describe, in general, the "net relative effect" of those variables on promotion.

Stories

Abbott advocates yet another approach to this problem, in this speaking for a large number of earlier analysts who have advocated, in one form or another, a focus on process, on the temporal dimension in which, as everyone recognizes, phenomena occur.

A process or narrative analysis has a story to tell. To continue using the language of variables (which, it should be obvious, becomes more and more inappropriate as we move away from simple causation models), this family of approaches treats the dependent variable, the thing to be explained, as something that comes about through a series of steps. It does not, as the cases and conjunctures approaches require themselves to assume, think of the result to be explained as having happened all at once. This shows up in several ways.

The analysis focuses first on discovering the sequence of steps involved in the process under study. The causal analysis takes the form of a tree diagram, showing how a case progresses from step to step in the story, each step understood as preceding in time the one that follows it. The treelike character of the analysis is not simply a useful visual convention. The analyst intends it to mirror how the result has "really" come about. The process is taken to be important to the result, perhaps even constitutive of it.

Causes may be seen to operate, but now it is possible to treat a given causal variable as operating in different ways (or indeed not at all) at different steps in the process. In an analysis of heroin addiction, race might be a crucial variable in explaining exposure to the possibility of using drugs, but once a person has started to use drugs, race might play no further part in affecting whether people so exposed in fact use drugs or, having used them, become addicted to their use (cf. Lindesmith 1948).

What is to be explained is typically more complex than the relatively simple outcomes measured in the approaches described earlier. Instead of an outcome described as a value of a variable (so many steps up in a hierarchy, so much more or less income), the outcome is described as a different form of organizational or individual activity, a different way of putting together a number of common and interdependent activities. Thus, in his classic study of embezzlement, Cressey (1953) describes and explains the genesis of the commission of an act of violation of financial trust; Lindesmith (1948) describes and explains the complex of activity that characterizes the behavior of opiate addicts.

Indeed, such analyses devote so much attention to how the result comes about that critics complain that the explanations are tautological (Turner 1953). That is, drug addiction becomes nothing more than the total story of the road taken to it. The criminal violation of financial trust is the story of how the embezzler came to embezzle. When you've told how it happened, you've said all there is to say.

That observation can be made as a criticism, but it can also be embraced as an advantage. (In the language of the computer hacker, it's not a bug, it's a feature.) The analyst is performing an operation Paul Lazarsfeld described as the "analysis of the dependent variable." Instead of what is to be explained being taken as given – e.g., variation in a person's class position or income, or the occurrence or nonoccurrence of a revolution – at least one major object of the research becomes the discovery of what exactly the end result is. Cases that look alike are inspected carefully to see how they may differ. Analysts look to discover subvarieties of what seem on the surface to be one thing. They are interested in the interrelationships between the elements of the dependent variable, itself seen as multidimensional, so that its character cannot be expressed as one number on a ruler.

A model of such an exploration of the dependent variable is Cressey's explanation of the way his study of the causes of embezzling became a study whose dependent variable was defined as "the criminal violation of financial trust." This shift in what his case consisted of is reminiscent of Walton's discovery that the Owens Valley story was not about a peasant rebellion, but rather about the changing relations between community and state. Later I will deal with the shift in Cressey's analysis further.

The research thus becomes, instead of the refinement of measures of association between independent and dependent variables, the story of how something inevitably got to be the way it is. Where the analysis of causes leads to a probabilistic statement of what might happen, and the conjunctural analysis leads to a description of all the things that must be present for a particular outcome to occur, the narrative analysis leads to what might well be called a tautology, the statement of a sequence in which is prefigured (to use Harrison White's evocative phrase) the end result. "In my end is my beginning."

Imagery

Behind all of these variations in analytic strategies, tactics, and goals lies a phenomenon Herbert Blumer (1969) habitually, even obsessively, called attention to: the underlying imagery with which we approach the phenomenon we study. What do we think we are looking at? What is its character? Most importantly, given what we think it is, is the way we study it and report our findings congruent with that character?

Abbott's intriguing discovery – that authors who relentlessly speak of the action of variables when they report "firm" results nevertheless start talking about real people when they have a result their analysis can't explain – reflects a problem in the congruence of their imagery with the world their work has revealed to them. These analysts envision a world in which variables do all the acting and interacting and produce a result they had foreseen. When it doesn't work out that way, they construct a more familiar kind of story, based on our common knowledge of the world, "common sense," in which people act the way people usually act.

Blumer thought, and so do I, that the basic operation in studying society is the production and refinement of an image of the thing we are studying. We learn a little something (maybe a lot, who knows?) about something we are interested in. On the basis of that little, we construct a pretty complete story of the phenomenon. Suppose we decide to study a city neighborhood. We might begin by consulting a book of local statistics (the Chicago *Community Fact Book* or the relevant census publications) and seeing what kind of people live there. How many men? How many women? Of what ages? What is their median education? Their median income? With this basic information, I can work up, in my mind, a complete, if provisional, picture of the neighborhood, deciding on the basis of the figures on income and education that it is a working-class neighborhood, using the age distribution to guess at the nature of family life, seeing it as an area of people retiring or getting ready to retire or, conversely, as an area filled with young people just beginning their families. I add the variables of race and ethnicity and my picture becomes more complete.

My picture is more than a compilation of statistics. It includes details that are not in the books and tables I consulted, details I have invented on the basis of what those books told me. I "know," for instance, what kinds of houses these people live in – I can practically see, as if in a photograph, the neat lawn with the plastic flamingos, the furniture "suites" from the credit furniture store and whatever else my stereotype of that kind of population produces. None of this is based on any real knowledge of the area I intend to study. It is imagery I have constructed imaginatively (or stereotypically) from a few facts. It includes, if I'm imaginative enough, the look of the streets and the smell of the kitchens ("Italians? Garlic!") and, if I'm well read enough in social science, the kind of talk that goes on over the dinner table ("Working class? Restricted code – a lot of grunts and monosyllables, à la Basil Bernstein").

Imaginative, well-read social scientists can go a long way with a little fact. Since, however, we claim to be social scientists, we don't stop with imagination and extrapolation, as a novelist or filmmaker might. We do a little checking to see if we're right. Research. We gather data.

Now, however, we enter another, more abstract, realm of imagery. This imagery has to do with the kind of causality we think might be operating. Imagery about kinds of causes has a more professional source. Do we think the phenomenon we're studying is totally governed by chance, so that a model of random activity is appropriate? Do we think it is partly chance and partly something more deterministic? Do we think it is a story? In other words, in thinking about the phenomenon, we include in the picture we build up some notions about the kind of conclusion we will draw about it, the kind of paradigmatic thinking we will assimilate it to. These paradigms come to us out of our participation in a world of professional social scientists.

Narrative styles of analysis devote a lot of time and energy to developing this imagery, which is another way of talking about the analysis of the dependent variable. Developing imagery is a process in which we try to understand what we want to understand better. We do not search for causes so much as look for stories that explain what it is and how it got that way. When an analyst of causes has done the job well, the result is a large proportion of variance explained. When an analyst of narrative has done the job well, the result is a story that explains why it is inevitable that this process led to this result.

Narrative analysis produces something causal analysts are suspicious of, and properly so, given their presuppositions and working practices. Any probabilistic causal analysis that produced a perfect correlation would be dismissed as necessarily containing sizeable errors. Researchers know that there is too much noise in their data, too many measurement and other errors, for perfect correlations to occur. They expect imperfect correlations, even if their theory predicts a perfect one. But, while they know that there is error in their data (the errors that stand in the way of better correlations), they do not throw their imperfect data out, for they don't know which cases or measurements contain the errors. To be honest, they include all the cases and thus guarantee a probabilistic result. This upsets narrative analysts who see the unexplained variance as a problem, not a natural feature of the landscape.

Narrative analysts, on the other hand, are not happy unless they have a completely deterministic result. Every negative case becomes an opportunity to refine the result, to rework the explanation so that it includes the seemingly anomalous case. A second way of dealing with anomalous cases, however, one which upsets probabilistic causal analysts, is to throw them out. Not exactly throw them out but, rather, decide by inspecting them carefully that they are not after all a case of the sort of thing we are explaining. Part of the process of constructing a narrative is a continuous redefinition of what the theory is explaining, of what the dependent variable actually is.

Cressey (1953:19–22) explains in detail why he redefined his dependent variable in the study of embezzling and what he threw out, as well as what he included that others might have left out, giving the category so constructed a new name, and in this way dealing with what might have been dismissed, from another point of view, as measurement error. He knew that

the legal category [of embezzlement] did not describe a homogeneous class of criminal behavior. Persons whose behavior was not adequately described by the definition of embezzlement were found to have been imprisoned for that offense, and persons whose behavior was adequately described by the definition were confined for some other offense.

The category he defined as the object of his study was the "criminal violation of financial trust," defined by the person first having "accepted a position of [financial] trust in good faith," and then violating "that trust by committing a crime." This defined a category of criminals that was homogeneous and that included people convicted of forgery, confidence game, and larceny by bailee who fit his definition but would have been lost if he had stuck to the legal definition. More important for the point I want to make here, it allowed him to exclude cases – which would necessarily have been included if he had stuck to the original legal definition – in which the prosecutors found it convenient to indict for embezzlement but which did not fit his definition. In particular, it allowed him to exclude violators who had accepted positions of trust fully intending to steal money the first chance they got, the explanation of whose behavior would be very different from the explanation of trust violation by people who had never intended to steal. Redefining the object of study, and eliminating cases, led to greater precision in the result.

Further problems

The chapters in this volume suggest some questions which deserve further study and analysis. Here are a few.

A major problem in any form of social research is reasoning from the parts we know to something about the whole they and parts like them make up. This is not a sampling question in the conventional sense. We are not trying to find out, by learning the proportion of cases which have property X in our sample, what the similar proportion is in the universe from which our cases come, or anything formally similar to that. Rather, we want to create an image of the entire organization or process, based on the parts we have been able to uncover. The logic of such an analysis is different. We ask: What kind of an organization could accommodate a part like this? What would the rest of the organization have to be like for this part to be what it is? What would the whole story have to be for this step to occur as we have seen it occur? I don't know anywhere that the logic of such reasoning has been fully worked out, although a start was made in Paul Diesing's book on social science (1971) some years ago.

Another problem has to do with the social organization of social science and the way different styles of analysis are related to styles of work and the practicalities of contemporary modes of research. Sociologists of science, such as Kuhn (1962), Latour (1987), Star (1989), and Fujimura (1987, 1988) [also see the literature cited by Clarke and Gerson (1990)], have created some tools with which to approach these questions. We understand a technical problem by seeing its place in the entire work process of that kind of science. Logical problems become understandable, and solutions to them can be found, in the social organization in which they arise.

For instance, causal analyses in sociology typically, though not necessarily, involve large numbers of cases, and that means, in today's versions of social science, doing large-scale surveys or using the results of such surveys as they are given to us in censuses and similar documents. The economics of large-scale data gathering lead to a host of problems. Take a mundane, but not trivial, example: interviewer cheating. Some survey interviewers do not conduct the interviews they turn in, but just fake them, in order to increase their earnings. Survey organizations have, of course, devised techniques to get this under control, but it can hardly be said to be a problem that is solved. Roth (1966) analyzed this as the "hired-hand syndrome," applying a simple result from studies of the restriction of output in industry: workers who have no stake in the eventual product of a work process will maximize what is important to them – income – rather than what their employers are after – accurate data. If that's the kind of data you have, then an emphasis on probabilistic styles of causal analysis is almost logically entailed.

Similarly, large-scale data gathering inevitably means, given the restricted economic base of social science research, collecting relatively small amounts of data about the many cases studied. Studies of process, on the other hand, are typically done by a single researcher spending long periods of time with people and groups, in the classical anthropological style. The economics are quite different; the researcher need only find enough money to support the necessary time away from other paying occupations. The trade-off for this style of research is the opposite of that typical of analyses based on variables and causes construed in variable terms: you know much more about fewer cases. Vaughan, in her chapter in this volume, makes the intriguing suggestion that the macro-micro "problem" of which so much has been made is really an artifact of styles of data gathering. It is hard to connect the two because survey analysts do not know as much about the many cases they gather as qualitative analysts do about the few cases they gather.

A final, and profoundly difficult, problem has to do with the ways we represent the knowledge our research produces (Becker 1986; Latour 1985; Kuhn 1962). Professional social scientists typically use only a few of the very large number of possible ways of representing social science results, those few being parts of "packages" of theories, methods, types of data, and styles of analysis and representation which have been conventionalized in some working group. The contents of the package are interrelated, so that using one portion more or less entails using the whole package. Sociologists who do certain kinds of statistical analyses have, for instance, learned a simple method of representing causal relations between variables, in the form of arrows with statistical coefficients attached. They find this an effective shorthand, easily understood by other adepts.

Like the other agreed-on parts of a scientific package, such conventions of representation facilitate sociological work. But they also hamper it because, while they make communication of some results easy and efficient, they make communication of other kinds of results difficult or impossible. The arrows that convey the results of causal analyses so well are not very good at communicating the complex interdependencies embodied in stories or in the visual materials (still photographs, film, and video) which social scientists are increasingly using (thereby finally catching up with the physical and biological sciences, where such materials have been routinely used almost since they were invented). But users of such methods have yet to develop the representational conventions which will make the communication of their results unproblematic.

These are problems for the future and for other conferences.

References

Becker, Howard S. (1986). "Telling About Society," in *Doing Things Together*. Evanston, IL: Northwestern University Press.

Blumer, Herbert (1969). *Symbolic Interactionism: Perspective and Method*. Englewood Cliffs, NJ: Prentice Hall.

Clarke, Adele E., and Elihu M. Gerson (1990). "Symbolic Interactionism in Social Studies of Science," pp. 203–14 in Howard S. Becker and Michal M. McCall (eds.), *Symbolic Interaction and Cultural Studies*. Chicago: University of Chicago Press.

Cressey, Donald R. (1953). *Other People's Money*. New York: Free Press.

Diesing, Paul (1971). *Patterns of Discovery in the Social Sciences*. Chicago: Aldine.

Fujimura, Joan H. (1987). "Constructing Doable Problems in Cancer Research: Articulating Alignment." *Social Studies of Science* 17:257–93.

    (1988). "The Molecular Biological Bandwagon in Cancer Research: Where Social Worlds Meet." *Social Problems* 35:261–83.

Kuhn, Thomas (1962). *The Structure of Scientific Revolutions*. Chicago: University of Chicago Press.

Latour, Bruno (1985). "Visualization and Cognition: Thinking with Eyes and Hands," pp. 34–69 in H. Kuclick (ed.), *Knowledge and Society*. New York: JAI Press.

(1987). *Science in Action*. Cambridge, MA: Harvard University Press.

Lieberson, Stanley (1985). *Making It Count*. Berkeley: University of California Press.

Lindesmith, Alfred (1948). *Opiate Addiction*. Bloomington, IN: Principia Press.

Ragin, Charles C. (1987). *The Comparative Method: Moving Beyond Qualitative and Quantitative Stratgies*. Berkeley: University of California Press.

Ragin, Charles C., Susan E. Mayer, and Kriss A. Drass (1984). "Assessing Discrimination: A Boolean Approach." *American Sociological Review* 49: 221–34.

Roth, Julius A. (1966). "Hired Hand Research." *The American Sociologist* 1:190–96.

Star, Susan Leigh (1989). *Regions of the Mind: Brain Research and the Quest for Scientific Certainty*. Stanford, CA: Stanford University Press.

Turner, Ralph (1953). "The Quest for Universals in Sociological Research." *American Sociological Review* 18:604–11.

10
"Casing" and the process of social inquiry[1]

CHARLES C. RAGIN

Linking ideas and evidence in social research

The biggest obstacle to clear thinking about "What is a case?" is the simple fact that the term "case" is used in so many different ways. It is used to refer to data categories, theoretical categories, historically specific categories, substantive categories, and so on. For this reason, it is difficult to reconcile the varied approaches to the question of cases represented in this volume. A wide array of possible responses to the question are represented, ranging from a bottom-up tale of discovery (Douglas Harper, Chapter 6) to a top-down discussion of how "worldly" conventions in the use of cases shape social scientific thinking (Harrison White, Chapter 3). There is common ground, but it is shrouded in fog.

Rather than attempt to delineate the many different meanings of the term "case" in a formal taxonomy, in this essay I offer instead a view of cases that follows from the idea implicit in many of the contributions – that concocting cases is a varied but routine social scientific activity. Implicit in this observation is the idea that the question of cases can be examined behaviorally and that it is possible to assess the conditions under which social scientists are compelled to delimit or declare cases. The approach of this essay is that this activity, which I call "casing," should be viewed in practical terms as a research tactic. It is selectively invoked at many different junctures in the research process, usually to resolve difficult issues in linking ideas and evidence.

It is impossible to do research in a conceptual vacuum. Whether it is viewed as given or socially constructed, the empirical world is limitless in its detail, complexity, specificity, and uniqueness. The fact that we can make almost any everyday social category problematic (e.g., family, community, social class, church, firm, nation-state) is testimony to the complexity of the empirical. We make sense of its infinity by limiting it with our ideas. In effect, theoretical ideas and principles provide ways

217

to see the empirical world and to structure our descriptions of this world. In this light, empirical research can be seen as culminating in theoretically structured descriptions – understandings that result from the application of constraining ideas to infinite evidence.

Theoretical ideas, by contrast, are relatively simple; the typical formulation embodies only a few principles. This apparent simplicity, however, cannot mask the complexity that derives from the fact that theoretical formulations are verbal and thus abstract, incomplete, and tentative. At best, theory provides an initial image, a vague starting point for looking at empirical evidence. Even though they are all that we have, theoretical formulations are remarkably feeble devices for structuring description – for generating the results of social science. Thus, we often use empirical evidence to articulate theories, to flesh them out, to ascertain their spatiotemporal limits and establish their scope conditions (Walker and Cohen 1985). In short, ideas and evidence are mutually dependent; we transform evidence into results with the aid of ideas, and we make sense of theoretical ideas and elaborate them by linking them to empirical evidence. Cases figure prominently in both of these relationships.

"Casing" as a research operation

For these reasons, consider cases not as empirical units or theoretical categories, but as the products of basic research operations. Specifically, making something into a case or "casing" it can bring operational closure to some problematic relationship between ideas and evidence, between theory and data. Casing, viewed as a methodological step, can occur at any phase of the research process, but occurs especially at the beginning of a project and at the end. Usually a problematic relation between theory and data is involved when a case is declared.

Some research appears to be atheoretical, and some researchers claim to be uninterested in theoretical ideas – to have little use for them. Such claims usually occur in research settings where the conventions of social science – established ways of seeing and doing – are wholeheartedly embraced. Social class is defined in terms of job characteristics; religion is defined in terms of church membership; society is defined in terms of the territorial limits on state coercion; community means location of residence; and so on. In short, conventionalized units are accepted as the proper way to structure description, and research can proceed along established lines. Many problematic relations between ideas and evidence are thus sidestepped. It is important to note that these conventionalized units are often "aggregative properties" (e.g., Lazarsfeld and

Rosenberg 1955:287–9) and are based on simple groupings of individual-level data. Many of the conventional units of social research are based on conveniently available individual-level data and depend implicitly on the assumption that the properties of individuals can be aggregated and then used to represent properties of more encompassing units. But using such data to concoct larger units such as social classes and religious groups avoids difficult issues in specifying (via theory) and then researching the institutional and organizational features of these groups – their more or less "global" properties. The individual-level variable (e.g., religious affiliation) is allowed to stand for the larger unit.

The nature and origins of these conventions for sidestepping are some of the primary concerns of Jennifer Platt (Chapter 1). When cases are conventions, casing involves invoking common practices, common conceptions, or commonly used units to accomplish vexing tasks. One alternative to finding the boundaries of a case inductively through empirical research is to resort to conventionalized ways of delimiting them. Douglas Harper's contribution (Chapter 6) illustrates this difference in the contrast between his research on the community surrounding Willie, the rural handyman, and his involvement in a collaborative research project on dairy farmers which involved communities defined according to formal political boundaries. Conventional casings simplify and bracket problematic relationships between theory and data; researchers accept them so that they can get on with other tasks.

More often than not, however, social scientists take theoretical ideas more seriously and give them an active role in framing research and producing findings. Most theoretical ideas are formulated in general terms and thus are applicable to some universe of cases. Sometimes these general claims are explicit (e.g., a theory of ethnic relations applicable to all ethnic situations), and sometimes these claims are taken to be general because a theory's scope conditions (Walker and Cohen 1985) have been left unspecified. Social scientists interested in testing theories that make general claims, either implicitly or explicitly, must seek to limit the uniqueness and specificity of the empirical world; it is necessary to place limits on detail and diversity. In short, the continuous web of human social life must be sliced and diced in a way compatible with the goal of testing the generality of theoretical ideas, and comparable objects of research must be established so that boundaries can be placed around measurement operations.

Thus, casing often creates objects. When the members of a generic empirical category (e.g., families, firms) are declared to be the relevant objects for a theoretical idea and thus "cased," researchers can manipulate them to address the theory's broad claims. This form of casing involves objectifying generic empirical units, setting them up to be viewed through blinders that hide all but their theoretically relevant, general features. To collect a sample of "families," for example, is to homogenize the members of the category as much as possible and to close off discussion of "What is family?" The problematic relation between theory and data that this type of casing resolves centers on the individuality, diversity, and specificity of cases. The casing operation washes empirical units of their specificity and leaves them manipulable. It makes only certain features relevant and thus allows viewing them in partial ways.

While theories are general and their claims often are broad, they are also vague, imprecise, and incomplete. It is rare that a theory's categories are well specified, and even when they are, specifications are contested. Consider Weber's specification of bureaucratic organization. A variety of controversies surround this term: what Weber really said, the relative importance of different features, the degree to which the different features must covary, which features must be present for an organization to qualify as bureaucratic, and so on. The point is not that we need greater theoretical clarity and specificity, but that we should recognize that there are practical limits on the degree to which verbal theory can be a precise guide to empirical research. Empirical research often proceeds without clear guidance from theory. It is not possible to construct verbal formulations that can embrace or contend with the complexity and diversity of the empirical world.

For these and related reasons, cases often must be delimited or found in the course of research. Theory provides a starting point (e.g., the idea of community, as in Douglas Harper's contribution, or the idea of a narrative, as in Andrew Abbott's contribution), but the guidance may be weak. Community, for example, must be found in the seamless fabric of social interaction. Where does it begin? Where does it end? Likewise, does a narrative start? When does it end? Vaguely formulated theoretical ideas take firm shape in cases that are pieced together inductively. Thus, casing often involves sifting through empirical evidence to define cases and thus bring a measure of closure to vaguely formulated theoretical concepts or ideas. Cases often must be found because they cannot be specified beforehand. In some research areas, delimiting the case may be one of the last steps of the research process. And once cases have been found, they may be used to refine or even refute the theory that provided the initial guidance.

Theoretical ideas are general and imprecise; they are also dynamic and ever-changing. They change through time, reacting to and back on the larger society and historical experience. Historically or culturally significant events and locales often stand out to us as objects demanding social scientific analysis. Why McCarthyism, and what was it? Why terrorism, and what is it? Sometimes these events and locales can be understood in the context of existing ideas, sometimes not. In either situation, the process of casing involves using and then elaborating theory.

When cases are made, the process of casing consists of matching ideas and evidence. The problem here is not that theories are vague and cases must be empirically discerned; instead the problem is one of proper identification. Either the case must be matched to the appropriate theory or its decisive theoretical properties must be specified so that it can be located theoretically, often generating new ideas in its wake. This type of casing often occurs near the end of the research process. It solves the problem of linking empirical evidence to ideas by specifying which ideas, among the many that are possibly relevant, to use. When none of the existing ideas can accommodate the case, it serves as a basis for elaborating or revising existing theory. In this process, some evidence becomes important or decisive, and other evidence is shunted aside and made irrelevant. Any new theoretical ideas that are generated alter conceptions of existing cases.

A brief illustration

The preceding discussion is exceedingly abstract. The best way to comprehend how casing pervades the process of social research and how it is intimately connected to the problem of linking ideas and evidence is to apply these notions to a case of social research – to link ideas about cases and evidence on casing. Consider Michel Wieviorka's research (Chapter 7). To illustrate some of the casings in his work, I approach his research, as described in his contribution, in a top-down fashion, beginning with the broadest casing:

(1) At the most general level, Wieviorka's research (1988) concerns social movements and is situated in that literature. Thus, from a textbook point of view, the largest relevant universe of observations is all social movements. This is the first casing; it establishes the research as a project directed toward a specific, conventional category of social phenomena – social movements.

(2) However, Wieviorka's main interest was in the new social movements of postindustrial society. Such movements are not based in the world of work and industrial organization, but in the world of culture, communication, and science. This is the second casing; a subset of social

movements is defined, historically and developmentally, and is placed in conceptual opposition to the social movements of industrial societies (e.g., workers' movements). This distinction, social movements of industrial societies versus those of postindustrial societies, does not enter directly into the empirical analysis; background understanding of the social movements of industrial societies is assumed. Thus, these cases (social movements of industrial societies) form an implicit point of contrast; direct empirical evidence on these movements is severed from the investigation.

(3) Among all the different social movements of postindustrial society, Wieviorka focuses on terrorist groups. This casing involves the selection of terrorist groups from among all the different kinds of postindustrial social movements. Among all these social movements, terrorist groups are likely to present certain features of postindustrialism in relatively extreme form. Thus this casing involves not selection on a random basis or on the basis of typicality, but on the basis of theoretical interests in cases which, because of their extremity, may be decisive for theory. Like the second casing, the third involves a theoretically motivated narrowing of the empirical focus and leaves the other side of the dichotomy (nonterrorist, postindustrial social movements) empirically silent. Both casings (2 and 3) are clearly motivated by theory; both involve a narrowing of focus that defines large categories of empirical evidence as secondary.

There is another important issue represented in the third casing, which was a pivotal issue in Wieviorka's research: the definition of terrorism. Obviously, one person's terrorist is the next person's freedom fighter. The identification of some groups as terrorist and others as not is politically charged. Different ways of defining terrorism clearly would lead to different "findings." For example, to accept the definitions of terrorism offered by political authorities (e.g., the U.S. State Department) would be to inject the concerns of these authorities directly into the analysis. An analysis of the features that terrorist groups share would expose the very characteristics that define them as terrorist according to political authorities (e.g., that these groups pose a threat to U.S. national security interests). Apparently, Wieviorka's solution to this problem was to start with relatively conventional definitions of terrorism and maintain the strong expectation, but not the conviction, that one or more of the groups he studied would be reclassified as nonterrorist once the analysis was complete.

(4) Wieviorka did not study all contemporary terrorist groups. For practical reasons, he could study a small subset. Thus, the next casing step involved the selection of specific terrorist groups for investigation.

While the universe of contemporary terrorist groups is not immense, practical considerations overwhelmed most other factors. Wieviorka chose a set of historically conspicuous and immediately available groups to study. He could not claim to have the universe, or a sample, or even groups that were especially strategic from the perspective of theory. It mattered most that they be generally acceptable as cases of terrorist groups and that they embody both the postindustrial elements critical to the second casing and the substantively important elements central to the third casing.

(5) Like all the previous casings, the next involved another narrowing of empirical focus. The main empirical units for analysis – the specific terrorist groups – were now selected. The next casing involved the specific empirical evidence to be collected. Conceivably, all evidence on these groups might be considered relevant to the study. Amassing and analyzing this great body of data could easily take several lifetimes. Wieviorka chose a different path using a novel casing strategy. The casing strategy he devised served to limit the data in a way that allowed Wieviorka to collect decisive evidence in a relatively efficient manner. As he details in his contribution, he confronted members of terrorist groups with representatives of a variety of other groups, including groups the terrorists claimed to represent and groups they claimed to oppose. In effect, these encounters, which are the smallest relevant analytic unit in his study, established different prisms through which different terrorists groups could be viewed.

(6) The next casing is one that emerged from Wieviorka's analysis of the theoretically structured evidence generated via the fifth casing. Before going into the details of the sixth casing and how it emerged from the analysis, I should note that this casing involved the inductive formulation of the concept of *inversion* as a defining feature of terrorist groups (see Chapter 7). This casing was both empirical and theoretical. It was empirical because the concept of inversion was generated from the evidence and provided a foundation for a sociological definition of terrorist groups. It was theoretical because it led to a new conceptual category and a new understanding of terrorism which had implications for postindustrial social movements in general.

Wieviorka's basic analytic technique was the method of agreement. With this method he sought to determine the theoretically decisive features of terrorist groups, which presumably would be present in all such groups. Fortunately, like virtually all researchers who work with small N's, he did not follow the method of agreement slavishly. First, there was no expectation that the theoretically decisive feature or set of features could be identified in a mechanical manner, by selecting from a tally of all the characteristics of all the groups the one characteristic that all groups shared. On the contrary, the expectation was that this decisive feature would be subtle, that in-depth knowledge of the cases would be required in order to be able to identify it, and that terrorist groups would display this feature in a "more or less fashion" – as empirical instances of an ideal typic construct (Ragin and Zaret 1983; Ragin and Hein in press). Second, there was no strong expectation that the feature or set of features identified as decisive would be truly universal among all the terrorists groups in the study. After all, the third casing, which narrowed the focus to "terrorist" groups, was clearly provisional. It was quite possible that included among the groups in Wieviorka's study would be those identified in the media or by political authorities as terrorist that, in the end, might not truly qualify as terrorist. The third casing was provisional because there was explicit recognition that the category *terrorist* as conventionally conceived was the object of political debate and controversy, not a refined theoretical category. Given the provisional character of the third casing, it would be foolish to search for universal features without also questioning along the way both the initial definition of terrorism and the categorization of groups as terrorist. It is common practice in small-N research to prune cases from an analysis, defining them as instances of something else in the process of refining theories and generating new conceptual categories.

In the end, Wieviorka's skillful application of the method of agreement led to a new sociological understanding of terrorism and a recategorization of one of the groups initially included as terrorist. The sixth casing thus involved a narrowing of empirical focus in the service of theoretical articulation.

There are additional casings in this study which could be addressed. For example, the concept of *inversion* has implications not only for terrorist groups, but for social movements in postindustrial societies in general, and for postindustrialism. While these additional casings are possible, the six discussed capture the essence of the view advanced here, that casing is a key part of the process of social inquiry. In each of these casings ideas and evidence interact. In each casing the empirical world is more structured by theoretical ideas. And in each casing more and more of the empirical world is pruned from the analysis.

Conclusion

The two main problems social scientists face as empirical researchers are the equivocal nature of the theoretical realm and the complexity of the empirical realm. As researchers our primary goal is to link the empirical and the theoretical – to use theory to make sense of evidence and to use evidence to sharpen and refine theory. This interplay helps us to produce theoretically structured descriptions of the empirical world that are both meaningful and useful. Casing is an essential part of this process; cases are invoked to make the linking of ideas and evidence possible. Casing is an essential part of the process of producing theoretically structured descriptions of social life and of using empirical evidence to articulate theories. By limiting the empirical world in different ways, it is possible to connect it to theoretical ideas that are general, imprecise, but dynamic verbal statements. In this perspective a case is most often an intermediate product in the effort to link ideas and evidence. A case is not inherently one thing or another, but a way station in the process of producing empirical social science. Cases are multiple in most research efforts because ideas and evidence may be linked in many different ways.

Just as researchers use cases to articulate theories, I have made a case of Wieviorka's research in order to articulate my ideas. One of the main conclusions from this case of research practice is that cases are dynamic. The initial casing of terrorist groups used by Wieviorka was discarded as a result of his analysis, and terrorist groups were recased using the concept of inversion. This fluidity of casing is a special feature of small-N research. Further, this feature explains why small-N qualitative research is most often at the forefront of theoretical development. When N's are large, there are few opportunities for revising a casing. At the start of the analysis, cases are decomposed into variables, and almost the entire dialogue of ideas and evidence occurs through variables (Ragin 1987, 1991). One implication of this discussion is that to the extent that large-N research can be sensitized to the diversity and potential heterogeneity of the cases included in an analysis, large-N research may play a more important part in the advancement of social science theory (Ragin 1987:164–71).

References

Lazarsfeld, Paul F., and Morris Rosenberg (1955). *The Language of Social Research.* Glencoe, IL: Free Press.

Ragin, Charles C. (1987). *The Comparative Method: Moving Beyond Qualitative and Quantitative Strategies.* Berkeley: University of California Press.

(1991). "Introduction: the Problem of Balancing Discourse on Cases and Variables in Comparative Social Research," pp. 1–8 in Charles C. Ragin (ed.), *Issues and Alternative in Comparative Social Research.* Leiden: E. J. Brill.

Ragin, Charles C., and Jeremy Hein (in press). "Methodological and Conceptual Issues in the Comparative Study of Ethnicity," in John Stanfield and

Rutledge Dennis (eds.), *Race and Ethnicity: Methodological Innovations.* Newbury Park, CA: Sage.
Ragin, Charles C., and David Zaret (1983). "Theory and Method in Comparative Research: Two Strategies." *Social Forces* 61:731–754.
Walker, Henry, and Bernard Cohen (1985). "Scope Conditions: Imperatives for Evaluating Theories." *American Sociological Review* 50:288–301.
Wieviorka, Michel (1988). *Sociétés et terrorisme.* Paris: Fayard.

Notes

Introduction

1. Special thanks go to Howard S. Becker and Mary Kate Driscoll for their supportive comments on various drafts of this Introduction.

Chapter 1

1. See Edmondson's valuable study for a general discussion of the rhetoric of sociology. Although her work is drawn on in this essay, our focus is more on the logical structure of arguments.

2. The examples chosen are pillaged for material relevant to issues in the use of cases. Although each of them is an excellent work of its kind, I have made no attempt to do justice to them as wholes. If the analysis sometimes appears critical, this is not intended to impute special weaknesses; it is likely that other works are much more open to criticism on the same grounds, and that some of the difficulties identified could hardly be avoided.

3. By great good luck, we have some historical material which throws light on the plausibility of this claim in relation to our particular example. Ernest Burgess initiated a restudy of Angell's cases. In this, one person reanalyzed Angell's cases using his concepts and methods of classification, another used his concepts but developed a rating scale for applying them to the data and a third (Robert Merton), who had not read Angell's book, devised his own concepts and procedures for analyzing the data. Angell was also asked to reclassify his own data, without looking back at his original decisions. Broadly, the outcomes showed questionable reliability in Angell's procedures. However, Merton arrived at a conceptual scheme which had a fairly marked similarity to Angell's. Given, however, that both used concepts like "social integration" which were in general use, one cannot take it that they were derived in a literally inductive sense from the data. Merton's concepts were to some extent different – and he did not end up with correct predictions in all cases, so the question of whether another theoretical schema could be equally good is left somewhat open. For more details of the restudy, see Platt (1987).

4. Interestingly, this creates problems about correlation. If a prediction has to be classifiable as right or wrong, the form "the more there is of a, the more there will be of b" is not sufficiently precise; particular values, or ranges of the values, of a and b need to be specified if they are put in quantitative form.

5. Note the implicit exclusion of southern areas as too dissimilar to be counted as represented.

6. Note the analogy with the ignoring of microlevel processes to which Abbott (Chapter 2) draws attention in rational-action explanations of emergent group outcomes.

7. For instance, people of C-D SES who belong to trade unions are assumed to vote more Democratic because there the worker "associates with, and is stimulated by, others of like predisposition," while those who belong to other associations, which have a majority of Republicans, are less Democratic because they "are naturally influenced by the higher prestige of the dominant group" (Lazarsfeld et al. 1944:147).

8. As Crompton (1990) has pointed out, the way in which these categories have been constructed draws to some extent on data about the cases of particular occupations, though she argues that he has been inconsistent in rejecting such case-study evidence, as irrelevant to the macrolevel with which he is concerned, when it has been put forward by critics.

9. Although the book does not say so, it might plausibly be suggested that a latent function of this is to persuade the audience he is addressing by choosing the kind of case with which it is at home. He does not need in the same way to persuade the Marxist friends and colleagues with whom, he makes it clear, he associates himself, while standard American quantitative sociologists do need persuasion.

10. The realist approach which Wright takes (Wright 1989:57–63) tries to deal with such issues, but suffers from the difficulty of showing the existence of "real" factors unless they make an empirical difference which can be seen as directly measurable.

11. Goldthorpe has taken a strong polemical position in relation to alternative interpretations of the issues with which he is concerned. His methodological strategy could be seen as fitting in with this, in that while the main body of the data gives heavy quantitative weight to his conclusions, he can also claim qualitative support for them against those who would find that more persuasive. It is interesting that he is so exclusively oriented to the sociological audience that he misses the opportunity to use the quantitative/qualitative distinction in ways which might help persuade a wider audience of his conclusions on equality of opportunity.

12. Harper (Chapter 6) in effect suggests that to use the author as case is a natural way of presenting ethnographic findings.

13. Cf. Kenneth Burke's idea of the "representative anecdote" and its use in the development of a vocabulary which may then be applied to the subject matter which it represents (Burke 1952:59).

Chapter 2

1. I would like to thank Charles Ragin, Howard Becker, David Weakliem, Claude Fischer, and Peter Abell for comments on this chapter. In particular, Howie's comments reminded me of the great Chicago tradition I had overlooked in early drafts, an oversight all the more surprising given the influence of that tradition on my substantive work.

2. I am ignoring here the problem that the case relation is not a mapping, a problem rising with particular force under the conceptual definition of "case." That is, "x is a case of y" can be simultaneous with "x is a case of z," and this may hold under a wide variety of relations between z and y. This is a most disturbing fact, but one whose implications would take me far away from my topic. Note, too, that even the subset definition of "case" is in fact subject to the same problems, for we do not have a well-defined, hierarchical set of categories for categorizing social entities. Jennifer Platt's essay (Chapter 1) considers these problems at some length, as does John Walton's (Chapter 5). Walton makes the important point that it is precisely in the reflection about what x is a case of that real theory arises.

3. While these papers are technically a random sample – my procedure was exactly as described – some readers might feel that I "just happened to get some articles that looked like this." In fact, other papers would have produced pretty much the same set of observations, although perhaps in different ways. Indeed, I would imagine that the overall balance – two papers taking a strong "population/analytic" view and one taking a more "narrative" one – probably overestimates the direct use of narrative in mainstream sociology.

4. Moreover, the action of the cases here is a peculiar one; they "vote with their feet." Note that this is one of the few actions always allowed to cases in quantitative approaches and that its results – selection bias – can vitiate such analysis altogether. An ironic evidence of disciplinary boundaries is the fact that the match-quality hypothesis is the standard theory of worker separation in economics (Mortensen 1988).

5. David Weakliem, who has commented on this paper with far better grace than I ever could have mustered in equivalent circumstances, makes this point in one of his comments: "Even when we spoke of variables as actors we had the idea of an underlying narrative, and the statements about variables were just a shorthand for this. Where the underlying narrative was not familiar, we tried to spell it out, which explains why explicit narratives appeared only for new ideas or results." Thus, narrative is indeed the level of "reality" (and hence a very necessary evil indeed) for which the rhetoric of variables is a shorthand. But note, as the singular noun implies, that the variables as actors permit only "*an* underlying narrative," not a variety of them.

6. The micro/macroimplications of the "case" concept are extensive, and I shall return to them later. But it is worth remark here that the approach taken by Pavalko means ignoring any microprocesses within cases (here the states) if those cases are emergents. Turnover is a good example. A state could change all its legislators over the 20-year period here studied, and still, if the determining contextual variables didn't change, the predictions wouldn't change. One legislator is a characterless rational chooser like another. Of course, the proper procedure is to get extensive microlevel data on each state to complement the extensive macrodata, but that necessity is a daunting one indeed. So one can easily understand why the concept of "case" assorts rather ill with micro/macro kinds of investigations.

7. One might adduce here the famous Heraclitean dictum about never stepping in the same river twice. But nonetheless, allowing temporal lines to distinguish cases seems a false procedure given our modern concepts of autoregression. Technically, the 369 "state-years" are regarded as independent not because the models are constructed that way, but because under certain conditions the equations for the temporal distribution reduce to that situation. One of the conditions is discussed by Allison (1982:82): the assumption that the vector of explanatory variables explains all variation in the hazard rate. Since this is unlikely, there will be serially correlated errors and problems of estimation. Pavalko has noted and discussed this problem (1989:601, note 5), although the caveats it raises disappear from her conclusion. The other condition is that of full rank for the matrix of explanatory variables, an assumption violated by any autoregression in the explanatory variables. Since the matrix includes repeated measures on substantive "cases" (i.e., states, here), this violation is virtually certain. (For example, whether or not the legislature is meeting follows a no-error autoregression scheme.) Econometricians have worried about this issue (Kennedy 1985:38), but it does not feature prominently in sociological discussions of event-history methods.

8. As David Weakliem has reminded me, this contrast is somewhat overdrawn. Even in the single-case-narrative view, we must disregard many things about the case because so much is known. And historians themselves, again as Weakliem reminded me, often have recourse to the "what would a reasonable person have done in the circumstances" argument, which I shall consider later.

9. Such methods do admit different narratives in a limited sense. In a system where two independent variables jointly determine a dependent variable, say with coefficients 0.2 and 1.0, a dependent value of 4.0 can arise from (20, 0), (10, 2), or (0, 4); the transformation takes all the points on the line $x_1 = 5k - 5x_2$ into the point k. But the narratives all have the same "causal shape," that is, the same coefficients. I am grateful to Peter Abell for demanding this clarification.

10. The move to the single-case narrative is thus not a move without its own problems, a point Jennifer Platt makes in Chapter 1 in her discussion of *The Jack-Roller*. As Douglas Harper argues in Chapter 6, we gain a great deal in terms of fidelity to the material, in terms of allowing material to develop its own structuring, when we move to single-case narrative. Harper's conscious choice of narrative presentation, however, elides the problems I have raised here – whether the plot of his trip to the apple harvest is not actually the intersection of a number of offstage plots, whether that plot really is more than a literary convention (i.e., a real social process), whether it really has a beginning and an end.

11. This does mean that the case/narrative approach often unjustifiably takes as unproblematic the structures (like monarchy) that make contingency important. However, these are usually ignored altogether in covering-law approaches, as in population/analytic ones. Thus neither side does well with structure and structural constraints or sources of those constraints. On the unreality of main effects, see the wonderful paper of Neyman (1935).

12. Stanley Lieberson's essay (Chapter 4 in this volume) concerns reasoning about cases in precisely this middle range. We differ considerably, however, on what to do about them. Lieberson's examples – drunk driving, losing one's luggage – are in fact not small-N situations at all. More importantly, Lieberson's entire analysis comes at the problem of small-N situations within the context of causal theory and population/analytic methods, as, indeed, do the arguments of Skocpol that he is at such pains to refute. I argue, however, that comparative narrative analysis can get us out of the small-N dilemma. To me the entire vocabulary of "causes," "interactions," "multiple causes," and so on seems inappropriate. [For a further analysis, see Abbott (1990).] John Walton (Chapter 5) clearly agrees. For him, reasoning about such cases is precisely the fastest way to think theoretically. And it is clear that Walton's conception of reasoning is fundamentally a narrative one: "At bottom, the logic of the case study is to demonstrate a causal argument about how general social forces take shape and produce results in specific settings."

13. Douglas Harper's essay (Chapter 6) underscores the traditional affinity of narrative, detail, and ambiguity as against causal analysis, generalization, and univocality. It is precisely this affinity that we must disassemble to advance sociological methods seriously. I am here arguing (implicitly) for the possibility of a narrative positivism, an argument I have made quite explicitly (e.g., Abbott 1988, 1990).

14. Claude Fischer has rightly pointed out to me that stage theories often have a strong whiff of determinacy about them. There is a sense that it is only a matter of time till the next stage arrives, and so on. In practice, some of the processes I have investigated might be thought of as determinate, others not. Most national professions eventually acquire associations, licensing, and so on, but many local medical communities never acquire schools or journals. As for the German musicians' careers, these vary in terms of pattern and in terms of how far through the pattern they manage to get. Nonetheless, as the most regular of "narratively conceived" processes, stage processes do partake of some of the determinacy of analytically conceived social reality.

15. A number of writers have been pursuing techniques of "narrative positivism." David Heise's work on events and responses to them attacks the problem from one angle. Peter Abell's homomorphic reduction techniques take another. My own use of optimal matching techniques is a third. One could also view the growing use of simulation models, by Kathleen Carley and others, as part of this development.

Chapter 3

1. I am indebted to Howard Becker for wise editorial guidance in this essay. I thank James Bennett, Martin Gargiulo, Shin-Kap Han, Wen-Rwei Hsu, Eric Leifer, Charles

Ragin, Marvin Reiss, Jae-soon Rhee, Ilan Talmud, Ronan Van Rossem, and Yuki Yasuda for comments on earlier drafts.

2. New Twentieth Century Unabridged.

3. One of the most thorough censuses ever, of goods and chattels as well as persons.

4. This pre-1905 work shaped his perceptions of Russian class structure which guided later action.

5. In ongoing affairs, actors are of course going to mix and match such institutional idioms for cases, as their situations permit and motivate [e.g., for a tribal context see Leach (1954), and for a bureaucratic context, see Simon (1945)] – even while institutional custodians may strive for monochromatic use.

6. I develop this at length elsewhere (White in press).

7. According to Berman (1983:part II), this study laid the ground for the dawning of a new order in European history around legal codes.

8. Udy (1970) offers a broad-based appraisal of this tension, which crosscuts government and economic realms.

9. As Berman's magisterial survey (1983) shows.

10. These may be in purely oral traditions of tribal era, as in the elaborate early Irish codes; see Patterson (1981).

11. Bloch (1977) traces the theme of identity-seeking in medieval law both through explicit forms such as trial-by-ordeal and through their reflection in emerging narrative genres such as romance.

12. Sociologists of science and ethnomethodologists (e.g., Cozzens 1989; Fleck 1979; Knorr-Cetina and Cicourel 1981) recently have begun such study.

13. I made one such effort, for the study of social mobility (White 1970); for follow-up, see Stewman and Konda (1983). Leamer (1978) is trenchant on the general problem.

14. Private communication, March 21, 1990, University of Sussex; her adaptation of a familiar phrase.

15. "From Aristotle to Hegel . . . the dramaturgical concept . . . crisis signifies the turning point in a fateful process that, despite all objectivity, does not simply impose itself from outside and does not remain external to the identity of the persons caught up on it" (p. 2).

16. A particular prosecution or study may of course be an effort to interdict or be a move toward identity: I spoke earlier of law as an institution.

17. Of old, projections such as these were by Roman aediles, from gazing at chicken gizzards; today, the equivalents are issued by economists, from the modern equivalent of gizzard-gazing, phrased in statistical studies (Leamer 1978).

18. Nohria (1990) presents a case study of technological innovation, which itself is a mixture of species, where the central figure, Michael Berlanger, is an entrepreneur of control, a master of timing. Anthony Caro (1974) portrays Lincoln Moses as adroit manipulator of New York governments and Lyndon Johnson (Caro 1990) as master finagler, first in Texas and then nationally.

19. Halevy's work should be recommended reading for current Eastern European parliamentarians.

20. "Voltaire's conviction that the period of Louis XIV was one of the few genuinely great ages of western civilization . . . Voltaire always insists that Louis XIV was the guiding spirit and prime mover" (pp. 16–17).

21. "The leaders of the school have produced a determinism in which Louis XIV, the most consequential personality in Europe, is little more than a proponent of principles that were opposed to the stream of history and bound to fail" (p. 110).

22. A case can be made that "individual" in this full sense can come to recognition only when the social reality permits a new concept of social environment: specifically, only with mobility among cities kept within an emerging class not bound on ethnic or kinship

grounds, and when such a mobility regime seizes upon a universalizing religion to bring its members into existence (Chesnut 1986).

23. The psychologist Gibson (1991) is trenchant on human perception of the physical environment. Baxandall (1975) shows how physical and social principles of perception combine in painting.

24. A study which itself should be geared to identity-forming!

25. For a useful overview of their theory, see Kreps (1988). His Chapter 14 suggests that their approach is a theosophy. For reality-oriented countertrends within economics, see, e.g., Grether, Isaac, and Plot (1989) or Zannetos (1966).

Chapter 4

1. I am indebted to William Alonso, Rogers Brubaker, John Campbell, William Kruskal, and Peter V. Marsden for stimulating discussions or comments on this topic.

2. This is different from historical or comparative analyses based on larger numbers, as, for example, in Isaac and Griffin (1989).

3. A brief history of earlier applications of this reasoning is given by Znaniecki (1934:236–8).

4. Following Marini and Singer (1988:347), by "cause" and "causal" they distinguish "causation from association, recognizing that causes are responsible for producing effects, whereas noncausal associations are not. Although causal terminology has been imprecise and has waxed and waned in popularity . . . the ideas of agency and productivity which it conveys have continued to be viewed as distinctive and important in social science."

5. It is not vital, for my purpose at this point, to define "small," "modest," or "larger."

6. Needless to say, determination of measurement error should not be made on the basis of whether deviations occur – all the more reason to expect rigorous procedures in both qualitative and quantitative analyses.

7. One cannot argue, by the way, that a new variable, combining being drunk and running a red light, could serve as a substitute for unmeasured interactions. This is because there would be no way of distinguishing such a combination from other combinations such as not speeding and running a red light, or for that matter a grand variable which includes all of the constants and the red-light variable.

8. Observe that were there to be a larger number of cases in Table 4.1, say 100, with 60 of them where Y is yes and 40 where Y is no, and where the presence or absence of X_2 is always in the form shown, whereas the other variables vary in a random way, there would be considerable confidence in the very same conclusion that is questionable with a small N.

9. In fairness, of course, the influence is tested if the constant is at a level where it is believed to affect the dependent variable.

10. To be sure, the method could still *possibly* work if all other conceivable causes of accidents were measured and recorded – a rather unlikely situation that requires exceptional good fortune in the recording of all possible causes and their precise measurement, for example, the exact speed of each car entering the intersection, and the speed and timing of cars entering the intersection from other points, all of the qualities of drivers who enter from these other points who did not have accidents, and so on.

11. This ignores the added problem when the small sample is not a random one, but is a selective set of cases.

12. For the most part, I would say that his approach is, however, a deterministic one. Particularly relevant is his treatment of contradictions (pp. 113–8). The emphasis is primarily on finding additional variables which resolve the contradictions and/or changing the delineation of the dependent variable. However, he does consider a type of statistical solution as well.

13. The Boolean methods proposed by Ragin (1987) advance our ability to deal with some of these problems, although they require a larger number of cases than are often used in these attempts to apply Mill's methods.

14. As for the former, Turner observes that the method of analytical induction is "ill-equipped to cope" with multiple causes (1953:609).

Chapter 5

1. For helpful suggestions on an earlier draft of this chapter, I am grateful to the editors of this volume, to various participants in the conference on "What is a case?" (particularly Jennifer Platt), and to Charles Tilly.

2. The question "A case of what?" is raised in most of the essays in this volume and is addressed specifically by Abbott (Chapter 2), Platt (Chapter 1), and Wieviorka (Chapter 7).

3. Jennifer Platt brought to my attention the connection between Znaniecki's methodological note and the case-study reasoning behind the larger study, as well as the remark by Burgess (cf. Platt 1988).

Chapter 6

1. An important exception was the fieldwork tradition as it developed during the 1920s at the University of Chicago's Department of Sociology.

2. VanMaanen (1988:49–51) does suggests that ethnographers who present their research as "realist tales" often do seek to present the point of view of their subjects. VanMaanen implies that the primary way this is done, by including lengthy quotations from subjects, is not the final word on the issue.

3. See Spradley (1970:74–6). During my research on homeless men I discovered that Spradley's categorization was a useful beginning rather than a final and complete linguistic system describing a closed cultural reality. In other words, I discovered additional "kinds" of tramps, and not all of Spradley's "types." Once again, we recognize culture to be fluid and only partially shared.

4. I note the historical and geographic limitations of my analysis. Particular climactic and environmental conditions, for example, made certain types of agricultural work available for certain categories of homeless during certain times of the year. The freight train – the usual mode of transportation for the western tramp – made him mobile, again in certain areas during certain times.

5. When I did my research in the middle 1970s there were estimated to be two to three hundred thousand homeless people in the United States. Homelessness was thought of as a social problem generally associated with the disease of alcoholism. The vast problem of homelessness in contemporary America (probably including ten to twelve times the number of homeless compared to when I did my research), most agree, is a problem which has developed at a structural level. I do not know what has happened to the rather fragile symbiotic relationship between the harvest towns in the Northwest and the tramp during this period of great change.

6. There may be organizational problems with such an approach. If we think of most sociological research emerging primarily from research universities with graduate departments, we recognize that divisions of labor on much research typically assign data gathering (often administering surveys, in person, through the mails, or over the telephone) to graduate students. The professor's role is usually limited to designing the study and the survey instrument, and analyzing the results. Surveys can be done quickly, and the results are more easily published than are the results of qualitative research. There is also the problem of time: research projects are funded by grants that have a short duration, which precludes *any* sociologist (whether professor or graduate student) from returning to the field after a survey is finished to do qualitative work. I think these (and related issues concerning "career work") push the discipline further and further into two camps: neither qualitatively nor quantitatively minded sociologists have the opportunity, let alone the predilection, to pause to really consider the benefits they might gain from working together.

7. See, for example, Suchar and Markin (1990) and Bunster (1977) for examples of case studies driven by photo elicitation methods.

8. Becker makes a point that overlies this idea. Becker suggests that when sociological writers use the passive voice and the third person they confuse the issue of human agency in social theories. For example, if a sociologist writes that a particular social action "is labeled," he or she has left out the important idea that someone has, in fact, successfully carried out the process of labeling. Similarly, if sociologists write that "social structures cause. . . ," they are, in fact, eliminating human agency from a circumstance that was undoubtedly caused by acting people. See Becker (1986:7–8, 36).

Chapter 7

1. Translated from French by Noal Mellott, CNRS, Paris.

2. Part of this program's results have been translated into English; see Alain Touraine, Zsuzsa Hegedus, François Dubet, and Michel Wieviorka (1983), and Alain Touraine, Michel Wieviorka, and François Dubet (1987).

3. Everett Hughes pointed this out in his presidential speech before the American Sociological Association (Hughes 1963).

Chapter 8

1. I thank Howard S. Becker, John Braithwaite, Frank T. Cullen, Emmanuel Lazega, Charles C. Ragin, Arthur L. Stinchcombe, Tony Tam, John B. Williamson, and the symposium participants for their useful comments on an earlier version of these ideas.

2. This definition is a variant of Schrager and Short's definition (1978). I have eliminated their reference to social and physical harm and added the violation of internal rules.

3. An earlier version of these ideas is available (Vaughan 1983:133–5).

Chapter 10

1. I thank Mary Kate Driscoll and Howard S. Becker for their many useful comments on this essay.

Index

235